Stanley Kubrick, Director

STANLEY

Revised and Expanded

A Visual Analysis by Sybil Taylor and Ulrich Ruchti

KUBRICK, DIRECTOR

by Alexander Walker

Weidenfeld & Nicolson
London

Dedication

Stanley Kubrick, 1928–1999
For Stanley Kubrick, whose permission and help in creating this book made it possible.

Acknowledgments

The quotation from A Clockwork Orange, *by Anthony Burgess, is reprinted with the permission of William Heinemann Ltd. and of W. W. Norton & Company, Inc., copyright © 1962 by Anthony Burgess.*

The cooperation of United Artists Corporation is gratefully acknowledged. All photographs from Paths of Glory, Killer's Kiss, *and* The Killing *are reproduced by permission of United Artists Corporation.*

The author and publishers are grateful to Columbia Pictures for all photographs from Dr. Strangelove, or How I Learned to Stop Worrying and Love the Bomb, *copyright © 1964 by Columbia Pictures; and for title page photo of Kubrick and photographs on page 6 and page 10, top right and middle row, copyright © 1964 by Columbia Pictures.*

The photographs on page 10, top left and bottom row, appear through the courtesy of Metro-Goldwyn-Mayer.

Photograph on page 374: Christiane Kubrick, September 1998.

We thank Alexander Singer for the photographs on page 9.

All photographs for Lolita *on pages 60–63 inclusive: LOLITA © 1962 Turner Entertainment Co. All photographs for* 2001: A Space Odyssey *on pages 164–180, and pages 225–227 inclusive: 2001: A SPACE ODYSSEY © 1968 Turner Entertainment Co. All photographs for* A Clockwork Orange *on pages 197–211 inclusive: A CLOCKWORK ORANGE © 1971 Warner Bros. Inc. and Polaris Productions, Inc. All photographs for* Barry Lyndon *on pages 235–263, and pages 228, 229 inclusive: BARRY LYNDON © 1975 Warner Bros. Inc. All photographs for* The Shining *on pages 268–308 inclusive: THE SHINING © 1980 Warner Bros Inc. All photographs for* Full Metal Jacket *on pages 316–343 inclusive: FULL METAL JACKET © 1987 Warner Bros. Inc. All photographs for* Eyes Wide Shut *on pages 344–361 and pages 230–232 inclusive: EYES WIDE SHUT © 1999 Warner Bros. Inc.*

Cover Credits: Front: 2001: A SPACE ODYSSEY © 1968 Turner Entertainment Co. THE SHINING © 1980 Warner Bros. Inc. EYES WIDE SHUT © 1999 Warner Bros. Inc. Back: Paths of Glory, *United Artists Corporation.* Dr. Strangelove, Or How I Learned To Stop Worrying And Love The Bomb, *Columbia Pictures. 2001: A SPACE ODYSSEY © 1968 Turner Entertainment Co. THE SHINING © 1980 Warner Bros. Inc. FULL METAL JACKET © 1987 Warner Bros. Inc. EYES WIDE SHUT © 1999 Warner Bros. Inc.*

Alexander Walker, Sybil Taylor and Ulrich Ruchti would like to thank the following individuals for their most generous assistance with many aspects of the text and illustrations.

At Warner Bros. Burbank: Judith Singer, Joe Hyams. At Warner Bros. London: Julian Senior, Savannah Brown, Gretchen Hines, Mary Conlin, Rick Senat, Lyn Jamieson.
In Beverly Hills: Jack Nicholson for permission to use hitherto unreproduced frame enlargements from The Shining.
On Mr. Kubrick's Personal staff: Anthony Frewin, Leon Vitali. Our heartfelt thanks too, to Jan Harlan.

And finally, the late Stanley Kubrick, who authorized this work and made available some illustrations, in colour and monochrome, from his personal archives.

We are grateful, as well, to our editor, Edwin Barber, who kept the faith throughout this sometimes complicated endeavour.

A CIP catalogue record for this book is available from the British Library

ISBN 0 297 82403 1

The text of this book is composed in Palatino with the display set in Perpetua
Composition by Trufont
Manufacturing by The Courier Companies, Inc.

Weidenfeld & Nicolson
The Orion Publishing Group
Wellington House
125 Strand
London WC2R 0BB

CONTENTS

Man and Outlook

Only a few film directors possess a conceptual talent—that is, a talent to crystallize every film they make into a cinematic concept. It is a skill that goes far beyond the mere photographing of a script, however cinematic the script may be in itself. It transcends the need to find a good subject, an absorbing story, or an extraordinary premise to build on. Essentially, it is the talent to construct a form that will exhibit the maker's vision in an unexpected way, often a way that seems to have been the only possible one when the film is finally finished. It is this conceptual talent that most strongly distinguished Stanley Kubrick.

But to say as much is only to restate the question this book seeks to answer: What is it that made Kubrick the kind of director he was? It even makes the task more difficult. Because almost every film Kubrick has directed has entailed constructing a new concept, he was a filmmaker who resisted the customary critical approach that tries to distinguish strongly linked themes in a director's work. It was wise even to avoid the head-on approach of question-and-answer with Stanley Kubrick. It was not one he readily submitted to or thrived on, for he knew the value of leaving the questioner, or viewer, unsatisfied, with an intensified curiosity about the complex forces shaping any action or individual.

Kubrick himself was a whole area of complex forces. Each film was a way of exploring the number of exciting possibilities it held for him at the time he decided to make it. Each film enabled him to extend his own investigation of himself by exhausting the area of research it opened up to his artistic and scientific imagination. This alone is one good reason why he was incapable of repeating a subject: it would mean repeating *himself.* And he simply did not have the time or the patience for that. Thus he was freed from the deadening demands that the film industry invariably makes on its most successful directors, or at least he did not give in to the demands when they were made.

Few directors have a temperament as strongly constituted as Kubrick's was to survive and create inside the industry without letting its enormous pressures rob him of his independence or impair his judgment. "Inside" is the key word here. If Kubrick kept himself to himself—and he increasingly did just that, making him one of the most elusive of filmmakers—it is not because he had any need to fear the kind of "punishment" that the movie industry still metes out even in these days, when directors have more creative freedom than ever before, to those who flout commercial imperatives in their pursuit of self-expression. Kubrick knew the laws that govern success or failure in this kind of world. He worked within them. As Hollis Alpert once put it, "He does not believe in biting the hand that might strangle him." Yet the fact remains that he succeeded in reconciling his own uncompromising requirements with those of the industry. On the strength of some dozen films, he has won a reputation for originality of subject and treatment that is rare among international film directors.

As well as his independence he kept his unpredictability. Each of his films, with only one exception, which he later disowned as not being "his" film, is stamped by its maker's evolving confidence in his own skill and by his curiosity in seeing how far he could extend it. He has always forced his reach to exceed his grasp. Other directors can justifiably boast of never underestimating their public. Kubrick's was a more characteristically private resolve: he never underestimated himself.

Such a man takes—and gives—immense pains in carrying out a resolve like this. To be part of his team was to surrender a part of one's life in a very real sense. Self-discipline in this kind of director demands a degree of despotism—basically benevolent, yet ruthless in never allowing anyone or anything to jeopardize the work of constructing a movie in his own image of it. His immense energy recharged itself on work. Beyond a certain amount of well-being and physical comfort, the customary social pressures or diversions outside work simply did not impinge on his creative priorities. In recent years he grew a ruff of black beard that added a visible dimension of inscrutability to a disposition whose self-sufficiency seemed at times almost monastic.

His curiosity about the world was unflagging; the capacity of a friend or associate to satisfy it was often less so. His conversation was endlessly interrogative. This was sometimes abrupt and disconcerting when rapid-fire questions pushed one up against the wall of one's own inability to come out with satisfying answers.

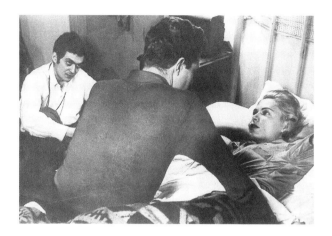
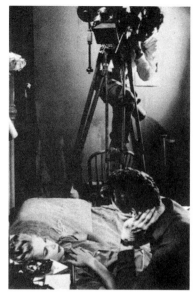

1955: on the set of Killer's Kiss

In part, Kubrick's insistence on tapping one's thoughts, on elicit-ing responses, was connected with an interest in communication that intensified over the years, until it occupied a major part of his life and, as we shall see, formed the central concern in several of his films. Communicating with Kubrick was a kind of "debriefing"—the military term is quite appropriate—for his need to inform himself fully before he made decisions was obses-sive. It follows that his range of interests was vast. An evening's conversation with him could cover such areas as optical percep-tion in relation to man's survival; the phenomenon of phosphenes (or "lights behind the eyes") and its connection with the "Star Ride" sequence in *2001: A Space Odyssey*; German thoroughness in building flash screens onto their coastal gun emplacements in Normandy so that the cannon fire would not be pinpointed by the enemy; compromised safety margins in commercial flying (Kubrick, a resolute nonflier, had been monitoring control-tower conversation at a nearby international airport); Dr. Goebbels' role as a pioneer film publicist; the Right's inability to produce dialec-ticians to match the Left's; Legion of Decency pressures during the making of *Lolita*; SAM-3 missiles in the Arab-lsraeli conflict; Irish politics and the possibility of similarities in the voiceprints of demagogues; and, of course, Kubrick's favorite game, chess.

Chess was the first of two lifelong obsessions he acquired from his father, a physician practicing in the Bronx, New York, where Kubrick was born in 1928. The second was photography. In

Kubrick's case, there appears to be a very strong creative link between chess and the camera—one is a mental discipline, the other an imaginative craft.

Chess in particular offers a clue to the elements that constitute Kubrick and helps to explain why he made certain films and not others—and why he made them in certain ways and not in others. For the thought that goes into moviemaking, both in the physical preparation of a production and in the conceptual structuring of the film, was closely related in the case of this director to the attitudes that chess playing develops.

"If chess has any relationship to filmmaking," Kubrick said, "it would be in the way it helps you develop patience and discipline in choosing between alternatives at a time when an impulsive decision seems very attractive. Otherwise it is necessary to have perfect intuition—and this is something very dangerous for an artist to rely on." It is hard to find the right criteria for making the dozens of decisions daily facing a director when they appear to have only small pluses or minuses attached to them. But the pondering of the choices, as in chess, enabled him, perhaps, to make more good ones than if he had impulsively reached for the first one that looked interesting.

Chess also sharpens one's awareness of the time factor. In tournament chess, a level Kubrick attained but stopped at, unwilling to make the total commitment required by serious championship play, the players are matched against a clock as well as against each other. There is a clear analogy between this rigorous framework and a film's budget and schedule, which relate to the time it will take to shoot. "You have a problem of allocating your resources of time and money in making a film, and you are constantly having to do a kind of artistic cost-effectiveness of all the scenes in the film against the budget and time remaining," Kubrick said. "This is not wholly unlike some of the thinking that goes into a chess game." The chessboard finds its way into scenes in several Kubrick films; and the narratives of *The Killing* and *Dr. Strangelove* are structured around the race against time and the consequences of "moves" made by the characters or by objects virtually independent of the characters. But whether there is this kind of internal evidence or not in a Kubrick film, its whole feeling suggests it has been shaped by a particular kind of mind, intuitively aware of choice, consequences, and the pattern of play—and chess has been a part of this conditioning discipline.

Formal education certainly provided very little of it. Kubrick at school was not even a "late beginner." Interestingly, physics was the most satisfactory among his subjects, in which he earned undistinguished grades, at Taft High School. Perhaps the failure of most of his teachers to hold his attention, much less ignite his imagination, helps account for the compulsive desire to connect with an audience that runs so consistently through his filmmaking. (Boredom taught him at an early age the distinction between artistic creation and public communication. Though this distinction is a primary concern of all filmmakers of stature, it is temptingly easy for a self-absorbed artist to lose sight of it.) The only instructor at Taft that he found stimulating was the English teacher Aaron Traister, who at least attempted to make Shakespeare's plays interesting; it was he who figured in a piece of photojournalism that Kubrick, spurred on by his father's gift of a camera, sold to *Look* magazine while he was still at Taft.

After high school graduation he quickly landed a job with *Look*. The magazine became for all practical purposes his university. "Four and a half years of working for *Look* magazine, traveling all over America, seeing how things worked and the way people behaved, gave me some useful insights plus important experience in photography." At the age of seventeen, in short, he had "backed into" the kind of opportunity that builds optimism and assists the belief that one can accomplish anything—a feeling that certainly doesn't hurt at this age. It also allowed Kubrick to save a few thousand dollars, enough to make a short movie called *Day of the Fight (1951)*, an example of photojournalism, on the middleweight boxer Walter Cartier. Filmed with a small, 100-foot daylight-loading Eyemo camera, it cost $3,900; RKO bought it for just a few hundred dollars more and played it at the Paramount Theatre in New York.

Fired by this first success, Kubrick quit *Look*. He was then twenty-one. His youthfulness was an important factor, for had he got his job on the magazine in his late twenties or early thirties, a much more usual age, he might not have found it so easy to leave such a good post; but his lack of family responsibilities at this age allowed him to pursue the far riskier livelihood of a filmmaker.

Kubrick's curiosity about the world, aroused by his experience with the magazine, now prompted him to get the education he had missed at Taft by monitoring courses at Columbia University. Among his teachers were Lionel Trilling, Mark Van Doren, and the classicist Moses Hadas. From this time on he became an omnivorous reader; in a sense, dropping out of school made him into a lifelong student.

The reading that influenced him as a child certainly wasn't done in the classroom, but at home, where his father's office shelves and bookcases held translations of European fairy stories, folk tales by the brothers Grimm, tales from Greek and Roman mythology, and other similar works. Because he read them at a formative age, they had, Kubrick acknowledged, a considerable effect on his filmmaking. They showed the inadequacy of naturalism as the mainspring of a plot. "Naturalism finally does not elicit the more mysterious echoes contained in myths and fables; these resonances are far better suited to film than any other art form. People in the twentieth century are increasingly occupied with magic, mystical experience, transcendental urges, hallucinogenic drugs, the belief in extraterrestrial intelligence, et cetera, so that, in this sense, fantasy, the supernatural, the magical documentary, call it what you will, is closer to the sense of the times than naturalism." His films show recurring evidence—sometimes in the selection of the main event; sometimes in the guise of a character, the concept of a set, the atmosphere of a scene—of this early, persistent interest in the symbolic analysis of society through its enduring myths and fables.

What place did films have in Kubrick's youth? During and after his stint on *Look* he used to haunt the Museum of Modern Art's film shows, going "as often as they changed the program." But his early curiosity was mainly about technique, not content. Editing in particular had exciting mysteries for a still-photographer bent on making movies. "The most influential book I read at that time was Pudovkin's *Film Technique*. It is a very simple, unpretentious book that illuminates rather than embroiders. It certainly makes it clear that the film cutting is the one and only aspect of films that is unique and unrelated to any other art form. I found this book much more important than the complex writings of Eisenstein. I think it's worthwhile for anyone interested in filmmaking to study the contrast between the films of Eisenstein and those of Chaplin, which is another way of referring to the difference between style and content. The greatness of Eisenstein's films represents the triumph of cinematic style over heavy-handed, often simple-minded content. Chaplin's films are masterpieces of content, taste, and sensibility over what is virtually a noncinematic kind of technique. If I had to choose between the two, I would take Chaplin: fortunately the two approaches are not mutually exclusive."

Nevertheless, one early memory of a film that impressed him because of a marvelous combination of music and action was the sequence of the Battle on the Ice in Eisenstein's *Alexander Nevsky*—a display he often alluded to in later interviews. But when his own film career was under way and he had cut his artistic teeth on technique, he speedily recognized the limitations of pure composition. Eisenstein's reputation as the master of montage probably influenced Kubrick later to give more and more attention to content. Although Kubrick did not acknowledge that the films of Fritz Lang that he saw—he liked in particular the Dr. Mabuse series and "M"—had any direct influence on him, Lang's concern with myth, legend, and the Teutonic unconscious seems clearly analogous to his evolving interests.

Kubrick's paternal grandmother had come from Romania and his paternal grandfather from the old Austro-Hungarian Empire. Whether these family origins played any part in determining the direction his tastes took is a matter Kubrick preferred not to speculate on. But he readily conceded that, of all the directors whose work he saw at this time, "I did very, very much like Max Ophuls' work. I loved his extravagant camera moves which seemed to go on and on forever in labyrinthine sets. The staging of these great camera moves appeared more like a beautifully choreographed ballet than anything else: a spindly waiter hurrying along with a tray of drinks over his head, leading the camera to a couple dancing, who, in turn, whirled the camera to a hussar climbing the stairs, and on and on the camera would go, all to beautiful music. I don't think that Ophuls ever received the critical appreciation he deserved for films like *Le Plaisir*, *The Earrings of Madame de . . .*, and *La Ronde*. When I went to Munich in 1957 to make *Paths of Glory* at the Geiselgesteig Studios, I found the last sad remnants of a great filmmaker—the dilapidated, cracked, and peeling sets that Ophuls had used on what would prove to be his last film, *Lola Montès*."

However, Kubrick was not aware that he derived an overwhelming experience from any particular film he viewed before striking out on his own movie career—except, he added dryly, from the *bad* films. "I was aware I didn't know anything about making films, but I believed I couldn't make them any worse than the majority of films I was seeing. Bad films gave me the courage to try making a movie."

But what he absorbed in movie theaters wasn't immediately apparent in his own films. After making a second short for RKO, *Flying Padre* (1951)—which was about a Roman Catholic missionary who got around his 400-mile parish in the Southwest by plane—Kubrick raised about $10,000 from his father and an uncle to direct his first feature, *Fear and Desire* (1953). He later described it today as "undramatic and embarrassingly pretentious." One suspects that he did not find it disagreeable to know that the only traceable print of it was in private hands and not easily available for public screening. It was the story of four soldiers lost behind enemy lines in an unnamed war and trying to find out who they were as well as where they were. A poet friend of Kubrick's, Howard Sackler, who has since become famous as the author of *The Great White Hope*, wrote the screenplay. "The ideas we wanted to put across were good," Kubrick said, "but we didn't have the experience to embody them dramatically. It was little more than a thirty-five-millimeter version of what a class of film students would do in sixteen millimeter." Nevertheless, its distributor, the late Joseph Burstyn, got it into art houses, where it collected an appreciative notice or two. It also provided Kubrick with formative experiences. One was the overriding necessity of a realistic and engrossing story. The other was the value of creative freedom. For even films financed by one's relatives can commit a director to burdensome contract stipulations.

But the greatest benefit of all was simply the experience of shooting a feature film. "The entire crew of *Fear and Desire* consisted of myself as director, lighting cameraman, operator, administrator, makeup man, wardrobe, hairdresser, prop man, unit chauffeur, et cetera. The rest of the crew consisted of a friend of mine, Steve Hahn, who was an executive at Union Carbide and who took his holidays with us and knew something about electricity; another friend, Bob Dierks, who was the studio assistant at *Look* magazine, helped me set up the equipment and put it away, and did a thousand other jobs; my first wife, Toba, who tried to cope with all the paperwork and minor administration; and three Mexican laborers who carried the cases around. Particularly in those days, before the advent of film schools, Nagras, and lightweight portable equipment, it was very important to have this experience and to see with what little facilities and personnel one could actually make a film. Today, I think that if someone stood around watching even a smallish film unit, he would get the impression of vast technical and logistical magnitude. He would probably be intimidated by this and assume that something close to this was necessary in order to achieve more or less professional results. This experience and the one that followed with *Killer's Kiss*, which was on a slightly more cushy basis, freed me from any concern again about the technical or logistical aspects of filmmaking."

Fear and Desire ran into postproduction problems of a technical nature that cost an additional $20,000. It never showed a profit on the investment; but its maker thought it expedient to get another film out quickly while it was still in the program at the Guild Theatre, in New York. Again with Sackler, he strung together some action sequences—they had to be reasonably cheap to shoot—and then filled in a story entitled *Kiss Me, Kill Me*, about a girl who is kidnapped by the sadistic owner of a dance hall and rescued from his clutches by a gallant young boxer. "While *Fear and Desire* had been a serious effort, ineptly done, *Killer's Kiss*, as it was later known, proved, I think, to be a frivolous effort done with conceivably more expertise though still down in the student level of filmmaking."

Killer's Kiss (1955) inevitably involved Kubrick in far more than editing—again in just about every technical job there is in filmmaking. Except for a few scenes with the boxer and the girl in their tenement rooms, which were shot in a tiny studio, it was all done on New York locations. It took twelve to fourteen weeks— "a generous time. But everything we did cost so little that there was no pressure on us—an advantage I was never to encounter again." The equipment was excellent—Mitchell and Eclair cameras, which were hired on a deferred-payment basis, as were laboratory, dubbing, and editing facilities. "All the dialogue was postsynched, which accounts for a slight zombielike quality to some of the acting. Money began to run out in the editing stage, and being unable to afford even an editing assistant, I had to spend four months just laying in the sound effects, footstep by footstep." Along with the main player, Frank Silvera, as the dance-hall boss, the cast worked for a pittance; Kubrick was surprised at how much actors would forgo just for the chance to act. It cost about $40,000, raised by Kubrick from friends and a relative, Morris Bousel, a Bronx pharmacist; but the final cost was $75,000, after deferred payments were made and union rates met.

To the limited number of critics who saw the film on release, *Killer's Kiss*, with its sense of violence and urban desperation, offered evidence of a highly original new talent, capable of refreshing the crime-film genre. However, Kubrick, still conscious of the film's limited intentions, or perhaps regretting a story fitted together for effect rather than content, stubbornly refused to acknowledge the values in it that others found. "It was John Grierson who said of von Sternberg that 'when a director dies, he becomes a photographer.' *Killer's Kiss* might prove that when a director is born, the photographer doesn't necessarily die. The only distinction I would claim for it is that, to the best of my belief, no one at the time had ever made a feature film in such amateur circumstances and then obtained worldwide distribution for it."

One of the most important consequences of having made this film was Kubrick's meeting with James B. Harris. Harris, also twenty-six, was, like Kubrick, passionate about films. (The mutual friend who brought them together was Alexander Singer, who had acted as stills-photographer on *Killer's Kiss* and has since become a director himself.) Harris and Kubrick subsequently set up a producer-director partnership that lasted for three films. Through his family's interests in TV and film distribution Harris was able to provide the finances Kubrick needed to buy a property and make a really professional film.

Their first film in partnership, *The Killing* (1956), is also the first on which Kubrick was proud to have his name. Critics have praised it chiefly for the brilliance of its construction, the precise working out of the racetrack robbery in it, and the way in which events that overlap in time are integrated into the suspense by audacious and ingenious flashback techniques. In view of this acclaim, Kubrick's comment is wryly amusing: "Jim Harris and I were the only ones at the time who weren't worried about fragmenting time, overlapping and repeating action that had already been seen, showing things again from another character's point of view. In fact, this was just the structure in Lionel White's thriller, *Clean Break,* that had appealed to us and made us want to do the film. It was the handling of time that may have made this more than just a good crime film."

Later, the importance of the story was to become a fundamental aspect of Kubrick's working methods. He was a filmmaker who put his trust in the old atavistic appeal of a story, in its ability to focus his own talent, retain the attention of his audience, and at the same time underpin his exploration of the areas of special interest within that story. In this respect he was a traditionalist, compared with avant-garde filmmakers who have freed themselves from the tyranny of the story by abolishing it. Kubrick acknowledged this was a strong temptation; but he was fond of quoting the passage in E. M. Forster's *Aspects of the Novel* in which this novelist and critic writes: "Neanderthal man listened to stories, if one may judge by the shape of his skull. The primitive audience was an audience of shock-heads, gaping round the camp-fire, fatigued with contending against the mammoth or the woolly rhinoceros, and only kept awake by suspense. What would happen next? The novelist droned on, and as soon as the audience guessed what happened next, they either fell asleep or killed him."*

For Kubrick, finding a story he wanted to film was probably the most important yet least successfully dealt with part of his work. The question "How did you find the story?" was to him

---

Aspects of the Novel (New York: A Harvest Book, Harcourt Brace Janovich, Inc., 1956), p. 26.

like asking, "How do you fall in love?" "I have always found it to be an accidental process, and never one which can be attacked head-on." He would ponder the opportunities a potential story contained for months before even beginning to do anything about it. "You must be receptive, certainly—but you have to reflect on them very realistically. Many apparently attractive stories mislead you by a narrative trick incapable of translating into a film." When pushed, he conceded that a story is a film's most artificial aspect, too, since a well-organized narrative is seldom met with in life. But naturalism, as we know, was not the frontier of Kubrick's interests; he continually crossed it. The story is one device for doing so. It satisfies the primal curiosity, a point often lost sight of in films; if the magical ingredients are present, the story also extends the imagination into the director's own sphere of concern. The excitement that the discovery of the right story released in Kubrick was intensely creative, as it drew on, added to and became converted into whatever other thoughts and interests obsessed him at that particular time. He set immense store on it. "Just as actors have nightmares that they'll never get another part, I have a recurring fear that I'll never find another story I like well enough to film."

E. M. Forster defined the story as "a narrative of events arranged in their time sequence." This hints at the special appeal *The Killing* probably made to Kubrick underneath its "good story." It posed the intellectually stimulating problem of dislocating the time sequence as the separate events overlapped in the racetrack robbery; and it offered him the emotional gratification of keeping the narrative pressing ahead in simple fulfillment of the audience's curiosity about "what happened next." This combination of intellectual precision and narrative satisfaction is one of Kubrick's strongest identity marks, as the analysis of his films will show.

The Killing was made for $320,000, a budget larger than the one before but still minute by today's Hollywood standards. Surprisingly, perhaps, it was shot entirely on film sets, except for scenes at the racetrack and airport. The largest set used was the racetrack betting area; this was made up of just a few wood-and-plaster flats, yet the film's air of total realism transfigures it. Now that his film had conventional Hollywood status, union regulations prevented Kubrick from doing the photography himself, and this led to a certain tension when his cameraman, a Hollywood veteran, objected to panning or tracking shots involving a twenty-five-millimeter lens, fearing that distortion would result. (The twenty-five-millimeter lens was the widest-angle lens available in

1956. Now, everyone tracks and pans with eighteen-millimeter, fourteen-and-one-half-millimeter, even nine-and-eight-tenths-millimeter lenses.) The confidence that his own thorough grounding in photography gave Kubrick now paid off; the tracking shots were perfectly realized using, at his insistence, the twenty-five-millimeter lens. The greater means at his disposal meant he was able to afford better actors than in *Killer's Kiss*, though, characteristically, he found at least one member of the cast, the wrestler who diverts the police by staging a brawl, in a chess club he often frequented on Forty-second Street. *The Killing* was the first film in which the satisfaction he took in directing extended to all the performances from his actors; there was not a weak one anywhere.

The Killing was followed by months of total indifference from Hollywood. Then Kubrick and Harris were signed to develop properties for Dore Schary, who was head of production at MGM. Kubrick prepared a script based on a Stefan Zweig story, "The Burning Secret," in collaboration with the novelist Calder Willingham; and when Schary lost his job in a company shake-out, and his protégés also left, it was with Willingham that Kubrick developed the scenario of his next film.

He reached back to a Humphrey Cobb novel whose story had fascinated him as a child. It was called *Paths of Glory*, and was based on a true incident in World War I. *Paths of Glory* had the obligatory obsessional element to grip Kubrick's imagination in its deep sense of injustice at the fate of three soldiers executed as scapegoats because their commandant had set his men an impossible military objective. Jim Thompson, the thriller writer who had coauthored the screenplay of *The Killing*, joined Kubrick on the new film and contributed, with Willingham, much of the fine dialogue.

But Kubrick controlled the overall construction.

The script was turned down by every one of the major Hollywood studios until Kirk Douglas agreed to play the main role. His fee claimed $350,000 out of the budget of $900,000, but without a star of his magnitude there would have been small chance of getting the film financed. It was made in Germany, partly for economy, partly because the story's anti-French bias made French locations inadvisable.* It is the first of Kubrick's

*French sensitivities about their World War I generals were still so raw that Kubrick's film was originally refused a French censorship certificate; the ban was relaxed only after President de Gaulle's retirement and death. The Swiss, too, banned it until the early 1970s, out of sympathy with their neighbor's feelings. Since many American army bases, at home and abroad, also banned the film, it seems that the nerve touched by *Paths of Glory* was militaristic rather than purely nationalistic.

major films, a totally confident advance from the action drama into the cinema of ideas and human values. Its performances were strong, subtle, and detailed; its visual impression of warfare at that period is still unequaled on the screen—no less an authority than Winston Churchill commended its authenticity.

Kubrick, however, tended to play down the technical virtuosity of the film as well as the difficulties of working in a foreign country with a crew who did not speak much English. (At that time far fewer American films were produced abroad than has become the case in recent years.) He says: "I had no qualms about the technical side of filmmaking; after all, I had done most of the jobs myself. The Germans were superb technicians, totally work-oriented." The German extras, however, were almost too fearless for Kubrick's liking. He had to keep reminding the hundred or so German police cast as French infantrymen that they were supposed to be raw troops under terrifying and unaccustomed fire. Only then did they get the knack of acting scared and stop performing foolhardy examples of physical courage that could have been dangerous; the shell holes they tumbled intrepidly in and out of were mined with explosives able to inflict severe burns. "For this sequence," he said, "we had six cameras, one behind the other on a long dolly track which ran parallel to the attack. The battlefield was divided into five 'dying zones' and each extra was given a number ranging from one to five and told to 'die' in that zone, if possible near an explosion. I operated an Arriflex camera with a zoom lens and concentrated on Kirk Douglas."

Another justly celebrated scene, General Mireau's first inspection of the "trench world" that forms so horrifying a contrast to the elegant château that houses the commanders, was done in a single long take. Both sides in the war, Kubrick explained, floored their trenches with duckboards because of mud; this historical detail made it a simple matter to lay the dolly straight on top.

As well as complete technical mastery, *Paths of Glory* (1957) showed Kubrick's developing authority with actors. While the cast of *The Killing* performed well without exception, they nearly all came from the sturdy, dependable ranks of Hollywood character actors. In *Paths of Glory* the stars have gained an extra dimension; the quality of Kubrick's intelligence is ingrained in their performances, in a superb alliance between their own skills and personalities and the photography, editing, and direction that the filmmaker has imposed. Critics generally agreed that Kirk Douglas surpassed himself as the humane Colonel Dax; much of this was due to the quality of the direction he received.* Kubrick

*Douglas has since shown himself oddly self-denying in *his* rating of his perfor-

totally dismissed stories that Adolphe Menjou, as the utterly corrupt General Broulard, was "difficult," resented his director repeating takes, and only grudgingly agreed to an additional reading after one *he* had considered his best. On the contrary, says Kubrick, Menjou was a consummate craftsman when it came to taking direction—and the fixed right-wing attitudes the actor held were not unhelpful in such a role.

Early in his career Kubrick had given himself a crash course in the theory of directing actors. "The equivalent to Pudovkin's book on film editing is a book oddly enough about Stanislavsky, not by him: *Stanislavsky Directs*, by Nikolai M. Gorchakov. It provides a very detailed and practical description of Stanislavsky at work on different productions. I would regard it as an essential book for any intending film director."

Kubrick asserted that it is the director's own imagination, the quality of *his* ideas, that plays the principal part in keying his actors to the pitch necessary for a good performance. "A director's job working with actors is much more like a novelist than the traditional image of a Svengali; it's essentially a problem of the right idea, the right adjective, the right adverb. These are the things that finally produce results. The right idea is like having the right tool for the job: you feel it as soon as you start work. Teaching actors how to act is something that should be done by somebody else." If actors performed better for Kubrick than for other directors, maybe the quality of the ideas he gave them was better. Invariably, he worked with professionals—actors who could "home" onto an idea he fed them, or hit the same mood intuitively, and who could generate subtle forms of feeling every moment the camera ws turning. Certain actors, Kubrick found, can do "a psychological rope trick," using their own taste, imagination, and judgment to come reasonably close to a characterization on their own. But even their awareness can be made much sharper by a director who is creating the right ideas for them and recognizes in which takes, or in which part of one take, they are at pitch. He did not allow people to "walk through" a rehearsal at 7:30 a.m. He wanted the real thing produced for his inspection—"otherwise," he said, "why are we rehearsing?"

In all his films he eagerly used technology to aid his actors, usually by expanding the time available to him for directing them. A Polaroid camera shot a scene for the lighting qualities,

---

mance. Interviewed by Michel Ciment in *Positif* (January 1970), he ranked *Paths of Glory* last of all the films for which he had a personal preference, after *Lonely Are the Brave, Spartacus, Champion, Lust for Life*, and *The Vikings*.

and after Kubrick scanned the instant print and issued any necessary instructions for adjusting the lighting effect he wanted, the time saved was at the service of his players. Time was more and more precious to him. A TV monitor accompanied rehearsals and shooting, allowing instant replay, and a close and trusted assistant videotaped players testing for parts, so that he could scan the results quickly and, if need be, painlessly at home.

Face-to-face encounters could be painful for Kubrick, especially with strangers, and it followed that the relationship he developed with his principal players was a process not just of directing them in front of the camera but of growing to know them over what was often a lengthy preshooting period. One feels he was prying them open for inspection. A part can often be made to follow a character trait. He certainly explored all the choices it offered, inventing, elaborating, selecting, rejecting. Intelligence or intuition was what he always hoped to find in his players: the often complex work of transferring ideas on the set, occasionally replaced by a kind of imaginative shorthand between director and actor, was thus made easier. The relationship eventually became so close that a code was elaborated in which Kubrick would say, when he wanted, for instance, a certain degree of smiling reaction, "I think that calls for a three and a half."

Some of those who have worked with him talk of Kubrick's preoccupation with finding "the moment" in every scene—the revelatory detail, be it a gesture, a look, the way a word was said, even an inanimate object, that electrified the effect of the playing. Comedy thrives on such moments; and more than anything else, one feels, Kubrick's success in finding them explains why he became such a brilliant director in that most difficult genre. If he worked his actors hard, it was usually in the mutual search for "the moment." But it was *cooperative,* this relationship; not dictatorial. "With Kubrick," says Malcolm McDowell, "you were encouraged to go out on a limb, often breaking away from the script (which had to be good in the first place, so that he had the confidence to roam free of it), but you always knew that he was there somewhere with you, sustaining and assisting you."

In spite of tremendous critical acclaim for *Paths of Glory,* Kubrick found his career stalemated by nonevents. It was now 1959. He had gone to Hollywood in 1958 and developed two scripts, an adaptation for Kirk Douglas and an original for Gregory Peck. Neither one was ever used. A contract to direct Marlon Brando in *One-Eyed Jacks* came to nothing but six months of frustrating, time-consuming discussions. Kubrick was finding out how Hollywood eroded a filmmaker's creative stamina by running him up deadends. Then came an emergency call from Kirk Douglas. *Spartacus* had run into trouble after its director, the late Anthony Mann, had fallen out with Douglas after only a few days of shooting. Douglas asked Kubrick to take over.

If any event decisively confirmed Kubrick's determination totally to control his own films—from inception to last shot, and then on through the promotional publicity to the premiere and even afterward—it was the experience of directing *Spartacus* (1960). He did not control this film; he was simply an employee who could be fired at the will of its star, whose own production company was making it. Nonetheless, things started off well. The early sequences of the gladiators training and dueling were rewarding to do, Kubrick said, perhaps because they were action sequences, not dependent on a screenplay whose dialogue and characterization the director regarded as poor for his purposes. He had criticized both and had believed his criticisms were accepted. After a few months' filming, however, it became clear to Kubrick that his suggestions for improving the script were not going to be adopted. Reasons for this differ, and Kubrick remained reticent about scraping away protective scar tissue. But one well-placed observer close to Kirk Douglas believes that the star at first accepted his director's revisions in the script until Howard Fast, author of the original novel, viewed footage from the film and told Douglas what a miracle it was he had found a talent like Kubrick. Though well-meant, it was tactless to give a star the impression that his film's success was largely dependent on its brilliant director.

Kubrick stuck out the difficult months that followed, unable to have any say in the script, but fearing that if he quit, someone else might make it worse, and vaguely hoping that at some stage, perhaps in the editing, it might be made better. He regarded it as his most difficult and fruitless period. A couple of years later he permitted himself a rather sarcastic reference to his powerlessness when Peter Sellers, in the character of Quilty in *Lolita*, lisps, "I am Spartacus; set me free." The experience had an annealing effect on Kubrick. He henceforth never relinquished the power of decision making to anyone—"a simple matter if it's in your contract, a great deal of trouble if it's not." Many filmmakers pursue the goal of artistic independence, but few with the tenacity Kubrick manifested after *Spartacus*. And later, of course, commercial success confirmed his independence.

It was while *Spartacus* was being painfully pushed forward that Kubrick and James Harris announced they had bought the screen rights of *Lolita*—for a reported $150,000 —and had engaged Vladimir Nabokov to write the screenplay. In view of thoughts he expressed at the time on adapting literary works, it was an odd choice for Kubrick. His preference had tended toward work that was little known, short in scope, but well furnished with psychological insights, so that the action could be justified—an important need for him. Now he committed himself to filming a book of worldwide literary acclaim, with a theme that defied the censors and, most said, even the filmmakers.

One element he certainly found appealing in the book was the obsessional quality of Humbert Humbert's love for the nymphet. The conventional love theme had so far had absolutely no appeal for Kubrick; he was basically a skeptic, not a romantic. But while exploring the bizarre he always liked to profit from the restraining discipline of the realistic and the conventional. Consequently, a forbidden devotion like that of Nabokov's hero, pursued under the surface of apparently orthodox society, put out ironic vibrations for him. "The literary ground rules for a love story are such that it must end in either death or separation of the lovers and it must never be possible for the lovers to be permanently united. It is also essential that the relationship must shock society or their families. The lovers must be ostracized. It is very difficult to construct a modern story which would believably adhere to these rules. In this respect I think it is correct to say that *Lolita* may be one of the few modern love stories."

He also believed it possible to devise a cinematic style corresponding to the book's erotic wit. He felt strongly that what could be described could be filmed. Recently he conceded that much less could be filmed in the mid-1960s and that *Lolita* would have been a different film if it were made today. The book's witty, allusive style encompassed material it was then imprudent to put on the screen or even imply. Moreover, some aspects of the film's promotion, such as restricting it in America to audiences over the age of eighteen, was interpreted less as appeasement to morality groups like the Legion of Decency than as an additional allure for those who expected to see sex-play between a grown man and a virtual infant.

False expectations did harm the film's reception to some extent, but in addition Kubrick had also to deal with the very real restrictions then imposed on the film industry. The Legion of Decency (which, much reformed in its ways, was renamed the National Catholic Office for Motion Pictures) was naturally concerned with the theme; its concern extended even to details like the scene in which a burial urn containing the ashes of Lolita's father happened to be placed next to a religious triptych. Kubrick was told that to juxtapose an illustration of Catholic piety with evidence of a cremation was totally unacceptable; and in the final print a photographic process had to be employed to blur the religious image. One can imagine from this example what a blast would have occurred had the film contained more overt sexuality. Kubrick commented:

"Naturally I regret that the film could not be more erotic. The eroticism of the story serves a very important purpose in the book, which was lacking in the film: it obscured any hint that Humbert Humbert loved Lolita. One was entirely satisfied to believe that he was erotically obsessed with her, and one believed his repeated comments that it would be necessary to get rid of her when she was no longer a nymphet. It was very important to delay an awareness of his love until the end of the story. I'm afraid that this was all too obvious in the film. But in my view this is the only justifiable criticism." (Again one notes his constant concern with justifying his effects.)

Some critics expressed the view that Sue Lyon looked too old for Lolita, but Kubrick rebutted this by pointing to the maturity of many an American nymphet of Lolita's age. Moreover, he pointed out as further justification of his casting, Sue Lyon bore a rather close resemblance to the nymphet named Annabel in the novel who seduced Humbert Humbert early in his life and whose spell, according to Nabokov, he managed to break by "incarnating her in another"—that is, in Lolita.* "I went to a party with Nabokov after the premiere," Kubrick said, "and he was very jolly and very flattering about the film in every respect. At no time during or after the production did he ever express any doubts about Sue Lyon looking too old."

The screenplay credit on *Lolita is* taken by Nabokov only, but Kubrick added many touches of his own sardonic invention. The entire table-tennis encounter between Quilty and Humbert Humbert in the opening sequence was his conception; so was the ironic scene showing Humbert Humbert soaking complacently in the bathtub while receiving his neighbors' condolences on his wife's death. Kubrick also encouraged Peter Sellers, as Quilty, to improvise the surrealistic scenes he figured in, under several disguises.

All this was in line with Kubrick's views on scripting, which had not changed much over the years. He always tried to get as complete a script as possible before shooting, allowing himself

---

*"I see Annabel in general terms as 'honey-coloured skin,' 'thin arms,' 'brown bobbed hair,' 'long lashes,' 'big bright mouth.'"—*Lolita*, by Vladimir Nabokov

the privilege of changing it as things evolve. The moment the actors began to play the scene was often the only time when the story's fullest possibilities became apparent; and he liked to be flexible enough to take advantage of this. "One has to work out very clearly what the objectives of a scene are from the point of view of narrative and character, but once this is done, I find it much more profitable to avoid locking up any ideas about staging or camera or even dialogue prior to rehearsals. I try to leave enough time between the writing of the script and the working out of the ideas of the scene, and the actual shooting of the scene, so that I can arrive in some way as an observer looking at something that has a degree of freshness to me. It's important to be able to respond to some extent in the way the audience will eventually respond."

Kubrick believed firmly in working out what his actors should do in terms of the scene, not the shot. He would sometimes alter what they did, in order to improve a shot—"but not too often, for things that are arranged for the camera generally result in cliché compositions." In other words, the visual aspect of an acting scene had to take second place to the performances. Since Kubrick learned to work fast on the visual side, and the new techniques already mentioned helped him, it presented no daunting problems for him; he was one of the very few film directors competent to instruct their lighting photographers in the precise effect they want: for a time he held a union card in New York as a lighting cameraman. But always in his work, achievement had to do with content, not effect. "The important thing is not to put the cart before the horse and to set things up for the camera before you've made something happen worth filming."

After *Lolita's* release the partnership with James Harris was amicably ended, for Harris wanted to direct his own films. Kubrick had gone to England to make *Lolita* on account of the funds that the financing company had available in Britain, and Kubrick continued to make his films there. Still, he never considered himself an expatriate American. With his aptitudes and craft rooted in communications media, he found it easy and attractive to keep in contact with the international film scene, and, indeed, with the larger world, from wherever he happened to be. (More often than not, a discussion with him was punctuated by the buzzing of his wristwatch alarm—or his "beeper"—announcing that someone, somewhere, was waiting for a call, or was ready to put in a call to him.)

But the change of work base had deeper effects on Kubrick. He lived in the English countryside, where time, energy, inspiration, and confidence cannot be eroded by too much contact with the world, especially the movie world; this provided him with a highly favorable psychological climate in which to function. His environment respected his privacy. Though he was remote from the Hollywood power struggles, the available mass media facilitated his spectator enjoyment of following these struggles, move by move, without submerging him in them. And finally, it allowed him to initiate action, rather than be on the receiving end of it. All these factors were important for a director determined to keep total control of his movies.

Until he moved even farther into the countryside in the 1980s, Kubrick inhabited a large house with a rambling family look to it, set in semirural Hertfordshire, about a half hour's drive from London. Built in a style of airy yet settled solidity, it suggests his sympathy for a Chekhovian life-style. He worked—until his death—from home. Elstree film studios were near this early residence. Kubrick's third wife is the painter Christiane Harlan, who has exhibited in London galleries and at the Royal Academy.* In the days when she was an actress in her native Germany, she played the frightened girl who is pushed out onto the stage to sing to the troops at the end of *Paths of Glory.* The Kubricks have three children.

From the moment he settled in England, Kubrick's permanent aides were few; one of them was his brother-in-law, another a son-in-law. This sense of a business center running imperceptibly into a family household probably gave Kubrick's creative life the kind of stability that was not easy to find in New York City or Beverly Hills (see page 10, Kubrick and his daughter). The flow of visitors who came by invitation was matched by the flow of films, old and new, sent for him to see in his home cinema —he rarely went to see them in London—and both visitors and films maintained the flow of that essential nourishment for Kubrick: information. Thus his ever-curious intelligence sharpened his protective life-style, while his relatively fixed abode supplied him with time for reflection, for "pondering the choices," which the hectic activity of wheeling and dealing in panicky circumstances denies many other filmmakers.

The Elstree lane he inhabited in the 1960's numbered several mansions with such monastic type names. No monastery had actually stood there but the ambience was appropriate for a man

---

*Kubrick's earlier marriages were to Toba Metz, at the age of eighteen, and later to Ruth Sobotka, a dancer at Balanchine's City Center ballet company, who made a brief appearance in *Killer's Kiss.*

whose style of working and living was to become even more secluded. The life of reflection, information, and stimulation that at any moment could be turned into action may have influenced Kubrick in fixing on some of his more recent film subjects. They came to him by more indirect means than the usual scanning of publishers' galleys for likely properties, they have crystallizing out of his more general concerns, rather than out of any specific need to find a story to do. In particular, they came from the wide diversity of material he read, all bearing on some area of interest. When his attention focused on a particular topic, he devoured all the relevant material he and his aides could lay their hands on. Other things, too, kept feeding his interest: a news item in a paper, a piece of information a friend sent him, a chance conversation with a visitor, a radio report. The phenomenon of finding all kinds of additional information flowing in coincidentally from all sides, like magnetized particles, once some main area of interest has absorbed one's attention, is not an uncommon experience among creative people in the arts or sciences; but Kubrick seemed particularly susceptible to it, perhaps because he arranged his life to facilitate it, and there is no doubt that it was a powerful factor in giving conceptual shape to the final film.

The strong interest he already had in the nuclear impasse was intensified in the early 1960s when he began subscribing to military magazines and other official or semiofficial publications dealing with the subject. "I started out being completely unfamiliar with any of the professional literature in the field of nuclear deterrence. I was at first very impressed with how subtle some of the work was—at least so it seemed, starting out with just a kind of primitive concern for survival and a total lack of any ideas of my *own*. Gradually I became aware of the almost wholly paradoxical nature of deterrence or, as it has been described, the Delicate Balance of Terror. If you are weak, you may invite a first strike. If you are becoming too strong, you may provoke a preemptive strike. If you try to maintain the delicate balance, it's almost impossible to do so because secrecy prevents you from knowing what the other side is doing, and vice versa, ad infinitum. . . ." This is the paradox that, once Kubrick perceived it from his involvement in the subject, inspired *Dr. Strangelove, or How I Learned to Stop Worrying and Love the Bomb* (1964).

More out of an interest in survival, rather than art, he turned to the Institute for Strategic Studies with the request for guidelines on more serious reading. In the course of his inquiries he asked the head of the Institute, Alastair Buchan, if he knew of any worthwhile fiction on the subject. Buchan, Kubrick recalled, mentioned the book on which he subsequently based his film. This was *Red Alert*, a straight suspense thriller by an English author, Peter George, who had been a Royal Air Force navigator. *Red Alert* contained two critical ingredients—a powerful story, which characteristically was what first caught Kubrick's interest, and a brilliant premise. In other words, its plot construction was logically justifiable, and this, to a mind like Kubrick's, rendered it doubly attractive. Even the premise had a Kubrick flavor—the impossibility of constructing a perfect plan, because, inevitably, every foolproof system has its built-in contradiction. Peter George had reasoned that although it is desirable to have a controlled nuclear-deterrent system that cannot be activated by middle-echelon officers, nevertheless a country's leaders cannot be the sole persons with the power to order a nuclear attack; they are far too conspicuous and hence too vulnerable. So the questions at issue were: How many other people were there with the power to issue the "Go" code? Where were they in the chain of command? And were there ways to launch weapons other than as instruments of national policy?

The film bore out the logical consequences of the premise. It took a situation that had been carefully designed to be fail-safe and turned it inside out, so that the man who sent the system wrong did so in a way that prevented others from setting it right again. But Kubrick did not get very far in constructing a serious suspense story for the screen. "As I tried to build the detail for a scene, I found myself tossing away what seemed to me to be very truthful insights because I was afraid the audience would laugh. After a few weeks of this, I realized that these incongruous bits of reality were closer to the truth than anything else I was able to imagine. And it was at this point I decided to treat the story as a nightmare comedy. Following this approach, I found it never interfered with presenting well-reasoned arguments. In culling the incongruous, it seemed to me to be less stylized and more realistic than any so-called serious, realistic treatment, which in fact is more stylized than life itself by its careful exclusion of the banal, the absurd, and the incongruous. In the context of imminent world destruction, hypocrisy, misunderstanding, lechery, paranoia, ambition, euphemism, patriotism, heroism, and even reasonableness can evoke a grisly laugh."*

Through Kubrick's temperament ran a strong fascination with

---

*A paradox borne out again and again by some of the extraordinary moments of nightmarish "comedy" that William Manchester reported in his analysis of the aftermath of the Kennedy assassination in *The Death of a President*.

the nightmare side of existence. He had a willingness to face the catastrophe he suspected to be imminent with an inquiring mind and release the pessimism he felt in savage laughter. Exactly what shaped this outlook is probably impossible to pinpoint precisely. One is tempted to seek its origin in the racial resilience of the Jews, whose historically helpless plight has given rise to some of the world's blackest humor. Kubrick, however, does not incline to this view; and certainly immersion in the film industry offers an artist enough occasions for acquiring a satiric cast of mind without his having to suffer additional persecution on account of his faith!

The world, as Horace Walpole said, is "a comedy to those that think, a tragedy to those that feel." And Kubrick appears to be a product of the creative tension between the two states of mind. On occasion, he spoke of Peter Sellers, who died in 1980, in terms that may very well have applied to himself. "Peter had the most responsive attitude of all the actors I've worked with to the things I think are funny. He was always at his best in dealing with grotesque and horrifying ideas. I've never felt he was as funny in conventional comedy roles; his greatest gift was for the grisly, horrifying areas of humor that other actors wouldn't think playable at all."

Comedy, for Kubrick, made it possible to deal with issues that would be unbearable in any other form. But such an attitude made his position exceedingly complex regarding some of the issues his films raise. Though he created two major films that leave no doubt about his basic attitude to war, he cannot be classified simply as a pacifist. His fascination with the subject also stems from the grotesque, often comic ways that war throws human nature into relief. He saw war as an irrational situation that swiftly forces attitudes out into the open, attitudes that in less critical times might take longer to develop and have to be presented on the screen in more contrived forms. Being the most extreme example of a pathological situation, war holds enormous dramatic attractiveness for Kubrick. The psychotic behavior need not be treated crudely; on the contrary, his films have proved what a wide range of ironic subtleties it is possible to explore. Preferably, though, the grotesque occurrence has a surrounding framework of realistic technical data or conventional social values; these set off the abnormalities of the situation and heighten the behavior of the characters. To keep one foot in nightmare and the other in reality, a director requires a very sure sense of balance. This Kubrick had to an exceptional degree. His skepticism about the upward progress of mankind, which sharpened the barbed pessimism of *Dr. Strangelove,* is linked with his own high regard for reason, logic, and precision—all qualities in dire jeopardy where the malfunctioning human animal is concerned.

The humanist in Kubrick hoped that man will survive his own irrationality; the intellectual in him doubted it. Both attitudes contributed to his choice of space exploration and man's first contact with extraterrestrial forms of life as the subject of his next film, *2001: A Space Odyssey* (1968). But no sooner has the "subject" been thus labeled than one has to qualify it. This is the "subject" as the casual eye might register the events in the film. In fact, Kubrick's chief concern in *2001* was with the concept of intelligence and its transformations. This enormously complex film does not date simply from the time Kubrick and his cowriter, Arthur C. Clarke, began to elaborate the narrative side. *2001* is the product of interests that were engaging Kubrick's attention in the years before a word of the screenplay was put on paper. The concept of communications was one of these.

On the most basic level, communications underpin the whole process of making a film. The organization of his film in the preshooting stage—never mind the task of communicating what he wanted it to say to future audiences during shooting—was a process that stretched every faculty Kubrick possessed. This was often where his team of collaborators felt the going was toughest. Some have formed the impression that shooting the film was actually a relief to Kubrick, for he strove for perfection in every memo, message, order, inquiry, suggestion, and revision he initiated. A man who makes communication a central feature of his working life will very easily extend it into the intellectual concept of his film.

Moreover, one of the additional working tools Kubrick used in recent years has been the computer. It saved him time and enabled him to predict the consequences of apparently equally attractive moves. Doing everything—from adding a column of figures to charting a film's critical-path analysis—the computer gave Kubrick a rational means of dealing with the constrictions of budget and schedule—and more, too. The prospect of programming a computer afforded him the satisfaction of organizing an intelligence fit for his needs—an intelligence without, he hoped, many common human shortcomings. Now a computer that plays a certain role in planning a film can very easily, by one imaginative leap, be cast in a major role *in* a film, especially if the film speculates on the relationship between man's intelligence and the way he has used his tools to embody and extend it. The stages by which HAL 9000 was promoted from a minor func-

tionary in an early draft script of *2001* to being an active protagonist in the finished film are things Kubrick preferred not to discuss. But of the underlying interest which HAL extends to sec-
tions of the film, Kubrick commented, "One of the fascinating
questions that arise in envisioning computers more intelligent
then men is at what point machine intelligence deserves the same
consideration as biological intelligence. Once a computer learns
by experience as well as by its original programming, and once it
has access to much more information than any number of human
geniuses might possess, the first thing that happens is that you
don't really understand it anymore, and you don't know what
it's doing or thinking about. You could be tempted to ask your-
self in what way is machine intelligence any less sacrosanct than
biological intelligence, and it might be difficult to arrive at an
answer flattering to biological intelligence."

With these interests so much a part of his daily activity,
Kubrick's imagination only needed a productive jolt to set it on
course for the "subject" of *2001*. "I had always been surprised at
how little interest anyone seemed to show in the quite
respectable and widely held view by scientists that the universe
was undoubtedly filled with intelligent life. As someone once
quipped, 'Sometimes I think we're alone, and sometimes I think
we're not. In either case, I find the idea quite astonishing.' The
reasons for believing we are not alone are quite compelling. First
of all, from spectrographic analysis of the stars we know the universe is made of the same chemical elements. Recent experiments
have gone a long way to confirming the theory that life was created by random chemical reactions which took place over billions
of years in the primordial soup. Now there are about 150 billion
stars in our galaxy, each star and sun something like our own.
And there are about 150 billion galaxies in the visible universe.
The formation of planets around a star is now thought to be a
common occurrence. So you are left with a staggering number of
possibilities for the formation of planets in stable orbits which are
not too hot and not too cold and from which it can be presumed
that life will eventually arise after a few billion years.

"Eventually biological life forms will develop and one of these
will be as ill-adapted to its environment as it is believed our
ancestors were. To these creatures intelligence will become an
evolutionary survival trait, and a process not entirely unlike our
own should follow. Having physical mediocrity as the sine qua
non for intelligence becoming a survival trait, these creatures will
probably channel their intelligence along the lines of the tool-
weapon culture and they will start on the relatively short road to

modern science. Since the age of the stars in the universe varies by millions of years, it is also reasonable to imagine intelligence far older than their own and possessing capabilities which to us would seem magical, even godlike."

Once this idea was started, the creative process of Dr. *Strangelove* repeated itself. Kubrick let the amassing of scientific data lead him on to a search for meaningful fiction. Arthur C. Clarke's writing supplied it, especially his short story "The Sentinel," which sketched the notion of a cosmic "burglar alarm" placed on the moon by extraterrestrial beings to forewarn them of man's approach.

Kubrick, as we have seen, already shared Clarke's belief in the power of myths and legends to set up echoes in human awareness. From the very start, even when the project was titled *Journey Beyond the Stars*, the pair were concerned to find a term for the film that would replace the overused and imprecise "science fiction." They came up with the word "odyssey"—"a space odyssey," said Clarke at a press conference, "comparable in some ways to the Homeric *Odyssey*." Given all this, it is not surprising that Kubrick cast his film about intelligence in the form of a myth—a "mythological documentary" is the term he was to apply to it—and gradually, unconsciously perhaps, and then with increasing awareness of their potential, drew on his other concerns and interests as he and Clarke developed the screenplay.

But what ultimately made the film unique was Kubrick's gradual perception of the perfect cinematic concept for the film as a nonverbal visual experience, one that would resist neat categorizing by dialogue or narration and, instead, penetrate an audience's consciousness at a deeper and more stimulating level. Most of Kubrick's earlier films had leaned upon the use of some kind of commentary or first-person narration, which he had used, he says, when it seemed necessary to compress and convey information of a kind that cannot easily or realistically be put into dialogue. Narration helped him put this across without having to slog through the conventions of a stage play.

Now, narration, and quite extensive narration, too, did exist in one early script for *2001*, dated mid-1965, some six months before shooting began. Most of it was in the "Dawn of Man" prologue. Yet the first words spoken in the finished film do not come until well after this sequence, and in all, there are only about forty minutes of dialogue. The early difficulty that narration presented was that to make the events remotely comprehensible to people with little scientific knowledge would require too much spoken commentary. Then, as he made the film, it came to Kubrick that words were actually working against the visual experience he wanted to convey. Kubrick had engaged Douglas Rain, a Canadian actor, to speak some narration for the film. But he kept postponing this as the conviction hardened that a nonverbal approach was the only appropriate one. Eventually, when Rain's contract was about to expire, Kubrick asked him, instead of supplying narration, to rerecord a part that had already been spoken by another actor, with not entirely satisfactory results. The part was that of the computer, HAL 9000. It proved one of the best choices Kubrick has ever made.

Not counting the time spent on preparing the screenplay, *2001* still took about two and a half years to make: six months of preshooting activity, four and a half months of filming with the cast, a year and a half working on the 205 separate special-effects shots. It absorbed the efforts of a vast team of technicians. And, characteristically, Kubrick took great pains to justify the elements in the film; consultations were held with nearly seventy industrial and aerospace corporations, universities, observatories, weather bureaus, laboratories, and other institutions, to ensure that the forecast of life in space in A.D. 2001 was based on information that already existed or could be predicted. The budget, originally six million dollars, escalated to ten and a half million. The reason for this was that the repertoire of special-effects techniques was inadequate to produce the shots needed, and equipment had to be designed and built, techniques experimented with, and all of this in an expensive film studio, rather than a factory or a laboratory. Obviously, budgetary increases resulted. But the film's profitability continues to grow. So does its extraordinary power to win adherents among the young—not by any means all from the "hippie" subculture so fond of the film's reputed (and overstressed) hallucinogenic properties. Many of the critics who at first failed to appreciate the film were later converted when, as Joseph Gelmis put it, "understanding became a function of the emotions, rather than one's reasoning powers."

Considering the scale of *2001* and his success in fulfilling his ambitions in making the picture, it was hardly a surprise when Kubrick announced in 1969 that the subject of his next film was going to be Napoleon. This film has not yet been made. The main preparation for it had been completed and a general staff of historians and researchers had supplied every relevant detail of what was envisaged as a huge canvas encompassing all the major events in the Emperor's life when the project was suddenly canceled for financial reasons. Hollywood's financial crisis of the late 1960s had shattered the confidence of some film companies as to their ability to commit themselves to a large-scale film, especially at a time when the small, youth-oriented picture was in vogue.

Fortunately, the disappointment over having to put off *Napoleon* until more propitious times did not last long. Almost on the rebound, Kubrick found the subject of his next film. The old self-responsive process led him to Anthony Burgess's novel *A Clockwork Orange*. First published in 1962, *A Clockwork Orange* deals with the future, an area that Kubrick made very much his own on the screen. The novel has been called the most cogent and terrifying vision of things to come since George Orwell's *Nineteen Eighty-four*. Like that book, it cloaks its prophecy about society's evolution in a good story—a persistent attraction for Kubrick. It takes the form of a nightmarish thriller narrated with vivid directness by Alex, the teenage antihero, whose generation of young hoodlums fraternizes in its own private language, called "Nadsat," and takes over society after dark, terrorizing town and country. Beneath the violence, though, the aim is satirical and even didactic. Burgess extrapolates a feature of contemporary life into the near future, certainly a couple of decades short of 2001, and exaggerates it in a savage, Swiftian way so as to reflect a distorted yet recognizable image of ourselves. Despite the stridently "pop" tone of the first-person narrative, the theme is a Christian one: redemption. The premise implied by the odd title is that it is far better for an individual to possess free will, even if it is exclusively the will to sin, than for him to be made over into a clockwork paradigm of virtue.

Seized by the State police after a particularly grisly bout of thuggery, Alex undergoes the "Ludovico Treatment," a savage system of aversion shock-therapy that reconditions his responses and turns him into a model but mindless citizen—in short, a "clockwork orange"; a mechanized being who only appears to be organic.

The interlocking ironies of humans who act like machines and a machine that is almost human have been already deeply implanted in *Dr. Strangelove* and *2001: A Space Odyssey*. And the overlapping "areas of interest" do not end there. Alex's fate continues Kubrick's concern with the ambiguous nature of science, whose capacity to enhance life is contrasted with the misuse men make of it to circumscribe freedom and even extinguish existence. The theme has the intellectual excitement Kubrick found stimulating; in giving shape to Alex's world, the imaginative possibilities—a sex-obsessed yet loveless society filled with the tensions created by the amoral young, their hostile but listless elders, and the repressive zeal of the authorities—were just the kind he could rework meaningfully in his own way. One of the problems confronting him was how to take an evildoer like Alex, who knows no remorse and experiences no love, for whom girls are simply objects to rape with "the old in-out-in-out," and turn him into someone who inspires pity, in the same way he evoked sympathy for HAL once the avenging astronaut had dehumanized what ought not to have been considered human in the first place.

Kubrick and Burgess shared the same involvement in what is perhaps the most ingenious feature of this novel: its creation of a teenager language, Nadsat, whose abusive terminology runs like a vocal manifesto of violence through Alex's unrepentant chronicle, giving it a quality of absolute and unashamed candor. Here, for example, is Alex's commentary on his arrest by the police: "All the time we were sirening off to the rozz-shop, me being wedged between two millicents and being given the old thump and malenky tolchock by these smecking bullies. Then I found I could open up my glaz-lids a malenky bit and viddy like through all tears a kind of streamy city going by, all the lights like having run into one another. . . . I knew I was going to get nothing like fair play from these stinky grahzny bratchnies, Bog blast them." Becoming easily intelligible through context and repetition, this language has the same purpose as the hypersophisticated whorls and loops of Humbert Humbert's erotic syntax in *Lolita:* it establishes a precise tonal connection between the hero and the audience. It continues the preoccupation with language that was noted earlier in the euphemisms of nuclear strategists, the professional offhandedness of the moon scientists, the paranoid officialese or bigoted malapropisms of the military mind in *Dr. Strangelove;* in short, Nadsat brought Kubrick back to "the magic of words," the ways of using vocabulary and locutions to show attitudes of mind and project states of heightened, sometimes irrational experience. Nadsat fulfills the same purpose. Its vocabulary is not without logic, but is derived from such roots as Russian, Gypsy argot, Cockney rhyming slang, portmanteau words, baby talk connoting a reversion to womblike pleasure, and onomatopoeic expressions that sound like the violence they describe. This "justification" for a language that at first seems baffling must have been an attractive feature to Kubrick.

The shooting schedule lasted through the winter of 1970–71. Kubrick used a compact and extremely mobile crew, for virtually all of the film was shot on location in and around London or at an old factory converted into a production headquarters and ad hoc studio. He made use of a conventional film studio for only a day or two, in order to shoot some special effects. Technically, this spareness seemed to signal a return to the stripped-down conditions of *Killer's Kiss*—with, of course, a much larger budget—and in the cutting Kubrick was engaged in finding out about the film he had shot and, by extension, about himself. The curiosity that served him in place of a need for community was the most driving part of his nature today. What he discovered and formulated into an experience became the film *A Clockwork Orange*.

As ever, Kubrick preferred to leave the film as the only real comment he could make on his work. The answers he gave to series of questions in an interview with this author in the spring of 1971 may not bear directly on *A Clockwork Orange*, the work then in progress. But they do indicate accurately how his self-scrutiny was linked in his mind with the process of creation. They reveal with almost painful honesty his refusal to argue from a preconceived theme or theory; they also show his fascination with the technical evolution of his craft as well as his consistent subordination of techniques to the need to communicate with people, hold their attention, and gratify their curiosity without abandoning his own vision. They confirm important aspects of his outlook and method; they convey information that may assist fledgling filmmakers, and do so with an evident honesty of self-response. They deserve quotation as evidence of the continuous process of exploration, hesitation, and conviction that makes Kubrick a major artist.

Walker: What attracted you to the subject? What do you hope to achieve with the film?

Kubrick: These are the questions I always find impossible to answer. I believe that the questions are asked with the hope of getting a specific answer like "This is the story of a man's search for his own identity," or any number of similar replies ranging from middle- to high-brow, with or without social conscience. I don't want to sound pretentious or cranky, but I think questions like that can only produce a reply which is either gimmicky or irrelevant. It comes down to about as much as saying, "*Hamlet* is about a man who couldn't make up his mind." Somehow, the question also presumes that one approaches a film with something resembling a policy statement, or a one-sentence theme, and that the film proceeds upwards like some inverted pyramid. Maybe some people work this way, but I don't, and even though you obviously have some central preoccupation with the subject, somehow when you're telling a story (and I know this sounds trite, but it's true anyway) the characters and the story develop a life of their own, and, as you go along, your central preoccupation merely serves as a kind of yardstick to measure the relevancy of what the imagination produces.

I also think that it spoils a great deal of the pleasure of the film for anyone who happens to have been unfortunate enough to have read what the filmmaker "has in mind." As a member of the audience, I particularly enjoy those subtle discoveries where I wonder whether the filmmaker himself was even aware that they were in the film, or whether they happened by accident. I'm sure that there's something in the human personality which resents things that are clear, and, conversely, something which is attracted to puzzles, enigmas, and allegories.

Walker: How deeply are you involved in the administration when you make a film like *A Clockwork Orange*—or indeed any of your films?

Kubrick: I am deeply involved in the administration, because it is in this area that many creative and artistic battles are lost. You've got to have what you want, where you want it, and at the right time, and you have got to use your resources (money and people) in the most effective way possible because they are limited, and when they are seriously stretched it always shows on the screen. Because I have to be, I am very interested in organizational problems, and the conclusion that I have come to is that the making of a film is one of the most difficult organizational and administrative problems to exist outside of a military operation. Running a business is unfortunately never a useful analogy because the key to the successful operation of all businesses is the establishment of routine and the breaking down of jobs into simple, definable, understandable functions which can be performed by normally adequate people.

Whereas in films almost everything is a "one-of" problem, it is almost impossible to establish a routine, and the work done is so diversified that if it were to be broken down as in a manufacturing process, you would need ten times as many people, which you could not afford.

Filmmaking violates the old adage that what is wanted is a system designed by geniuses which can be run by idiots. It has always been the other way round with films. However, I keep trying and keep coming up with new systems, new means of displaying information, remembering, reminding, following up. I risk my popularity with some of my department heads by continually pressing home the point that merely giving an order to somebody is only a fraction of their job, that their principal

Man having his responses mechanically conditioned: Malcolm McDowell (with his director) begins the grueling scene in A Clockwork Orange *where Alex, the young thug, is given the Ludovico Treatment to turn him into a model citizen.*

responsibility is to see that the order is carried out accurately, on time, and within the budget.

Walker: Can you give me an example of some of the systems you used in *A Clockwork Orange*, on the production side—to find locations, say, in a country to which you are a relative stranger?

Kubrick: Apart from all the normal procedures you'd expect your art department or production office to come up with, such as going out and looking, it seemed a logical idea on *A Clockwork Orange*, since it was necessary to find modern architectural locations, to go through the appropriate magazines and literature. I purchased ten years of back issues of three different architectural magazines and spent two solid weeks with my art director, John Barry, turning and tearing out pages. The material was put into a special display file, manufactured by a company in Germany,

(Left) As in his first film, so in his latest, Stanley Kubrick supervises every detail personally.

(Below left) Trapped by the Cat Woman wielding a bust of Beethoven, Alex counterattacks with a gigantic sculptured phallus. Kubrick spent most of a day filming the bizarre duel, much of it with a camera hand-held by himself (seated at left), moving round and round with the weaving, thrusting combatants in furious 360-degree circles until they almost collapsed from exhaustion.

(Below right) Kubrick, behind the cone of lights, prepares the sequence in A Clockwork Orange *where Alex and the Cat Woman (Miriam Karlin, on the right) fight to the death.*

called Definitiv. The system encompassed various signals, colored, alphabetical, and numerical, which were displayed when the file was hanging in a rack. These signals allowed the material to be cross-referenced in almost an infinite number of ways.

Walker: I am sure you know how much time and trouble some filmmakers put into the credit titles of their films. With your emphasis on the visual, how do you feel about this?

Kubrick: I never worry about the main titles. I have seen some very clever ones which I have admired, but I think that clever main titles are just a waste of money and a disservice to the film. I have a very simple-minded point of view, in that the first shot of the film should be the most interesting thing that the audience has seen since it sat down. In addition to winning the audience back from the credits to the "anticlimax" of the film itself, clever titles mean animation, trick effects, opticals, and usually a very expensive designer; and this means they cost a fair amount of money. I would rather put the money into the film itself.

Walker: It seems to me you approach the task of editing your films with as much involvement as, if not more than, the actual shooting, is this so?

Kubrick: I love editing. I think I like it more than any other phase of filmmaking. If I wanted to be frivolous, I might say that everything that precedes editing is merely a way of producing film to edit.

Editing is the only unique aspect of filmmaking which does not resemble any other art form—a point so important it cannot be overstressed. (I know I've already stressed it!) It can make or break a film.

The basic equipment I use is two Steenbeck editing tables and a Moviola. I use the two Steenbecks for selection, and by having two of them I can continuously look at the film without waiting for the last roll to be taken off and replaced by another. I don't feel too guilty about having the two Steenbecks, because their combined rental cost is only a small fraction of the daily interest charges which exist on the production loan of even a small film during the editing phase of a production. I find the Steenbeck marvelous for selection. It allows the fast-forward and reverse and runs very quietly at normal speed. But for the actual cutting of the film and the handling of small bits of film, the Moviola is far superior, for all of its noisy, clattery, old-fashioned self.

When I am editing, I work seven days a week. In the beginning I work ten hours a day, and then as we get closer to the deadlines I usually push that up to fourteen or sixteen hours a day.

Walker: You have shot virtually all of *A Clockwork* Orange on location. Can you tell me what special equipment you made use of?

Kubrick: There is some marvelous sound, lighting, and camera equipment available today which makes it possible to shoot anywhere on location without suffering any disadvantage in comparison with working in a studio. This means that one can benefit from realistic surroundings and cut costs significantly.

Specifically, on the photographic side, one now has lightweight fiberglass blimps which allow hand-held sound takes, ultrafast lenses (f. 0.95) which permit shooting under extremely low light levels, and extremely wide-angle lenses (9.8 millimeter) which allow long shots in even the most confined rooms.

Sound recording has traditionally been the reason why people have thought it necessary to work within the soundproof walls of a film studio. But sound technology has advanced more strikingly than any other technical side of filmmaking. Aside from lightweight portable sound recorders which can be slung over a shoulder (formerly a sound truck with a man inside served the same purpose), there is a diverse range of microphones which allow excellent recordings to be made under the worst conditions. We had a scene in *A Clockwork Orange* that took place under the Albert Bridge. The traffic noise was so loud that you had to raise your voice just to be heard in a conversation, but with the aid of a Sennheiser Mk. 12 microphone no larger than a paper clip, stuck into an actor's lapel, it was possible to produce a sound track which had only a very pleasant hum of activity in the background.

As for lighting, I should say that eighty-five percent of *A Clockwork Orange* was lit either by replacing normal light bulbs in existing lighting fixtures with photo floods, or by the use of very lightweight Lowell 1,000-watt quartz lights, bounced off either ceilings or special reflective umbrellas. At other times it was necessary to use brute arcs for which there is no substitute when large expanses have to be lit at night, or when a one-source light effect has to be achieved in a large interior.

Style and Content

Without *Fear and Desire* and *Spartacus*—the one film an initial practice piece and the other an assignment picture he virtually disowned—each of the films of Stanley Kubrick has a strong, unifying aspect. But it would be rash to say that all of them bear witness to strong, unifying themes. Kubrick clearly did not work thematically, with deliberate intent, from one picture to the next. He worked by discovery. He worked by accidentally happening on a subject, usually one with the lure of a good story; then, by pondering the problems and possibilities it offered for development, he conceptualized a way of telling the story in film terms that fit it with imaginative precision.

He also worked by "surprise," in the sense that Cocteau has used the word. And Cocteau borrowed it from Diaghilev, a creative autocrat, in some respects like Kubrick, who employed it in the impresario's challenge, *"Etonne-moi."* Kubrick guarded the element of surprise, of revelation, in his films, for his own sake as well as the audience's. He wanted the unfolding films to surprise *him*, too, which is why he avoided saying much about them before they were made. Prior discussion might exhaust the power of suggestive thinking, just as deciding a camera setup too early could curtail the development of a scene.

Even on a film like *Spartacus,* where he was not only a hired hand but a tied one, he was able to convey an unmistakable sense of his own fascination with the possibilities the film had, but which were never realized in Dalton Trumbo's banal and sentimentalized script. Significantly, these moments occur where the script merely indicates action—and where the action ties up the star, to the director's distinct advantage. One such scene permitted Kubrick to deal with the techniques of gladiatorial training and the scientific emphasis on reducing men to being efficient killing machines. Others occur in the battlefield perspectives at the end; resting his camera on an Olympian cloud, Kubrick surveys the rival armies of Romans and Spartacists with a detached, aesthetic appreciation that anticipates his later fascination with the order, precision, and lethal beauty of Napoleon's maneuvers in classical warfare.

Much that is integral to Kubrick's movies comes from the way his compulsive curiosity pushes radically different subjects into his own areas of interest. Perhaps *Killer's Kiss* came low in his own estimation because it reflected so few of his later interests. But it is an oddly compelling work that tells much about the young Kubrick and explains why he stirred up immediate critical notice. The story, as he has said, was deliberately built around surefire action sequences. Yet what critics sensed as novel in this modest film were precisely those moments of rest when nothing visibly happens on the screen, but Kubrick's camera (operated by himself) brings people or objects into meaningful relationship and seems to make everything "happen." The young boxer, at the start as captive as his own goldfish in the bowl in his dingy tenement room, sits out the last hour or two before his big fight; across the courtyard a lighted window reveals a girl getting ready for her night's stint at some treadmill job. One life can look through the New York darkness into another life, yet the two lighted squares of glass only emphasize the couple's apartness. They are unaware of each other to the point of invisibility, each self-isolated, virtually imprisoned in lives that are soon revealed as humiliating and hopeless.

What is immediately evident is Kubrick's talent for lighting and photographing a scene so as to abstract its latent emotional value. He trusted to the power of the lens to crystallize moods and confer values on objects. *Killer's Kiss* has more shots of objects with affective associations, like the mental inventory that the hero makes of the girl's bedroom while she sleeps, than any later Kubrick film. It is an accomplishment that clearly derives from his years as a photojournalist. *He* was quickly and increasingly to make it serve his attitudes to events in a film, not substitute for them. Perhaps a lingering connection with the magazine photo-essay later made him disparage his achievement in *Killer's Kiss. He* was soon to insist that style is attitude, not applied photography.

The other striking feature of the film is its tone, one of urban loneliness, almost melancholy. Its three main characters—Davy, the boxer; Gloria, the girl; and Rapallo, a brutish dance-hall owner infatuated by her—are people defeated by life.

Lighting and grouping: Kubrick establishes character
and mood by using sharply defined areas of
illumination and shadow to set people in relation to
their environment or to each other—(left to right) the
boxer's loneliness in Killer's Kiss; the husband's
subservience to his wife in The Killing; The Killing's
criminals huddled together in conspiracy (see General
Ripper "lost" in his own fantasy of Communist
conspiracy in Dr. Strangelove, page 131); Humbert
Humbert's fearful isolation in a motel room.

Professional failure, family tragedy, a kink of nature have them
trapped. Davy's career is on the skids; Gloria's life as a dance-hall
hostess is a kind of penance for her sister's suicide; Rapallo's
slightly sadistic passion turns to crazed despair when Gloria
walks out on him, and he is driven to kidnap her. Beaten people
in the penumbra of the underworld, they foreshadow the gang of
small-time crooks taking their last chance to make it big in
Kubrick's next film, *The Killing.*

But *Killer's Kiss* adds a dimension of poetry to its characters'
desperation by the way it interlocks their fates. While an action-
thriller on the surface—fast, violent, charged with suspense
and physical climax—its undertones are as disturbing and
omnipresent as one of those self-fulfilling curses laid on the vir-
tuous characters in a German folk tale from the brothers Grimm.
The story readily resolves itself into the archetypal fable of a
maiden rescued by a valorous knight from the clutches of an ogre
whose obsessive love for her she cannot return. And the impression of a fable is strengthened by an extraordinary sequence in
which the girl tells Davy her life story; this is a harrowing tale of
Gloria's devotion to a sister who trades her gift as a ballet dancer
to marry a rich man and support her father, and who kills herself
after her father's death, since she has nothing left to live for. As
Gloria tells what amounts to a complete short story, Kubrick's

camera shows the sister (played by Kubrick's second wife, Ruth Sobotka) dancing a sad, haunting *pas seul* before an unseen audience. By the laws of logic, Gloria's flashback has no right to be in *Killer's Kiss* at all, for throughout the film it is supposed to be Davy who is telling the story in flashback. It was put in, says Kubrick, to add interest to Gloria's character and also as a tribute to his wife's talent. Yet it works poetically in the traditional way that a character in a folk tale or fairy story can embellish the tale by embarking on his own narrative within the framework of the main tale.

Kubrick referred at times to his early love of fables and fairy tales; and his belief in the energizing power of myth to work on our unconscious or touch the memory trace of our race finds a place in several of his movies. It is implicit in the whole concept of *2001;* and to discern its early manifestation in *Killer's Kiss* is not overfanciful. It even shows up in *Lolita,* itself based on a novel by a writer powerfully attracted by the creative force of myth and legend. Indeed, *Lolita's* story of a girl abducted from her true lover by a wicked ogre has a slight but eerie similarity to *Killer's Kiss*. Humbert Humbert driving to Quilty's mansion, vengeance-bound at the start, emerges out of a ground mist that might have drifted over from German legend. "I pushed the front door," Nabokov writes at this point, "and, how nice, it swung open as in a medieval fairytale." Kubrick follows to the letter a novelist's direction that was so congenial to his own temperament and, how nice, even improves on it by permitting a glimpse of Quilty's home, with its machicolated roof like that of an enchanter's castle.

Something else seems to connect *Killer's Kiss* with this insubstantial world of suggestion. Its actual events of boy meeting girl, girl being abducted, boy getting her back again, cover at least a few days—and Kubrick's early skill in editing turns them into a tight, dynamic story; yet all seem to happen within the ambiguous time span of a dream that may have lasted only a few min-

Realism in lighting: *Kubrick's early preference for light that comes from a natural source, generally an overhead lamp, is simple and brutal in effect. From left to right, pictures 1, 3, and 4 are from* The Killing; *picture 2 from* Killer's Kiss. *The meeting that takes place directly under this source of light, which increases the sense of confrontation, is a favorite Kubrick composition. (See* Paths of Glory, *page 75.)*

utes or a few hours. Davy, at one point, has a premonitory dream, or nightmare, which the camera records by traveling down straight, endless streets photographed in negative, the onward impetus recalling the low-flying B-52s' mission of destruction in the last reels of *Dr. Strangelove* and the cosmic ride in *2001*. Dawn, dusk, and darkness, the times when one is most aware of one's loneliness, are used by the director-photographer to light his moods as well as his locations. And the fatalistic sense of trouble that comes from involvement with total strangers is fixed almost tangibly in this world where it is either nighttime or else light is just breaking or just fading.

Kubrick's handling of action is also masterly. The sequence of Davy being chased by Rapallo's men begins with the boxer dwarfed by perpendicular blocks of riverside warehouses, like a mouse in search of a hole; the camera rises with him as he scales a fire escape, and the chase again becomes horizontal as Davy scuttles round the perimeter of a vast expanse of rooftop. Kubrick keeps his camera immobile, watching him, catlike. The subsequent fight between him and Rapallo reveals Kubrick's early flair for the grotesque. Boxer and gangster confront each other in a bizarre, cramped storeroom full of naked and partly dismembered tailor's dummies. They lunge at each other—Rapallo with an ax, Davy with a pike—but sometimes each repels the other

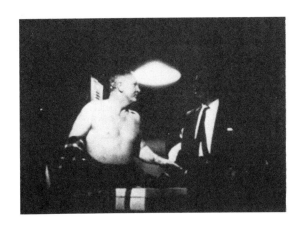

with a fusillade of limbs and torsos. The sense of amputation that
surrounds the men conveys a savage suggestion of what such
jousting may do to *their* bodies, while the impassive nudity of the
dummies contrasts with the sweaty, panting desperation of the
humans.

Halfway through *Killer's Kiss* is a sequence that rewards
detailed analysis. It is the murder of the boxer's manager by
Rapallo's henchmen, who have mistaken him for Davy. Here is
early evidence that Kubrick can build a sequence like a chess
game; one move determines the next, and that one a still later
move, until out of a coolly manipulated consecutive structure
there is created a cumulative menace.

Davy is waiting outside the dance hall for Gloria to join him
with her final paycheck; then they aim to leave New York for
good. Suddenly, by a quirk of fate, two drunken conventioneers
playfully filch the boxer's scarf, and he takes off after them in
their clownish retreat up the street. Meanwhile his manager
appears, having arranged to bring over Davy's share of the earn-
ings from his last fight. He stations himself against one half of the
plate-glass door leading to the dance hall, and waits for his
friend. Gloria, after an angry, inconclusive interview with
Rapallo, comes down the stairs and, not finding Davy, takes up
her stance against the other half of the door. She and the manager
do not know each other. Kubrick's camera looks obliquely down
at their backs from the top of the inside staircase. One of
Rapallo's henchmen descends the stairs to tell Gloria, in dumb
show through the glass, that her boss wants another word with
her; actually, it is just a trick to get her out of the way while he
and a buddy rough Davy up. The camera is still at the top of the
stairs as Gloria reenters the lobby. WATCH YOUR STEP, says a notice
suspended over the steep staircase—a touch Kubrick swore was
already a feature of the location he used. As Gloria passes the
camera we see that the henchman has taken her place outside, his

back to the plate glass, beside the unsuspecting manager; he has, of course, been mistaken for Davy and will soon be beaten to death out of sight up a back alley while his giant frightened shadow is seen writhing expressionistically on the alley wall.

This smooth manipulation of the action, pure movement without a word spoken in our hearing, has a preconceived pattern and a tense symmetry that characterize moments of climax in later Kubrick films. It directly anticipates the very last shot of *The Killing;* the armed FBI men advance with synchronized caution toward the robber, who stands, his will for flight paralyzed, outside the airport's plate-glass doors, which the agents proceed to open in balletic unison. Kubrick's camera has already an impulse to seek order and balance in what it frames as a visual equivalent of the mechanistic way that human behavior interlocks and settles people's fates.

The Killing attracted Kubrick both for the good story it tells and for the test of telling it. Other features, too, made it ideal for his temperament. It is the story of a racetrack robbery which takes Time—abstract and capitalized—and reorders it as the plot

Composition in depth: In moments of crisis in his films, Kubrick tends to compose his action in depth, framing it in narrow but natural confines. The boxer, pursued by the gang in Killer's Kiss, *runs toward the stationary camera through the "bolt holes" of New York's back streets. (See Colonel Dax's purposive march through the trenches, advancing into a highly mobile camera, in* Paths of Glory, *pages 78–79, to lead his men over the top and into battle; and the astronaut in* 2001: A Space Odyssey, *page 172–173.) But the hero is usually speedily diminished again by his environment, whether a battlefield or . . .*

dwells on the different parts of the robbery assigned to each of the gang. It is like playing chess against the clock, for the robbery has to be carried out within very tight limits of time, precisely within the start and finish of the seventh race, the $100,000 Lansdowne Stakes, at one mile. Actually, the limits are extended a little. The gang gains time by shooting down the favorite horse in mid-race, thus delaying the payout to bettors and giving Johnny, the ringleader, an additional few minutes to hold up the cash office. But the sense of action synchronized against measurable time (and distance: one mile) is deftly conveyed, projected into the events so accurately that one can tell to the half-minute when the racehorse hits the turf with a bullet in its flank.

Yet all perfect plans are only as foolproof as the people who execute them. Humbert Humbert in *Lolita*, thinking wishfully of his wife's demise, reflects, "No man can bring about the perfect murder: chance alone can do it." In Humbert's case, chance co-operates to an ironic degree, but in most cases it frustrates the grand design. It is characteristic of Kubrick that while one part of him pays intellectual tribute to the rationally constructed master plan, another part reserves the skeptic's right to anticipate human imperfections or the laws of chance that militate against its success. Kubrick, for example, praised the novelist Peter George, who coauthored the screenplay of *Dr. Strangelove*, for inferring the premise on which the nuclear fail-safe system must be based: that there must be people other than the ones in the top echelons of command who know the "Go" code. But once this premise is noted, it suggests an inherent human weakness in the system; and it is this weakness that *Dr. Strangelove* exploits so savagely.

Moreover, accurate prediction is an essential part of the film-making process, particularly in the preproduction stages. It is one into which Kubrick put fanatical effort. His films, as has already been noted, have used computers in the planning stages, to determine, among much else, the critical-path analysis of the projected

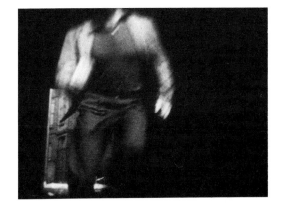

. . . the skyline of warehouse roofs.

film. So it is no wonder that the "perfect plan," whether it has to do with criminal conspiracy to rob a racetrack, with nuclear strategy, or with film production, occupies so much of a mind already intellectually absorbed by it. Of course, the computer that goes wrong, as HAL 9000 does in *2001*, is only the most sophisticated example of an old human mistrust in perfection. *The Killing* is the first Kubrick film to make this interest dramatically apparent. It is constructed on a parallel pattern. While a "flawless" scheme is pushed forward step by predetermined step, at the same time chance, accident, and irrational forces lodged in its executors are bringing about its failure.

The viewer realizes the film's full cinematic originality only when the racetrack robbery begins. Instead of crosscutting between the parts of the raid that are overlapping in time, Kubrick films one part as it is carried to its climax, then puts the clock back several hours and takes another part to *its* climax. At 2:30 p.m. on the day of the race, for example, the massive wrestler hired to stage a brawl in the betting area leaves his chess club, after making arrangements for his coming spell in jail; at 4:23 p.m. precisely, with cops clinging to every limb, he is dragged away while Johnny is given the chance to slip unobserved into the now unguarded cash office. Then we flashback to 11:40 a.m. that same day, as the hired marksman leaves his farm, arrives at the track, brings down the favorite at 4:23½ p.m. exactly, only to be lying dead himself at 4:24 p.m., when the tire of his getaway car is punctured by a "lucky" horseshoe—the first of those chance accidents—and a policeman shoots him. We flashback to 2:15 p.m. that afternoon, and Johnny's story is taken to its climax as he holds up the cash office wearing a rubber clown's mask—another bizarre Kubrick touch—and throws a kit bag

52

stuffed with bills through the window. Not till the raid is all over and the crooks are assembled, waiting for the payout, do we learn what happened to the loot after this point. "Nobody saw the bag come through the window," says one of the gang, a venal cop, and a brief, laconic flashback shows him stowing it away in his waiting patrol car. It has the conclusive force of perfect logic.

The parts of the film before and after the raid have their particular style, too. Instead of using the dynamic cutting and the multiple cliff-hangers of the central episode, the members of the gang are introduced in vignettes that fit together like jigsaw pieces, until the larger plan of which they are part begins to emerge. These scenes are written like good memoranda; they look simple, but they say much. As well as establishing motives—a sick wife, gambling debts, a man's need to gain status in the eyes of his trampish wife—they hint at weaknesses in character or relationships that will bring the whole scheme down. The trampish wife, for instance, weasels the plan out of her husband and blabs it all to her boyfriend, a rival hood; he, in turn, stages his own "killing," which goes fatally wrong and leaves nearly everyone full of lead, stiffening almost visibly like wet cement sacks on the floor of the dingy living room where he has ambushed them before the share-out.

Kubrick's often repeated "corridor" compositions: the hallway of the dance hall, where a murder is lined up by one precise move after another; and the nightmare street ride taken by the sleeping boxer, both in Killer's Kiss. *(See the astronaut's psychedelic ride down the space corridor in* 2001: A Space Odyssey, *page 175;* Mandrake's walk down the hall in Dr. Strangelove, *page 147; and the next page.)*

A director like John Huston, involved in the loyalties of the furtive underworld he exposed in *The Asphalt Jungle,* would probably pay respect to the courage of men of action, even when they are criminals. He might allow all of them some individual decency in death. Not Kubrick. His criminals are as human as Huston's, and even more subtly individualized, but he stays detached, cynical. Like a psychologist supervising a devilishly constructed maze, he knows it does not pay to get too fond of the rats. The sense of detachment is underlined by the use of a disembodied narrator to introduce each conspirator and tell us who he is, what he does, and also the day, the hour, sometimes even the minute, of some action or encounter involving his part of the master plan. He keeps temporal tabs on his characters and ticks off the countdown with fateful precision. In this, one hears the echo of *The March of Time* technique—so aptly named in this case—which Louis de Rochement extended into feature films like *The House on 92nd Street* and *Naked City.*

It may be pertinent to note that Kubrick's first short, *Day of the Fight,* was deliberately aimed at the same market as *The March of Time.* Of course, his fondness for narrative exposition cannot be explained this simply. Kubrick, it is worth remembering, belongs to a pretelevision generation whose sense of drama was still shaped to some degree by the aural impact of radio. Narration is a strong identity mark of his films. It is one way, as he once

Depth and symmetry: *the horses' stalls in* The Killing; *Humbert Humbert observing the mysterious car that always keeps an unsettling distance from him and Lolita; the the marksman's targets in* The Killing, *popping bizarrely up at the start of a sequence; the last shot in the same film, showing FBI men advancing in synchronized motion on the beaten crook as the targets come to life.*

remarked, of cutting directly through stage convention and conveying essential information without tedious use of dialogue or other expository scenes. One grants him this. Yet the narration, usually brief and resonant with foreboding even when it has a ticker-tape succinctness, as in *The Killing*, is like an aural note he strikes to which he tunes the rest of the film. It teases the expectations of an audience by the intimations of menace, mystery, or doom, as in the opening phrases of *Dr. Strangelove.*

The casting and acting in *The Killing* mark an impressive advance from *Killer's Kiss*. Not that the latter is badly acted. Kubrick really underrated it when he referred to the slightly "zombielike quality" conferred on the acting by postsynching. His own ear was too well tuned to let him do a botched job. With the exception of Frank Silvera, as Rapallo, the members of the cast of *Killer's Kiss* do not do much evident "acting," but they have the right weight and quality for the small-time people they portray. In *The Killing* the casting was more ambitious, and the partnership with James Harris provided more cash to pay some of Hollywood's sturdiest character actors. The lived in faces of the aging crooks—the only young, virile figure is, significantly, the rival hood—need only an overhead lamp bulb and the simplest of camera setups to give a contour of reality to scene after scene. And the dialogue by Jim Thompson, author of thrillers about desperate, obsessed people, like *The Getaway* and *The Killer Inside Me*, provides Kubrick with openings into character that his camera can enlarge revealingly. From a man who starts off boasting that criminals are artists admired for their daring, Sterling Hayden, as Johnny, adroitly scales himself down into a deflated dummy as he sees his suitcase full of dollar bills upset at the airport by one of the film's chance accidents, involving a runaway lapdog—the least successful "accident" because it is seen coming a long way off—and the loot being blown literally out of his grasp in a blizzard of money. Best of all the players is Elisha

Cook, Jr., as the little racetrack clerk desperate to impress his shrewish mate, and Marie Windsor, who plays his wife. Kubrick, with *Lolita* to come, is already very much at home with this kind of pathetic infatuation. A whole marriage is laid bare as the cheap, worthless wife peels off her false eyelashes in front of her husband as unconcernedly as if they were her gloves. Their relationship could be the subject for an entire film. From Kubrick, it draws only a subjective note, when his camera, after dispassionately scanning the bodies of the men killed in the gangster's ambush, adopts the unsteady viewpoint of Cook lurching across the room homeward bound, mortally wounded, to wipe out his treacherous wife. For a moment or two, we have left the privileged enclosure of all-knowing, all-seeing observers and become

The time element: simultaneous events in time in The Killing. *Kubrick "puts back the clock" as each portion of the racetrack robbery reaches climax, and begins again on the next. Repeated shot of dray horses hauling the starting gate into position provides a time check or an "edge" to each cliff-hanger episode: the brawl at the bar (top right) which keeps the cops preoccupied as the marksman (middle right) prepares to shoot down the favorite horse, thus delaying the payout and giving Johnny (bottom right), in his bizarre clown's disguise, the necessary time to hold up the pay office. Repeated shots also occur in* Paths of Glory *(see pages 73, 77), where Kubrick shows the simultaneous lives being led in trench and château by giving the action of the former, cutting to binoculars through which the general is looking at this action, then coming back and enclosing the general's world with more action in the trenches, which, in turn, leads into the binocular framing again.* Dr. Strangelove's *action (pages 128–131) happens in three distinct locations, War Room, B-52, and air base, each remote in space from the other, but all linked by the temporal continuity of events until the final H-bomb blasts, triggered by the Doomsday Machine, unite them in an overall apocalypse and, appropriately, the end of all temporal relevance.*

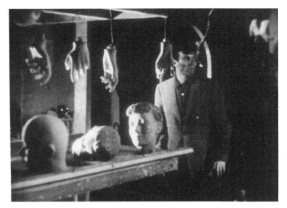

part of one pathetic man's tragedy. Kubrick carries us powerfully along the impetus of Cook's homicidal advance—his stumbling return to his own apartment, his wife's desperate kidding, her panicky attempt to ignore his plight ("You look terrible," she snarls as blood seeps through his shirt), and, finally, Cook's pumping slug after slug into her while a parrot in the cage he has upset squawks out its own alarm at this mild man transfigured by murderous hate, by "the killer inside me," as Jim Thompson calls that other self which stirs in the human consciousness. To find another scene as grotesque and horrifying in Kubrick's work, one had to wait for *Lolita*.

Kubrick acknowledged with regret that when he made *Lolita* it was not possible to portray Humbert Humbert's obsession on the screen with all the physical eroticism suggested in Nabokov's novel. The problem was more social than aesthetic. Public opinion was not ready to let the screen follow perversion into the same arcane areas open to a writer; even the novel *Lolita* had been rejected by many good publishers in New York and London as too risky, and was only brought out after much defensive use of "authoritative" critical opinion vouching for its artistic integrity. A film version started with this handicap. The only real physical intimation in the film of Humbert Humbert's sexual enslavement by the nymphet Lolita occurs in the visual metaphor that backs the credit titles. A girl's foot and leg are extended imperiously into the frame and a man's hand receives the limb in a kind of loving clasp while his other hand wedges lint between the toes and fondly enamels the nails.

Instead of sensuality, the pilot light that burns through the rest of the film is ironic comedy. If the screenplay necessarily omits the physical lusting, Kubrick and Nabokov deserve credit for sticking so closely and successfully to the comedy of a man trapped between a voracious mother and her precociously seductive daughter, struggling to free himself from the clutches of the

Kubrick's surrealism: Parts of tailors' dummies provide a bizarre environment in Killer's Kiss *and suggest what horrors of amputation the men fighting with pike and ax may inflict on each other.*

one to attach himself concupiscently and pathetically to the other. On this level, *Lolita* is extraordinarily successful. Its dialogue respects the psychology of the novel, while Kubrick sharpens the comedy by his casting of the principals and by the intelligent direction he gives them and their response to it.

A critical controversy has raged over the film's construction. Some critics call the opening sequence a serious error. They complain that by letting Humbert Humbert kill Quilty at the start, the film sacrifices the hideous pathos that his revenge contains when it follows Quilty's seduction of Lolita, as it does in the novel. This sequence certainly involved a major decision for Kubrick—an agonizing one, too, to deprive oneself of a perfect climax by transferring it to the prologue. Yet the film as a whole gains from that opening on several grounds. One is the peculiar tone Quilty's murder immediately gives the movie. It is a mood of brilliantly organized black comedy, happening in a world that is realistic enough to contain terror, pain, and death, yet fantastic enough to surprise and amuse. The baroque rooms of Château Quilty, the gloomy air of "the morning after," the dust sheets under which the owner, then yet alive, is discovered like a premature "stiff" in his own shroud, the whole debris of orgy and

Bodies after the mayhem in The Killing *stiffen into the lifeless image of disposed-of dummies. Men behave like robots, and robots have the appearance of men. The mechanism that distinguishes the two stops with death, but even in life it shades human reactions into mechanistic responses. (See* Paths of Glory, *page 102* Dr. Strangelove, *pages 128–129; 2001, pages 170–171.)*

Birth of an obsession: Humbert Humbert sees Lolita for the first time . . . the monster in a drive-in cinema terrorizes Humbert, Lolita, and her mother— compressed into a few brief sequences are the object of desire and the figure of supernatural horror as Kubrick establishes the fairy-tale trio of hero, princess, and ogre beneath the erotic surface of Nabokov's novel.

decadence marvelously assist the grotesque comedy. (It also usefully removes Lolita from the "normal" world, where film censors might expect Lolitaphiles to do their hunting.) Vaguely aware of menace somewhere in his vicinity, the bleary-eyed Quilty temporizes with Humbert Humbert in a variety of ways. He kids. He playacts, putting on a Gabby Hayes accent when required to read out, in verse, the confession Humbert Humbert has penned for him. He starts a nervy game of table tennis (a favorite Kubrick pastime with *his* houseguests), in which the relationship between him and his future killer is broken open by the pit-pat of the ball, and then shattered completely by the sudden crash of Humbert Humbert's gun, amplified to bone-jarring volume by the emptiness of the house.

There is another good reason, besides black comedy of the most inventive, subtly played kind, for Quilty's muzzy-minded horseplay. In the novel, he and Humbert Humbert never meet face to face till the showdown. In the film, they are introduced early on. Had the retribution come at the end of the film, it would have been harder to explain Quilty's failure to recognize Humbert Humbert and guess what was coming to him. Logically, he should still have done so in the film; but one fails to notice this slight cheat when death comes before introductions. With Quilty's demise—sheltering from a hail of bullets that perforate the innocence of a Gainsborough-type painting behind which he

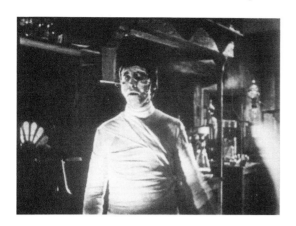

crawls, lugging his wounded leg behind him as a final horrifying detail—the film flashes back to "Four Years Earlier," and *Lolita* proper begins. The result, as Kubrick foresaw when he decided to shoot the film this way, is to exchange the suspense of waiting for fate to overtake Quilty for the suspense of waiting, in the book, for Humbert Humbert to bed down with Lolita. This gives Quilty a much greater role in the film than in the book. He appears throughout in the multifaceted impersonations of Peter Sellers: first as his bland yet sinister self eyeing people as if he were casting them for parts in a private orgy; then in Sellers' dexterous improvisation as the cop at a police convention, prying into Humbert Humbert's private life with garrulous innuendo; finally, in the most bizarre shape of Dr. Zempf, the college psychologist, unnerving Lolita's stepfather-lover with vaguely couched threats of exposure. The director and his star play the Quilty character as if he were a fugue, producing inspired passages of inventiveness yet always integrating him with the rest of the film. Kubrick deserves more credit than he got at the time for placing a surrealistic figure so firmly in an otherwise realistic film; and it is this coexistence of reality and fantasy that powerfully anticipates the style of *Dr. Strangelove.*

The film of *Lolita* reinforces the black fairy-tale aspect of the novel out of Kubrick's own admitted fascination with "magic," especially its darker sides. Apart from the atmosphere in the prologue, already referred to, when Humbert Humbert enters Quilty's Gothic mansion as if it were an ogre's castle, one early sequence sums up the erotic relationships in classic fairy-tale terms. This is the scene at the drive-in cinema where the introductory "shock" cut of a monster in some horror film rears above the watching Lolita and Humbert Humbert, confronting them with a menace that the as-yet-unmaterialized threat of Quilty will turn into a real crisis when the evil spell he throws over Lolita enables him to carry her off in the traditional way of horror-film

monsters. The trappings and lighting of horror films, weird attendants, transformations into different shapes, unexpected materializations and disappearances accompany Quilty through some of his main sequences, most strikingly in the prologue but also in the comic-macabre scene when Humbert Humbert returns home late at night to discover Quilty, as Dr. Zempf, awaiting him in a darkened room in a pose that already conjures up the sinister, chair-bound presence of Dr. Strangelove.

The director is not so successful with another risk he took—reducing the novel's eroticism—for without evidence of Humbert Humbert's carnal obsession, audiences might assume that he is simply in love with Lolita. The nymphet philosophy, spelled out succinctly early in the novel, had now to be conveyed by looks: Humbert Humbert glancing over his book at Lolita twirling a hula hoop around her desirable pubescent hips; his fixated eyes peering satyrlike through the decorative foliage at a college dance; and the reflex action at the drive-in cinema, where the horror movie brings him and his loved one (and, alas, her mother) physically together for a moment's shared fear. Where it should have been gradual and cumulative, the rhythm of eroticism has here had to be sudden and conclusive. It is too sudden. And it is not really conclusive enough. No sooner is Humbert Humbert's more than ordinary interest in Lolita established than certain aspects of the film throw doubt on its being a profane passion. The insistently lush "Lolita theme" music smacks of love, not lust. And the music "leads" some scenes. The shot of Humbert Humbert burying his face in the pillow on the nymphet's deserted bed after her mother has packed her off to summer camp loses its desperate pathos in a backwash of melodiousness.

What preserves the truth, if not the taint, of the relationship, is Kubrick's handling of his cast. True to his belief that actors are allies in a film's success, he adopts a self-effacing camera style. He uses noticeably long takes, but often very simple setups. The

Surreal elements amidst Lolita's realism: Humbert Humbert arrives in the Gothic shambles of the ogre's castle (top left); under the enchanter Quilty's spell, Lolita has the frozen look of a fairy-tale princess (middle left); horror materializes out of an apparently secure environment as doctors detain the hero and try to pronounce him insane (bottom left).

More use of Kubrick's Gothic techniques and lighting in Lolita: Quilty in the "transformation" of Dr. Zempf awaits Humbert's return to his darkened house. (See Dr. Strangelove, *pages 134–135.)*

camera stands there, usually with the characters in medium shot, while the actors play an often lengthy scene involving quite intricate dialogue and interplay of emotional nuances. He lets the rhythm of a performance do the "planting" of a point, an end that is more usually achieved by cutting.

Shelley Winters, as Lolita's mother, gives what is possibly her best film performance. She is a potent mixture of bossy momism, ten-cent intellectualism, women's club energy, and sexual thirst. From the first genteel chime of her doorbell at Humbert Humbert's arrival, Kubrick helps project her as a beady-eyed epitome of the all-American matron-vampire; playing up to her personable prospective lodger by praising the rudimentary nature of the bathroom plumbing as if it, too, were proof of old European values, she leans in the doorway, barring his departure, while her well-preserved body assumes a provocative posture almost as a reflex action. James Mason, a sharp, sardonic, intelligent actor, conveys the undertones of Humbert Humbert even if he is denied the obsessive notes.

Sue Lyon has the "eerie vulgarity" and provocative whine of the novel's Lolita. That she may look "too old" in some scenes merely emphasizes the discrepancy between the mind's eye, to which the novel is directed, and the more literal camera's eye as it registers the authentic way American adolescence annihilates the pubescent gap between childhood and adulthood. Sue Lyon does not violate the nymphet theme, even though she may occasionally look older than some people expect; and when violated herself at the end, pregnant, married, and beginning to assume her mother's blowsy vulgarity, she has a commonplaceness totally appropriate for Mason's flood of grief, guilt, and remorse.

Kubrick turns the necessity of not showing the pair of them in bed together into a virtue by substituting slapstick for seduction and forcing the man to sleep on a folding cot—a typical piece of antihuman mechanism—which he has ordered to be sent to their motel room as a "cover" for his intentions. Moreover, the myth of Lolita's sexual innocence is exploded by her own confession in the morning, before she and her stepfather presumably have sex together. Afterward, when she has learned of her mother's death, her childish weeping is used by Kubrick to purge the relationship of sexual content and key the second half of the film to a new note of sadness, disenchantment, and frustration, as Lolita turns from desirable love object into infuriating bitch.

Two scenes are particularly characteristic of what Kubrick brought to the filming of Nabokov's novel. One is the bizarre "happening" of Lolita's mother's death, by a chance road accident, just as she has made the discovery that her second husband is a "monster." At first the scene follows Nabokov closely. Humbert Humbert is fixing a drink, while considering what story to spin his wife to allay her alarm; when the phone rings, he calls up to his wife, whom he left locking herself in her room. "There's this man saying you've been killed, Charlotte." So she has. By suppressing the event and inserting only the effect, the movie conveys the sense projected in the novel of the world moving suddenly an inch or two from under one's feet. But Kubrick tops the disconcerting effect of random tragedy—though a tragedy so completely in line with Humbert Humbert's wishes— by the irony of the next scene. The new widower, minutes after the accident, is soaking in the bathtub with his martini floating beside him, as he accepts condolences from the neighbors with a contentment that they take to be shock. What makes this marvelously funny is the absolutely normal act of taking a bath set within the completely incongruous tragedy that has just struck. It foreshadows the way *Dr. Strangelove* builds comic effects out of the ironic incongruities of actions and circumstances and the disparity of causes and effects.

Kubrick brings his own characteristic feeling to another scene through the way he "magnetizes" particles of madness to come rushing out of a seemingly normal environment. It occurs when a group of calm, methodical night doctors at the hospital suddenly jump on Humbert Humbert when he flies into a panic on learning Lolita has fled from her bed with a mysterious stranger (Quilty). "Get a straitjacket," cries one man in white with lustful eagerness. Flat on his back, with people holding him down at every extremity and one medic spotlighting the white of his eye with a surgical light, Humbert desperately tries to prove his sanity by snatching at the most English brand of understatement. "I really ought to move on now," he murmurs. It is the same sharp use of language and locutions played against the grain of an event, in this case the man's pinioned position, that Kubrick developed into the vastly sophisticated verbal comedy of his next film.

If social pressures and film-industry prudence compelled Kubrick to jettison the erotica of *Lolita*, he gained powerful compensation by the chance it allowed him to formulate his flair for grotesque comedy. With *Dr. Strangelove* he extended his talent beyond one man's obsession into the collective folly of mankind.

Paths of Glory

Paths of Glory is Kubrick's graduation piece. Before he made it, he had the reputation of an interesting newcomer who used highly original techniques to refresh the Hollywood thriller. After it was produced, he was recognized as a significant American director. It revealed a talent able to work in a tradition of individual statement—and, indeed, able to work in Europe, too, for there were far fewer expatriate directors or "runaway" productions being set up on the Continent then. And the era and milieu of the film, the 1914–18 conflict, brought an American filmmaker face to face with the challenge of a particularly European experience beyond the direct recall of all but a few of Hollywood's veteran directors. The fact that some favorably compared the film to the work of Max Ophuls is one measure of Kubrick's growth as an artist.

But even more impressive is the humanist response that beats like a pulse through a brutally cynical story, lifting it out of its particular place and time. *The Killing* had its limits inside a genre crime story; and though it stretched them imaginatively, it remained a heartless illustration of criminal ingenuity and its unforeseen consequences. *Paths of Glory* finds Kubrick dealing in the wider realm of ideas with a relevance to man and society. Without casting off any of his innate irony and skepticism, the director declares his allegiance to his fellow men.

The film has sometimes been compared to *All Quiet on the Western Front,* which Lewis Milestone made in 1930. This is a natural, yet a misleading, comparison to make. Both are American films that sink their national identity into a depiction of "foreign" combatants in World War I—in Milestone's film, the Germans; in Kubrick's, the French. Both are unsparing with their battlefield detail. But Milestone argued that the good man's only response to war is pacifism; his film's emphasis on sacrifice in battle is what keeps his protest reverberating still. It shows lives wasted. Kubrick's film, on the other hand, takes its stand on human injustice. It shows one group of men being exploited by another

General Broulard's arrival at the château.

group. It explores the social stratification of war. No man's land is not really the great dividing barrier between the two sides in *Paths of Glory*; the "two sides" actually wear the same uniform, serve the same flag, and hold the same battle line, though in vastly differing degrees of comfort. The actual division, the deeper conflict, is that between the leaders and the led. It exists whether there is a war or not, but a war situation widens the division fatally. Only by implication is *Paths of Glory* a protest against war as such; it is much more pertinently an illustration of war as the continuation of class struggle. The paths of glory in the title are not the ones that lie across the battlefield; they are the avenues to self-advancement taken by the generals in command, with the utmost indifference to the fate of the men in the trenches.

The film's brief and brilliant opening exposition prepares all the other moves that follow. A narrator sets the war-front scene in a few communiqué sentences as General Broulard, played by Adolphe Menjou, arrives at the grandiose château commandeered as field headquarters by the French. This masterly casting of Menjou confirms Kubrick's instinct for an aspect of filmmaking that often predetermines much of a film's effectiveness, before the camera starts turning. From the first second of his entry—he hands his hat to his aide without a glance toward him, confident that the man knows his place and will be standing there—Menjou radiates the air of someone used to warming both

Kubrick shows Broulard leading Mireau morally astray in a winding choreographic pattern (see page 14) as he suggests an attack on an impregnable enemy position. Human lives are adjusted to fit the policies of leaders.

The trench world: Kubrick cuts from the elegance of the
military Establishment to the reality of war.

hands before the fire of human life. His acute-angled glances shot
from under hooded lids play off chillingly against the carefully
cultivated air of bonhomie with his crony and subordinate,
General Mireau.

Equally indicative of the moral ambiance is the physical setting. The château is a place of order and elegance—all mirrored
walls, shining parquet, baroque furnishings, and palatial staircas-
es—yet somehow corrupt and eerie, like a vampire's castle in the
old High German cinema.

The use Kubrick makes of such a set was to occur again in his
later films—most strikingly in *Lolita*, which opens, like *Paths of
Glory*, in an eerie and decadent mansion, cavernous and deserted
except for the two protagonists, Quilty and Humbert Humbert,
who proceed to lead each other through the baroque furnishings
in a way that recalls Mireau and Broulard. And although the
keynote is black comedy in *Lolita*, whereas it is ironic tragedy in
Paths of Glory, the impression both films convey is that of an
obsession which will overwhelm and destroy those who feed on
it. In the opening scenes of *Lolita* it is the resolution of an obsession—love of a forbidden kind—which Kubrick makes us witness. In *Paths of Glory* it is the sowing of an obsession—ambition
of a monstrous degree. In both obsessions, needless to say, lies
death.

The visitor proposes, ever so subtly, for the good of morale
back home, an attack on a German emplacement that is clearly
impregnable. As Broulard perambulates beside the ambitious
General Mireau (played by George Macready) in ever more
winding circles among the gleaming furniture, Kubrick's camera

General Mireau's machinelike incitement to the troops:

"Hello, soldier! Ready to kill more Germans?"

"My wife . . . I'm never going to see her again. I'm going to be killed."

"You act like a coward!"

starts moving too, duplicating physically the devious moral seduction of Mireau away from all reality and reason. The deal is closed as Mireau agrees to order the offensive that will decimate his men but perhaps capture the hill and gain him promotion. It is partly the tone of cynical decadence, the baroque decor, and the camera's labyrinthine movements that have prompted the comparison between Kubrick and Ophuls.* The comparison is valid, yet largely irrelevant. Kubrick's camera follows character —the character of two corrupt militarists—rather than the stylistic example Ophuls set in the cinema.

Since Kubrick was a director whose attitude to a subject formed his style, he resisted getting involved too early in the visual possibilities of a sequence. But throughout *Paths of Glory* the moral content of a sequence has its effect on his choice of camera technique. In this respect, it is a far more complex film than those of his earlier American subjects, which depend primarily on the action content of the story. The château scenes with the devious commanders in *Paths of Glory* are shot with a continually curving mobility; the trench scenes force the camera to follow, without choice, the shape of the dugout maze that has conditioned men to obey; and the scenes of court-martial and execution have a geometrical rigor that reflects the predetermined verdict and the preordained fate of the accused men.

In contrast, Kubrick maintains an honest directness of camera angle to characterize the relationship between the ordinary men in the line and Colonel Dax, who is a man of moral conscience. Dax belongs to the trench world, which is the polar opposite of the château society. When General Mireau visits Dax in his

---

*Partly, too, Kubrick's placing of Ophuls at the top of his list of directors whom he particularly admired, in a *Cahiers du Cinéma* interview, July 1957.

Lighting and space sharply define the physical reality of Dax and his world. Mireau views the objective from a safe distance. Mireau's view (below), through binoculars, one of the devices Kubrick uses to emphasize war as a spectator sport for the high command.

*Direct confrontation in contrast to the château's
labyrinthine machinations. The brutal responsibility of
the plan is passed on to Dax—the man who will have to
carry it out.*

dugout, he moves, ill at ease, through the tortuous trench system,
stiffly complimenting soldiers with hollow exhortations to valor;
but Dax, taking the same route before the attack, moves like a
man among his fellow men. His military obedience has a place in
it for human values; he is the only officer who has not let a gap
develop between himself and his men. Kirk Douglas's strong
bone structure and physique, so often used to give his screen
roles a barely suppressed threat of violence, serve here to give a
dimension of moral stature as he stands up for the rights and
lives of his men. But Dax is a soldier, too. When ordered by
Mireau to lead the attack on the enemy emplacement, known as
Ant Hill, he protests passionately—but he obeys.

The cynical calculation of the potential casualties that prefaces
this offensive is almost a pilot study for *Dr. Strangelove*'s nuclear
overkill. Five percent killed going over the top, says Mireau,
another five percent as the advance starts, "let's say another
twenty-five percent in actually taking the Ant Hill—we're still
left with enough men to keep it." Such mental arithmetic resembles General Turgidson's call for all-out nuclear war on Russia in
Dr. Strangelove, on the ground that retaliation will mean "only ten
to twenty million people killed, tops, depending on the breaks";
the difference is simply that the Bomb makes multiplying easier.
Mireau's calculation of casualties also has its cynical concomitant
in reverse, after the raid has failed; the angry, humiliated general
now demands the lives of hundreds of his own men before the
firing squad, so as to "encourage" the others. Gradually the numbers of scapegoats are whittled down, like a business deal being

Dax orders a reconnaissance of no man's land . . . but it ends with the Lieutenant killing one of his own men and hiding his responsibility for it.

Corporal Paris: "You ran like a rabbit after you killed Lejeune."
Lieutenant Roget: "I don't like your tone. You're speaking to an officer, remember that."

A single source of illumination intensifies the bluntness of the encounter (see The Killing, *pages 48–49. See also page 131).*

Day breaks with Dax passing on orders, giving his men encouragement. Kubrick shows the noninvolvement of the leaders, who drink to a success for which others will spill their blood.

done between him and the more politically prudent General Broulard. The "hundreds" become "dozens," and finally "one man from each company, three in all." This reductio ad absurdum could not be more horrifyingly rendered.

The gathering enormity of the affair is rendered audibly in the echo effect taken on by the voices of the bargaining men. Kubrick will use a similar hollowness, presaging doom, in *Dr. Strangelove*. But something else can be detected as well, a minor but telling Kubrick characteristic. This is General Mireau's shortness of breath, which lends to his character at this point a panicky indignation, part anger at the catastrophe, part fear that his own faux pas will be revealed. While it is dramatically right in this context, the kind of asthmatic fear the sound embodies, the sense of entrapment and enclosure, seems to have a special appeal for Kubrick. Claustrophobia is the last thing one is prepared for in the infinity of space, but the breathing of the astronaut marooned outside his craft in *2001* is the only audible sound at that point in the film and it illustrates his sense of isolation more dramatically than would any music score.* A man as protective of his private

---

*Composer Alex North contributes a wry memoir in this respect in *The Making of Kubrick's* 2001, edited by Jerome Agel (New York: Signet Books, New American Library, 1968), p. 199.

Trench: Dax's walk to his battle position . . . gives Kubrick's ever-tracking camera, as it retreats before him or now and again assumes his subjective point of view, the chance to express the documentary feel of this confined and seemingly endless world of the common soldiers.

life and guarded about his personal independence as Kubrick is particularly alert to situations in which one might no longer be in full control; this awareness has made him sensitive to, and predisposes him to use, these highly appropriate sounds of unease.

The most justly famous sequence in *Paths of Glory* is the attack itself and the prelude to it. It has all the shattered details of old World War I photographs and an emotional thrust that rides on the shock waves of slaughter. Kubrick's subjective camera "stands in" for Dax as he strides through the endless, wormlike trench. The waiting infantry making way for him (and the camera) look in the flat gray light like figures in stone relief already carved into the plinth of a war memorial. Soldiers loom like apparitions through the smoke, or dust, at the far end of the trench. Now and then a mobile overhead camera keeps the grim-visaged Dax under dispassionate scrutiny while the pace of his inspection builds up a purposive momentum. Then the attack! It is a marvel of composition in depth and detail. The movement is now sideways, keeping pace with the packs of crouching men scurrying like rats up and down the inhuman contours of the shell-pocked ground, shrouded in smoke one second, showered with earth, shrapnel, and debris the next. On and on and on they go, in an animated mural of death. The sound of battle has a dreadful distinctiveness, too. Like all Kubrick's movies, *Paths of Glory* uses sound to emotionally supplement per-

Dax reaches the end of the trenches and . . .

*for an instant Kubrick conceals unnervingly in the dust
what lies ahead, but as the leader goes over the top, the
screen opens up from the constricted trenches to show the
horizontal panorama of blind destruction.*

*Kubrick keeps zeroing in to close-ups of the horrified Dax
as the camera, hand-held by Kubrick, follows the horizontal sweep of the battle. (See page 20.)*

ception. Over the noise and panic shrills the call-to-duty piping of Dax's whistle. A zoom lens operated by Kubrick himself continually "homes" in on Dax, catching his growing despair as the thinning ranks of the living betray both the failure of the attack and the lack of support from the French soldiers in the other trenches, who are unwilling, or unable, to advance through the German firepower. A furious Mireau orders his own artillery to fire on these "cowards," but he is met with the artillery commander's refusal except on written orders. Mireau snaps, "If the little sweethearts won't face German bullets, they'll face French ones."

Cut instantly to the château. The random slaughter of the battlefield is succeeded by selective killing through court-martial and execution. As Broulard says, "Soldiers are like children. They need discipline." The discipline he recommends is "shooting a man now and then." The isolation of ordinary soldiers from the officers who command them is emphasized throughout *Paths of Glory* in a variety of ways. It is explicit not only in the main story but also in the well-integrated subplot, in which a cowardly lieutenant, ordered to make a reconnaissance sortie into no man's land before the attack, sends a soldier out in front of him, panics when the man does not return, and then thoughtlessly kills him

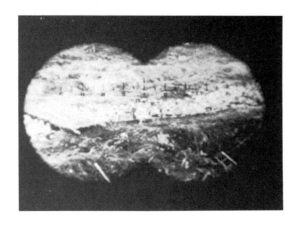

Back to Mireau's view of the attack: "Where in heaven's name are they?" he storms. "Miserable cowards, they're still in the trenches!"

"Order the seventy-fives to fire on our positions."
Soldier: "I can't do that, sir, without a written order."

A dead body prevents Dax from returning to the attack. From the battlefield Kubrick cuts directly to the château and a furious Mireau.

Confrontation after the failed attack. Mireau demands scapegoats and is opposed by Dax.

himself when he lobs a grenade into the dark at the imagined foe. He later tries to conceal his criminal callousness by condemning the one eyewitness to the deed as one of the three scapegoats picked for execution. The gap between leaders and led is implicit in the film's settings as well; it has already been noted how the characters belong either to the château or to the trenches, with Dax the only man straddling the two worlds. But there is a third visual device that Kubrick uses, to the extent of making it almost a leitmotiv. This is his repeated framing of a view of no man's land, or the actual battle, inside the double lenses of a pair of field glasses. The binocular effect is employed no fewer than four times. Each time it allows the military command to look on what are (or will be) the horrifying consequences of their orders without suffering the moral responsibility of physical involvement. Apart from Dax, the commanders' role is limited to that of spectators. (General Mireau does intervene in the action, it is true, but only to order gunfire on his own troops.) Protocol also makes them voyeurs at the execution of the scapegoats; the huge château in the background appears to observe the deaths in the morning with the same chilly aloofness. And General Broulard

*In cramped, dark quarters, Dax puts hope into the
accused. Kubrick cuts to the inhuman immensity of the
château, in which the environment created by humans
also controls humans.*

even improves on this detachment—for, his foxy nose scenting
the risks of involvement in even this formal encounter, he makes
up his mind not to attend the court-martial, thereby effectively
putting the consequences of his strategy right out of sight.

Paths of Glory opens with the blare of the "Marseillaise" behind
the credit titles, but despite the brazen orchestration it has an
ironically hollow ring. The citizens' song has become the anthem
of an Establishment that uses men for its own cynical ends, in
war as in peace. And war gives the leaders an advantage in permitting them to take shortcuts to power and privilege that need
at least the plausible processes of government in peacetime. A
well-aimed bullet is the extreme sanction of the Establishment;
war facilitates it.

The court-martial, at which Dax, a lawyer in civilian life,
defends the three accused men, is a mockery of justice. Kubrick
shoots it in a way that emphasizes the inhumanity inherent in the
ritual. The camera tracks laterally along behind the officers of the
court as the prosecutor makes out a case as if the result was a
foregone conclusion—which indeed he knows it is. Then it
repeats the movement in parallel fashion, though this time
behind the accused, as Dax makes his plea. Symmetry is all. The
guards' rifles are grounded and angled at precisely the same
degree; the three accused men are so symmetrically positioned
that one half of the white, gleaming, light-filled hall looks like a
mirror image of the other. Such inflexible lines have something
sacrificially ritualistic about them.

One of the strongest impressions *Paths of Glory* leaves on a

viewer is the extreme mobility of Kubrick's camera. In sequence
after sequence the arrangement of the shooting angles is planned
with a view to the camera's participation in the action. Kubrick is
extraordinarily successful in inventing visual movements that are
the equivalent of the drama created by events or latent in the
atmosphere of a scene. The lateral movements already described
in the court-martial sequence, the horrifying horizontal advance
of the camera in line with the no-man's-land battle, along with
the "zooming" incursions into the midst of the carnage and the
long backward track of Dax's trench walk are all ways of visually
dramatizing what is happening. They are also ways of relating
the viewer to the space on the screen by involving him in that
space—moving him through it. Far more than in the earlier films,
Kubrick is at pains to ensure that the mechanical factor does not
stand as a barrier between the spectator and the film. And in
2001: A Space Odyssey he was to use such movements extensively
with the same aim in mind.

In the court-martial sequence Kubrick employs a visual device

Stiff and statuesque compositions emphasize the feeling of legal hypocrisy as the examination proceeds. Humans are shown as pieces in their own games.

Judge: "The indictment is lengthy and there's no point in reading it. The charge is cowardice during the attack on Ant Hill."
Major Saint-Auban: "Did you advance? How far?"
Private Ferol: "To about the middle of no man's land, sir."
Major Saint-Auban: "Then what did you do?"
Private Ferol: "Well . . . I saw that me and Meyer—"
Major Saint-Auban: "The court has no concern with your visual experiences!"

Major Saint-Auban: "Did you urge your comrades forward?"
Private Arnaud: "Most of them died as they left the trenches."
Colonel Dax to Arnaud: "Aside from your sad failure to utter battle cries, was your behavior different from the others'? Is it true that you have been designated a coward by lot?"
Judge: "It's accepted practice in the French Army to pick examples by lot."

Colonel Dax: "Corporal Paris . . . why didn't you leave
the trenches?"
Corporal Paris: "Major Vignon was shot, and he fell on
me and knocked me cold."
Judge to Paris: "Have you any witnesses?"

that crops up in other films—*The Killing, Dr. Strangelove*—for various reasons. This is the repetition of an image or a series of images. His repeated use of the "binocular" image has already been referred to. In the court-martial section of the film he starts off the testimony of *each* of the three prisoners with the *same* visual composition, a high-angle shot of the stiffly aligned soldiers placed geometrically on the chessboard floor of the huge salon. He then comes in to show us the prisoner facing the camera (the judges), and the soldiers behind him, so that the man appears to be clamped between the jaws of a vise. The camera then cuts between close-ups of the prisoner, the judges, and General Mireau. The separate human individuals are all caught in the same machinelike action.

The whole execution scene continues the buildup of formal procedure, only now it is pierced through and through by the piteous spectacle of the condemned men, one insensible and tied to a stretcher, one crying and being comforted by the whining pieties of a priest, and one resigned and somber. Their plight is contrasted with the rigidity accompanying the execution of the

Major Saint-Auban: "And I submit that that attack was
a stain upon the flag of France, dishonoring every man,
woman, and child in the French nation."

Dax's movement is filmed in severe geometrical lines as
he is caught between the accused and the accusers.
Colonel Dax: "Gentlemen of the court, to find these men
guilty will be a crime to haunt each of you to the day you
die! I can't believe the noblest impulse in man, his compassion for another, can be completely dead here.
Therefore I humbly beg you . . . show mercy to these
men."

Judge: "The court will deliberate."

sentence—the stiff ranks of soldiers, the upright execution posts, the monotone beat of the drums, the two statuesque generals, Broulard and Mireau, the cart waiting with the caskets. The silence after the shots is suddenly filled with birdsong, a kind of gentle "Amen," brutally truncated by a cut to the château and Mireau's relishing remark, "The men died wonderfully!" as he butters his breakfast croissant. Condemned men, of course, get fed. Generals go to watch executions on an empty stomach: it sharpens their appreciation.

The firing-squad scene is all the more stark at first viewing because Kubrick has previously, and very subtly, aroused false expectations that Broulard will intervene at the last minute to halt the affair. The night before, Dax has gone to the château to make a last plea for mercy. Characteristically, the camera finds the generals and their guests in the middle of a waltz and sidles deferentially in a smooth arc round the perimeter of the parquet until an aide informs Broulard of the colonel's arrival—and then, unhurriedly, it sidles back again, playing up the feeling that men die at dawn, but generals dance at night. In the hush of the library, the self-possession of the urbane Broulard, who has treated Dax's plea almost as a faux pas in military protocol, is severe-

Space, light, and shadows: Kubrick focuses on the confined agony of men awaiting execution.

Priest: "Have faith in your creator, my son. Death comes to us all."

The atheist attacks the priest and is knocked against the wall.

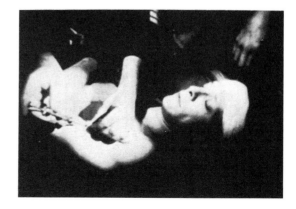

Those who trap the prisoners are caught in their own patterns. The mechanical convolutions of the dancers echo the choreography of the film's opening sequences (pages 68–69) as Dax confronts Broulard with Mireau's error.

Tables turned: Broulard quits the library and Kubrick repeats the high-angled composition of the final shot on page 83, when it is Dax's turn to leave.

The château presides over the execution of its victims. The camera, as it once moved through the trenches, now gives way before the prisoners advancing to their deaths.

ly shaken, just as he is about to return to his guests. As Broulard places his hand on the doorknob, Dax reveals that Mireau was ready to order artillery fire on his own men. The door snaps closed, betraying the snap of surprise in the general's mind. Menjou (Broulard) blinks—one of the most potent of his battery of fastidious effects. He sees the risk of scandal to the high command. By using a slow fade-out after the message has got through to Broulard, Kubrick implies that military vengeance will now be tempered by expedient mercy. Throughout the rest of the film he has frequently used direct cuts from sequence to sequence. This device, not so commonplace in 1957 as it has since become, stretches the story line out tight and confers an inexorable logic on events. But Kubrick avoids it at this point, and allows the scene to fade on a close-up of Dax's face and a shot of Broulard impassively taking his leave of Dax, a stratagem that adds doubt to the suspense about the execution, which follows. Of course, the finality of the act, without the anticipated reprieve, is another well-planned device. We realize over the generals' breakfast that what Broulard decided was not to save the three scapegoats but to add a fourth to them—Mireau, whom he now throws to a court of inquiry, although with the fair certainty that he will "honorably" blow his brains out before things get that far. The outrage to human decency is compounded to the utmost limits when Broulard offers Dax the expendable general's job, with a congratulatory murmur at having intrigued so well for it. With this cynical old man's utter inability to tell the difference between an act of humanity and a bid for promotion, *Paths of Glory* delivers its final moral shock.

Kubrick's problem now is how to end the film with some sense of catharsis. He solved it in an allusive, indirect way that intensified its deeply humanist resonance. By a deliberate change of key,

he puts an unfocused but powerful emotional experience in the place of the austere cynicism of the rest of the film. As Dax returns to his quarters after his interview with Broulard, he stops momentarily in the doorway of a tavern, where a captured German girl is being made to sing to the troops. With obvious distaste he sees the muddled animal sentiments on the faces of men whose comrades have been shot like pigs a few hours earlier. If Broulard was wrong when he quipped, "There's nothing so *stimulating* to a soldier than seeing someone else die," then these men whistling lecherously at the frightened girl also give the lie to Dax's faith in humanity. The girl is coerced into nervously starting a song. Gradually she asserts herself through the wolf calls, and though the words are in German, their undertones of memories of homeland and loved ones soften the battle-hardened soldiers and set them humming the melody. Dax's mind ceases to judge them. The sound reaches his heart as a guarantee of their basic humanity. He carries it within him, sustaining him, as news comes that the army has been ordered to the front. Man is capable of the noblest as well as the basest of emotions. "We know," wrote Hollis Alpert, who found this moment profoundly moving, "that Colonel Dax and his soldiers have made their odyssey and returned home safely."

Paths of Glory is a film held so truly on course and with such a confident balance between characters, casting, and moral and physical ambiance that its ideas on inhumanity and injustice permeate dramatically, not didactically, the nature of the events. It has not one weak sequence. If the scenes describing the three condemned men's captivity are cruder than the rest, this is because the emotions conveyed are cruder than those underlying the sophisticated double-talk of the generals—and also because the American accents of the cast are more obtrusive in their

Mechanical precision of the ceremony of death. The feeling of inevitability is complemented on the sound track by the repeated refrain of drums. "Aim!" Drums stop . . . birdsong ascends . . .

the shots ring out.

From the sound of bullets Kubrick cuts ...

... to the sound of breakfast.

attempt to portray French peasants or the middle class. All the same, Kubrick and his coscenarists, Calder Willingham and Jim Thompson, do come up with a crudely effective irony, as when one of the victims laments that a common cockroach will be nearer his wife than he will because "we'll be dead, it'll be alive." And his comrade squashes the cockroach with the quip, "Now you got the edge on it."

Paths of Glory is the first Kubrick film in which the characters' relationship to their surroundings is more than physical. The architecture embodies them and their follies in a metaphorical sense, too. There was no real architectural design in either *Killer's Kiss* or *The Killing,* though it has been noted how the camera singled out everyday objects in *Killer's Kiss* and used them as visual shorthand comments on the inner lives of the boy and girl. But in *Paths of Glory,* and even more in *Dr. Strangelove* and in *2001,* the sets for the first time assume a dynamic role as part of the total concept, usually a role that is hostile or cynically disposed to the

General Mireau: "I'm glad you could be there, George. These things are always grim, but this one had a kind of splendor. The men died wonderfully!"

human fates that are being settled under their shadow. In each of these three major films the principal setting is one which the dominant regime has constructed in its own image, rather in the way that Hitler's growing pretensions to extend his rule over space and time in his "Thousand-Year Reich" were encapsulated in the architecture designed and, in some cases, built for him by Albert Speer.* The château in *Paths of Glory*, the War Room in *Dr. Strangelove*, and the Wheel in *2001* represent Kubrick's most distinctive ways of using a created environment to contain, define, *and dominate* the protagonists. *Paths of Glory* enables us to pick this characteristic out very clearly. As well as being a simpler film, architecturally, than the later ones, it contains a distinctive example of how Kubrick repeats a setup in order to emphasize the relationship between the men and their setting. The first time this occurs is when Colonel Dax demands the right to speak out in defense of the men who have finally been selected as scapegoats: he exits through the tall doors at the extreme right of the "frame," and the heavy elegance of the walls and ceiling bears down on his isolation. Virtually the same composition is used later, in the château library, when Dax turns the tables on General Broulard by revealing Mireau's duplicity, and his military superior bows out through the door to go back to his ballroom guests, with an ominous pensiveness. This composition occurs a third

---

*Speer's memoirs, *Inside the Third Reich*, made a strong impression on Kubrick when he read them, and one can easily see why in the story of a "superman" regime brought to ruin by a self-fulfilling curse, by the many black-comedy moments, and especially by the way Speer confirms Kubrick's thesis about the gulf that modern technology creates between reality and the fantasy of those who control it.

Broulard springs a trap on his fellow general.

Kubrick again uses the overpowering composition to suggest a man who is checkmated—Mireau retires beaten.

The final cynicism: Broulard offers Mireau's job to Colonel Dax.

Kubrick changes emotional gear. Dax looks into the window of a tavern to see a German girl ridiculed by his soldiers.

time when General Mireau in his turn is made a scapegoat by Broulard at the breakfast table and, choking with fury and fear, walks through the right-hand door, a departure that has the finality of a last exit into the wings. Kubrick's attitude to architecture reflects the influence of certain Teutonic traits in his work, for the creation of an architectural ambiance that is far more than surface effect and penetrates to the inner meaning of the action is one of the strongest characteristics of old High German cinema, the cinema in existence before Hitler killed it. Of course, Kubrick had a German art director in *Paths of Glory;* and another designer who was German by birth, though British by adoption, was his associate on *Dr. Strangelove.* But his awareness of the metaphysical sense of the setting derives from his own nature, rather than reflecting the national characteristics of his collaborators. The realist tradition of the American cinema counteracts any danger of his being pulled into mere decorative expressionism or baroque effects for their own sake, in the German manner. In the same way, his brilliant use of lighting effects—a skill that has obvious links with German directors like Fritz Lang and Paul Leni—is tempered by his insistence that the illumination must issue from a realistic source. *Paths of Glory* shows us fully for the first time the concern with space and lighting that Kubrick was to build more and more organically into his movies.

Paths of Glory is a realist's view of war, not a propagandist's. As has already been remarked, it is not a film against war, except in that it depicts the horrors of war. Dax executes orders that horrify him and leads an attack that he knows is bound to fail with

immense loss of life. But the point is, he *does* execute the orders and he *does* lead the attack. The fact that the story portrays an incident in the 1914–18 war helps Kubrick's intentions. For there are wars and wars. World War I was, according to historical consensus, one of the most unnecessary conflicts ever fought—a war without a just cause, breaking out almost by monstrous accident and achieving almost nothing except the conditions for the next world war. The madness of nations and their leaders characterized it; no "moral" struggle, such as underlay World War II , can be discerned in it. A frame of reference like this is highly sympathetic to a man of Kubrick's temperament, for individual acts performed inside a situation of lunacy take on his peculiar reverberations of irony, cynicism, and doom. Democratic government is a bad springboard for human drama; unjust or insane conditions are better forcing beds for the protagonists. *Paths of Glory* profits directly and indirectly from this condition of collective insanity in which the actions of the principal characters are attuned not only to the inequalities that prevail among men when the world is at peace but also to the insanity that breaks loose in wartime.

In the latter respect, only the scale differentiates it from the war world of *Dr. Strangelove*. A more colossal series of insane events demands a more grotesque cast of obsessed characters. And instead of revulsion at the way the generals in World War I sacrificed their men for political reasons, a kind of helpless laughter is the only appropriate response to the enormity of the holocaust as world leaders prepare to sacrifice the very existence of the human race. "The visual concept of, say, a 'Summit' conference and a hydrogen bomb exploding one city is only taking *Paths of Glory*'s contrast of the château and the trenches a stage further," analyzed Gavin Lambert in *Sight and Sound* in 1957. It was an astute and, as it turned out, prescient observation.

As she sings a simple song of home, the soldiers' response restores some of Dax's faith in the universal emotions of his fellow men.

Aware of man's manifold sentiments . . .

Dax returns to the front.

Dr. Strangelove,

or How I Learned to Stop Worrying and Love the Bomb

The feature of *Dr. Strangelove, or How I Learned to Stop Worrying and Love the Bomb* which grows with repeated viewings is how Kubrick's precise intention in making the film is perfectly matched by the sureness of his effect. Ultimately the most critical decision he made in approaching the subject of nuclear destruction came from his perceiving how comedy can infiltrate the mind's defense mechanism and take it by surprise. For in self-protection we have learned how to shut tragedy on this scale, or even the intimation of it, out of our thoughts. Kubrick spoke of how he became struck by people's virtually listless acquiescence in the possibility—in fact, in the increasing probability—of nuclear war, by either design or accident. *Dr. Strangelove* was undertaken with the conscious aim of sounding an alert that would startle people into a response and even resistance to such a fate. And laughter, not for the first time, was the device selected to penetrate the soundproofing of the paralyzed will. The largely unimaginable prospect of the extinction of the human race is turned into the satirical embodiment of its leaders' collective madness. The fantasy of nuclear destruction, which, like death itself, we never think of as happening to ourselves in our lifetime, is turned into the comic reality of actors giving inspired performances—"inspired" by their material and director.

As for Kubrick's basic ingredient of filmmaking—the story—it, too, is brilliantly developed in ways that heighten and extend the theme. The look, the sound, and even the sequence of events leading to the global holocaust all create a suspense plot that has room for grim realism and grotesque humor, close-packed and often side by side. The theme of communication is again central to the whole construction of the film and the working out of many separate scenes in it. Time and space, too, are as much a part of it as they were in *The Killing*—indeed, *Dr. Strangelove* might appropriately be subtitled *The Overkill*—and Kubrick

Dr. Strangelove *strikes its note of doom from the opening narration: "For more than a year, ominous rumors had been privately circulating among high-level Western leaders that the Soviet Union had been at work on what was darkly hinted to be the Ultimate Weapon, a Doomsday device. Intelligence sources traced the site of the top secret Russian project to the perpetually fog-shrouded wasteland below the arctic peaks of the Zhokhov Islands."*

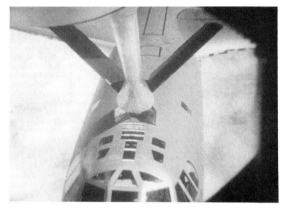

Title sequence of melody "Try a Little Tenderness" is suggestive of the conflicting demands of destruction and security. A nuclear bomber is refueled from the mother aircraft in flight.

Man's radar technology, designed to safeguard him against surprise nuclear attack; the film sets up the ironic theme of the fallibility of men and machines.

imposes even more rigorous restrictions on himself than he did in the earlier film.

What happens in *Dr. Strangelove* is confined to a few hours and to three highly localized settings. Each setting, moreover, is sealed off from the others. One is a locked office on an air base commanded by a psychotic general; another is the cabin of a B-52 H-bomber captained by a moronic pilot; and the third is the underground War Room at the Pentagon, dominated by a manic warmonger and his malignant counterpart, a power-mad nuclear strategist. Insanity is sealed in with the characters; they are locked into their "cells," just as the fate of the peoples they rule or represent is locked into the events. Once again we note Kubrick's fondness for using the feeling of helplessness which is the peculiar fear that follows from being "locked in" by certain physical circumstances or emotional situations. For a picture that illustrates the end of the world, the actual areas involved are absurdly small. The old scientific boast of "Give me a place to stand and I shall move the earth" has been succeeded by the new scientific reality of "Give me a place to sit down and I'll destroy it."

The characters in *The Killing* generated the suspense that comes from working to the clock in a concerted effort; those in *Dr.*

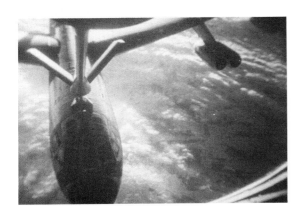

General Ripper tells Group Captain Mandrake a red alert
has been declared. The telephone, a primary instrument
of communication, allows one man to extend his insanity.

The B-52 crew: men not conscious of the sophistication of
the machinery they have created, a theme Kubrick is to
develop further in 2001. The unbelievable happens. The
B-52 is put on attack.

Strangelove generate the nightmare that comes from working against the clock while suffering a total disruption of communication. The chief area of communication that has broken down is, of course, in human sanity. Both films convey Kubrick's unmistakable intention of measuring off minutes from an allotted time.

The timing starts in *Dr. Strangelove* with Kubrick's favorite device, the opening narration, which is factual and ominous. This sets the mood, with a foreboding account of mysterious Russian construction work in the polar regions, work whose purpose no one knows. What is being constructed is, in fact, the Doomsday Machine—the nuclear booby trap that an attack on Russia will automatically trigger. The significance of this is not revealed until late in the film, just as the revelation of the purpose of the Jupiter mission in *2001* is delayed. At a first viewing of the film one may not make the connection. No matter. The right intimation of mortality has been sounded.

The following sequence, over which the credits appear, is a visual metaphor for the theme that whets expectations the way the emblem of Humber Humbert's "enslavement" did in *Lolita*. Two planes rock gently together in midair, a B-52 bomber being

refueled by the tanker aircraft, the sexual implication impishly emphasized by the music, "Try a Little Tenderness." This concept was Kubrick's, though, as he recalled with wry amusement, one of the world's leading nuclear strategists later said it reminded him less of copulation than of a mother giving suck to her infant. Maternal or erotic, the image anticipates the sexually based human motivation for the coming destruction. It is an Air Force general's paranoid anxiety about the waning potency of his "precious bodily essence"—he blames it on an international Communist conspiracy to poison the drinking water—that makes him activate the "Go" code, sending B-52s winging off to Russia to destroy the poison at the source. And in the false dawn of hope at the end of the film, the prospect of renewing the human race by bringing together carefully preserved males and temptingly selected females is what boosts the virility of another general and reconciles him to the slaughter. This irony—that the sexual neuroses of two militarists should be at the heart of the holocaust—is only the first of the disparities that *Dr. Strangelove* points up between the smallness of the cause and the enormity of the result.

Communications: General Turgidson's mistress takes a
call from the Pentagon summoning him to the gathering
crisis . . . while General Ripper, at the air base, uses his
address system to seal himself off from reach.

In the B-52, the crisis manual is followed step by step,
further locking the men into their destiny.

The course is set.

The film begins with almost lethargic calm in each of the three main locations. At Burpelson Air Force Base, the computers, making their debut in a Kubrick film, produce a murmur of order and routine, which is suggested, too, in the politely deferential attitude of Peter Sellers, playing Group Captain Lionel Mandrake of the Royal Air Force, as he leans fondly over these banks of brain-children. Physical posture plays an important part in *Dr. Strangelove.* More than in any of his other films, Kubrick uses it to split open character for our inspection. Since the characters are caricatures—though they are never without their human dimension—the way their bodies are used, photographed, and edited in the film indicates their incipient or active insanities.

The madness already resident in General Jack D. Ripper, Mandrake's commandant at Burpelson, played by Sterling Hayden, is embodied partly in the actor's performance, but the way he is photographed, frequently in close-up, often from slightly below his jutting cigar, suggests a man totally sunk into his obsessional view of a world which he believes is polluting his bodily essence. General Ripper has turned a deaf ear to all but his own paranoid voices. Hayden plays out his dementia with the stage-by-stage methodology of a military rule book. Sellers, on

*Sealed into his own madness, suggested by Kubrick's use
of confined space and low-angled view of brooding
mania, General Ripper informs Mandrake that the alert
is his own invention.*

the other hand, is encouraged by Kubrick to be a foil, both physically and verbally, of slow-burning comprehension. "Oh, hell," he
murmurs in well-bred irritation when Hayden tells him that the
nuclear alert which has just been sounded by him is real. "Oh,
hell, are the Russians involved?"

Having sounded the warning, Kubrick now moves smoothly
on to second base—the B-52 bomber on patrol, part of the
twenty-four-hour airborne alert. Again the narrator is briefly
introduced with facts and figures on this kind of nuclear guard
duty. The bland, soothing voice—a kind of ur-HAL—relieves us
of any insecurities by its total reassurance. Somebody up there is
on guard. But when we see *inside* the plane, dementia tightens its
grip, for human beings are operating on a level of sophistication
many IQs below that of the machinery they are nominally con-
trolling. The B-52 crew is not only listless, it is mindless as well,
leafing through *Playboy*, riffling card decks like lazy riverboat
gamblers, while the apelike impression made by Slim Pickens, as
their captain, is amply confirmed by his name—Major Kong.

And yet, as is characteristic of all of *Dr. Strangelove*, these
grotesques exist in an environment of painstaking realism. The
B-52 cabin is a detailed replica of an actual bomber. The events
inside it are filmed with no more lighting sources than one would
expect a real plane to furnish. It is when the nuclear alert sounds
that this documentary detail is suddenly convulsed by demoniac
forces. The machinery takes over. The spinning counters, revolv-
ing numbers, and clicking codes on a multitude of automated
dials lock in the crew's fate, and ultimately the world's, as the
bomber heads for Russia. HAL 9000, the computer conspiring

The Circle of Fate in the War Room. Like the judges at the court-martial in Paths of Glory, *this group of leaders sits in judgment on men's lives.*

against his "masters" in *2001,* is only the sophisticated Big Brother of these mute instruments in *Dr. Strangelove.* They set Major Kong's old Deep South blood tingling at the thought of the glory mission. Clamping on his Stetson, he sets the bomber on target to the strains of "When Johnny Comes Marching Home." "There'll be some important promotions an' citations when we come through this," he promises the crew.

The prologue is over. The war posture, at once antic and appalling, has been struck. And the cast of humans is about to be absurdly dwarfed by an escalating calamity beyond their control. Kubrick now begins the process of incongruity and disparity of events which structures the rest of the film. It is done by injecting actions that would be perfectly normal, even insignificant, in ordinary situations into the Ultimate Situation that shapes up as the B-52 nears its bombing zone.

Confront a man in his office with a nuclear alarm, Kubrick has said, and you have a documentary. If the news reaches him in his living room, you have a drama. If it catches him in the lavatory, the result is comedy. Which is exactly where General Buck Turgidson happens to be when the message comes through to him—human necessity interrupted by human destiny.

George C. Scott's portrayal of Turgidson is an excellent example of how Kubrick gets his peculiarly manic effects in this film by collaboration with his cast. Scott brings many an inventive trait of his own to the part of this Pentagon "hawk"; his complacent slapping of his bare tummy, as he leaves his mistress's bed to join his President in the War Room, is like a man sounding his own war drum. But Kubrick, too, "creates" Scott's performance. Again and again Turgidson is "frozen" in some extraordinary posture, usually resembling that of an ape or jackal, either by having the camera cut away from him in mid-grimace or else by holding the camera on him while the actor petrifies himself into

President Muffley shows a realistic concern at the grow-
ing crisis: "Obviously the work of a psychotic."

But the military mind will not admit it.
Turgidson: "I wouldn't be too hasty, Mr. President."

The grotesque inappropriateness of Turgidson's
simple-minded response is captured by Kubrick's long
take of George C. Scott's contortions.

Major Kong, elated by the discovery of the pleasures of
the survival kit: "one .45 automatic; two boxes of ammu-
nition; four days' concentrated emergency rations; one
drug issue containing antibiotic pills, morphine pills, vit-
amin pills, pep pills, sleeping pills, and tranquilizer pills;
one miniature combination Russian phrase book and
Bible; one hundred dollars in rubles; nine packs of chew-
ing gum; one issue of prophylactics; three lipsticks; three
pair of nylon stockings. Gee, a fella could have a pretty
good weekend in Vegas with all that stuff."

some subhuman attitude. This gives the impression of a gargoyle animated by its own wound-up dementia or a jumping jack-in-the-box of manic impulses, tics, spasms, and reflexes. The effect is in total contrast to the massive, brooding psychosis of General Ripper. In both cases, Kubrick adapts his editing and his cast's acting to outwardly embody the inner humors of the characters.

As the crisis grows, the scene expands—into the Pentagon War Room. This is one of the most functional and imaginative sets ever designed for film. It was created by Ken Adam, a German-born architecture student, whose designs for other movies did much to create the larger-than-life feeling of the James Bond films. It is no accident, therefore, that we see shades of Fritz Lang's work, especially *Metropolis*, in this cavernous design. But what is specifically characteristic of Kubrick is the logic and rationality in the set. He and Adam chose the semitriangular shape, since Kubrick liked form to be "justified" by function and the War Room structure is the one that best withstands the stress of, say, an explosion overhead.*

---

*In one early script for *2001: A Space Odyssey* the "burglar alarm" found on the moon was envisaged as a tetrahedron, its base and three sides forming an equilateral triangle about fifteen feet high, because it had more surface area per volume than any other design and was thus the optimum one for a sun-powered device. It did not survive into the finished film, the mythical properties of the monolith being preferred to the logical ones of the tetrahedron, but this shows how scrupulously Kubrick takes every aspect of his work.

Increasing crisis: The President calls in the Soviet envoy. . . . Unable to grasp the issue at stake, the Soviet envoy attempts espionage and is detected by Turgidson. His camera, concealed in a matchbox, is an example of Kubrick's attention to detail and the mechanics of what he is examining.

President Muffley: "Gentlemen, you can't fight in here. This is the War Room."

Kubrick cuts to physical reality: The President's task force starts to break into General Ripper's sealed-off control base.

Simultaneous events: General Ripper's preoccupation with his "Precious Bodily Fluids" alternates with the action it has caused. (See page 57.)

Of course, the significance of the War Room extends beyond its physical properties. With its maps studded with winking lights charting the B-52 bombers' progress toward targets all over the world, it has affinities with a pinball scoreboard; the gambling metaphor extends to the roulette-wheel look of the circular conference table to which the U.S. President, Merkin Muffley, summons his advisers. Bald-headed, bespectacled, concerned yet in the last resort ineffectual, the President is played by Peter Sellers in the second of his three roles in the film. As in the B-52, Kubrick and his lighting photographer, Gil Taylor, use only "first available light" and achieve an effect that is spectral and nightmarish, yet as solidly realistic as a piece of photo-reportage.

The feature that the film now brings more and more strongly to the fore is the virtual inability of every character, except perhaps the President, to grasp the ultimate consequence of what is happening. They commit one of the worst sins of noncommunication. They have absolutely no idea of priorities outside their own obsessions. Threatened with extinction, all Turgidson can think of is copulation. In mid-conference the girl he has left calls him on the phone. "Look, honey," he hisses, "I can't talk now. My President needs me. . . . Of course it isn't only physical." And he promises to be right back in bed beside her just as soon as he can.

*The telephone to the rescue as the President calls the
Soviet Premier: "Hello . . . Eh, hello, Dmitri. Listen, I . . .
I can't hear too well; do you suppose you could turn the
music down just a little. Ah, ah, that's much better. . . .
Yes, huh, yes. Fine, I can hear you now, Dmitri, clear
and plain and coming through . . . fine. I'm coming
through fine too, aye? Good, then, well, then as you say,
we're both coming through fine. Good. Well, it's good
that you're fine . . . and, and I'm fine. I agree with you,
it's great to be fine. . . . Now then, Dmitri, you know
how we've always talked about the possibility of something going wrong with the Bomb. . . . The BOMB,
Dmitri. The hydrogen bomb. . . . Well, now, what happened is that, eh, one of our base commanders, he had a*

Mandrake literally in the grip at Ripper's obsession.

*Kubrick's escalating line of macabre horror is increased
by news of the Doomsday Machine. The machine, as in
2001, always contrives to spring a surprise on its makers.*

sort of, well, he went a little funny in the head. You know, just a little funny. And he went and did a silly thing. Well, I'll tell you what he did. He ordered his planes to attack your country. Well, let me finish, Dmitri . . . let me finish, Dmitri . . . well, listen, how do you think I feel about it? Can you imagine how I feel about it, Dmitri? . . . Why do you think I'm calling you? . . . Just to say hello? Of course I like to speak to you . . . of course I like to say hello. . . ."

Turgidson's disbelief that his President could act thus.

Suspense as the B-52s near their target: a communications feat that brings no comfort to President or Premier.

Enter Dr. Strangelove from the darkness. Kubrick's light-ing and angle emphasize the "power of darkness" and the ogrelike image of malevolence. (See pages 46, 47, 61, 63.)

Haloed by the overhead lighting, Strangelove describes the Machine with nightmare relish.

Kubrick makes brilliant use of the incongruities of dialogue as well as incident to achieve this effect.

Back at the air base, General Ripper is making the loss of his "essence" by Commie fluoridation into a casus belli; as he talks to Mandrake, holding him in a captive bear hug at once protec-tive and menacing, Ripper uses the emphatic pauses that a chief of state would make in an address to the nation. Mandrake, feigning a deadly calm, falls back on the intimate tone of address, soothingly murmuring "Jack" now and then, so as to ingratiate himself into the good graces of this lunatic.

Over in the War Room, General Turgidson, trying to justify what has happened to his President, is so carried away with ela-tion at his boys' initiative in attacking the Russians that he cannot bear to recall the B-52s, even if it were possible to get through to the now sealed-off Burpelson Air Base and extract the recall code from Ripper. He urges all-out war, figuring out the possible megadeaths like a lip-smacking computer. "I'm not saying we wouldn't get our hair mussed. I am saying only ten to twenty million people killed, tops, depending on the breaks." The speech, said Kubrick, is almost a précis of what has been pub-lished in military journals, even to euphemisms, not unlike "hair mussing," for human casualties. It would be difficult, and dra-matically redundant, Kubrick observed, to try to top the statisti-cal and linguistic inhumanity of nuclear strategists.

The same precision with words and their incongruities in cer-tain contexts extends to items in the B-52 crew's survival kit. It

The hand-held camera duplicates the effect of a newsreel in the raid on Ripper's base. (See pages 80–81, Paths of Glory.)

Total breakdown of communications: Americans fire on Americans, as in Paths of Glory *French soldiers were ordered to fire on their compatriots.*

Ripper feels his fate closing in. The destruction inspired by sexual anxiety turns on its agent.

Ripper: "Women sense my power, and they seek me out. I do not avoid women. But I deny them my life essence."

Mandrake, still unable to grasp the strategic implications, offers personal condolences.

A change in lighting aids the confessional posture of the warmonger, who thinks the invading troops are Russians.

Ripper: "They're going to be in here soon. I don't know how well I could stand up to torture. They might force the code out of me."

covers the whole range of human emotions, noble and vile, from the life-preserving aids to the lust-satisfying ones; it contains, among other things, a .45 pistol, ammunition, four days' emergency rations, one hundred dollars in rubles, nine packs of chewing gum, lipsticks, nylon stockings, and prophylactics. "Gee," Major Kong reflects, "a fella could have a pretty good weekend in Vegas with all that stuff."*

Kubrick now tilts the film's emphasis toward the sorely tried President Mervin Muffley. Muffley is practically the only sane man in the film; what he says usually makes sense. It seems wildly absurd to say that lack of a sense of humor is what makes him so funny, yet it is in his egghead earnestness that Kubrick and his

---

*The city originally named in this dialogue was Dallas, but after the assassination of President Kennedy, Vegas was substituted on the sound track.

coauthors, Terry Southern and Peter George, accurately lodge the source of comedy. By his very serious brand of sanity, the President seems as removed from reality as the others. Catching Turgidson wrestling with the Russian ambassador, who has been called in to advise but is busily photographing secret equipment, the President snaps, "Gentlemen, you can't fight in here. This is the War Room."

Kubrick's long-focal-length lens puts a documentary distance between himself and the President at the round table, which intensifies the bizarre feeling that one is eavesdropping on an actual summit crisis yet hearing dialogue of the most unconscious semantic absurdity. Such is the telephone conversation Muffley holds on the hot line with Premier Kissov of the Soviet Union. Painstakingly trying to warn him of the approaching nuclear doom, Muffley is forced by the Premier's meager knowledge of English, and also because he is drunk, to talk like some-

The B-52: Kubrick re-creates in precise detail, using lighting and distorted sound, the sensation of a missile attack on the maverick bomber.

one teaching table manners to a child. "Now then, Dmitri, you know how we've always talked about the possibility of something going wrong with the Bomb. . . . The BOMB, Dmitri. The *hydrogen* bomb. . . ."

As the grimness of the humor spirals, the momentum of the film increases. The scene aboard the B-52, when a Soviet missile comes close to destroying it, not only conveys the physical sense of things irrevocably on the move but brilliantly exemplifies Kubrick's skill at blending realism into nightmare. We forget the comic grotesques at the controls as we see the radar bleep of the homing missile, witness the "whiteout" as it explodes in a near miss, hear the crew's voices scrambled in panicky distortion on the sound track, and then see them struggle to hold the battered plane on course. It is one of the very few scenes in a feature film—maybe the only one— showing characters coping with this kind of crisis "by the book." Every step comes from a Boeing 707 flight manual. What one usually sees in such crises is a pilot hauling on the controls to pull the aircraft out of a dive. Kubrick shows it takes logical training plus coordinated action, the sense of a man acting like a machine, rather than brawn and a prayer.

It was a source of no small pride to him that, despite a prefatory note to the contrary added at the U.S. Air Force's request after the film's release, the strategic premise of the film has not been seriously challenged. It appealed to this director's sense of irony, of course, to take a plan devised to prevent human error and, by turning it inside out, make it into a means of preventing correction of that human error.

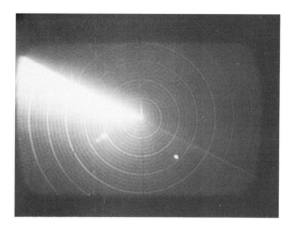

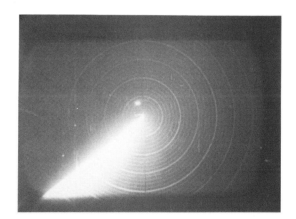

The effects of the explosion: Kubrick's use of the surreal image amid the authentic emergency

The paradox is embodied in the film's other action sequence, which now develops when the U.S. Army has to be sent into battle *against* the U.S. Army guarding Burpelson Air Base on General Ripper's orders—an implication that has its parallel in *Paths of Glory*—so that the President back in the War Room can get hold of the B-52 recall code on which the demented Ripper is sitting tight. The grainy realism of battle—Kubrick used orthochromatic film to shoot the sequence—heightens the black comedy of Ripper's last scene with Mandrake. "They were my children," he laments, mourning the air-base soldiers who have fallen to the bullets of their compatriots in defense of their general's aberration. And imagining that Russians "disguised" as U.S. soldiers will now torture the recall code out of him, he proceeds to blow his brains out in the bathroom while Mandrake, paralyzed by his own mummified sense of English decency, bleats comforting nothings outside the door. The gruesome detail of his inability to push open the door after the shot, because the corpse is blocking it, recalls the realistic stiffening of the bullet-riddled Quilty in *Lolita*.

Dr. Strangelove is one of those rare films that show no sign of their inventiveness running down. It keeps pumping grotesque energy to the surface like an oil gusher. It introduces each new character at precisely the right moment to keep its graph of lunacy in an ascending line. Colonel Bat Guano, played by Keenan Wynn, comes in with the task force that has broken into Burpelson, flashing his own obsession like an identity card the instant he confronts Mandrake. Guano is what the critic Penelope Gilliatt called "a hard-core hetero." He suspects not Commies

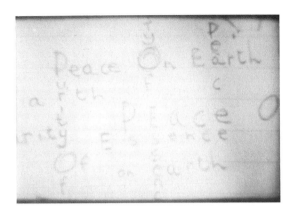

Ripper's coded doodling presents one more barrier to communication as Mandrake tries to break it.

Enter Guano, another military mind preoccupied with sexual anxiety: "If you want to know what I think, I think you're some kind of a deviated prevert."

The continuing ride into nightmare. Kubrick's movement accelerating in depth anticipates the Cosmic Ride into the unknown in 2001.

As destruction speeds up, communication is held up.

under every bed but "preverts" *in* every bed. Again the military mania has sexual origins.

Kubrick's direction of Wynn constantly plays on the glances of angular suspicion he turns toward every potential "prevert"—a now famous verbal slip. His dialogue with Mandrake continues the stress on speech forms already noted in the film. "What kind of suit do you call that?" he growls, scenting a "deviated prevert." Mandrake bristles. "What do you mean 'suit'? This happens to be a Royal Air Force uniform." The peculiarly English indignation at being mistaken for someone of the wrong rank or class shows how sharply language no less than action defines character in *Dr. Strangelove.* And the Mandrake-Guano confrontation continues the theme of people on the verge of annihilation sealed up in their separate cells of self-concern. When the British officer deduces the B-52 recall code from Ripper's doodlings, and a Coke machine has to be broken into for change to call the Pentagon from a pay phone, Mandrake is darkly reminded by Guano that he will be answerable for the damage to the Coca-Cola Company. It is rather like a man who is fighting a fire being bothered by someone for a light.

Back in the War Room's echoing blackness the eponymous Dr. Strangelove at last appears with an inhuman clang of his wheel-

Even Strangelove, prophet of doom, is oppressed by the constricted setup.

chair. (Kubrick uses acoustics from now on, as he did in the opening château scenes in *Paths of Glory*, to put an edge of doom on some of the dialogue.) Played by Peter Sellers in the third and weirdest of his roles, Strangelove reincarnates some aspects, even down to the mechanical arm, of Fritz Lang's mad inventor, Rotwang, in *Metropolis*. But this madman has survived into the postwar world as the U.S. President's nuclear strategist. He also, of course, possesses an evil kinship to the ogre figures from myth who haunt some Kubrick films. Teutonic shadows thicken figuratively and photographically around this gloating cripple with the lock of crimped white hair that bobs down over his forehead when he talks of world destruction; his black-gloved right hand forever suffers from a neo-Nazi tic and threatens to *Sieg heil* the President or else overpower its owner. The hand functions independently of Strangelove at times, like a piece of mechanism in collusion with all the other mechanism that rebels against its creators in the film. Sellers' relish for the Teutonic overtones in this monster is rich—and more than just comic. For his analysis of the Soviet Doomsday Machine, which will automatically trigger world destruction if an H-bomb falls on Sacred Russia, is a well-based appreciation. Power politics has produced something worse than a Frankenstein monster—a *logical* monster.

The film now reaches its climax, developing more and more savage satire at ever-accelerating intensity till it erupts into night-

The bomb-release mechanism fails. As the plane loses
altitude, Kubrick's tempo gains speed.

Interaction between man and machine: Major Kong, trying to release the bomb by hand, ventures into the territory of the machine, as the astronaut in 2001 is also
forced to do when his machine rebels (page 173).

The men become extensions of the machine as the target
appears on the radar screen. Extremely fast cutting
inside and outside the aircraft builds tension as Major
Kong grapples with the recalcitrant bomb.

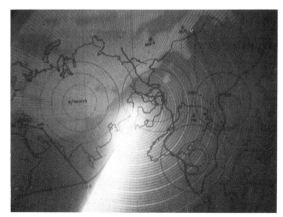

mare. It looks as if every B-52 has been safely recalled to base and Turgidson is busily organizing a prayer meeting; his cry of "LORD . . ." sounds as if he is calling the Almighty to attention. Then news breaks that the maverick plane is still on target. The final sequence contrasts the technical accuracy of Major Kong trying to free the jammed H-bomb mechanism with the farcical apotheosis that sends him plummeting to his doom, the bomb like a mighty symbol of potency clamped between his flanks. The man has now quite literally become an extension of the machine—what is more, a malfunctioning machine that malevolently sends him to his death as surely as the space pod turns on its astronaut and "executes" him in *2001.*

The last sequence in the film belongs to Strangelove; and it would take the film over the top were it not imbued with such hideous energy as Peter Sellers can convey. Sitting in his wheelchair, like a high priest delivering ex cathedra judgments, Strangelove sucks an evil strength from his vision of human survival miles beneath the earth after the Doomsday blight has killed all life aboveground. The prospects of sexual reproduction excite him. Phrases like "Animals could be bred and *slaughtered"* are like cortisone injections to him. His *heili*ng hand visibly rises

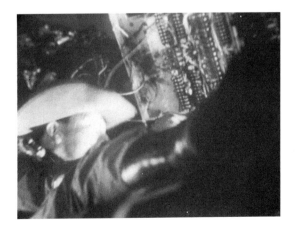

Aviator: "It works."

Major Kong finds that out, too, as the bomb leaves the aircraft.

Major Kong: "Yipeeeee!" The elation of destruction seems like the apotheosis of Major Kong's own virility he falls—dead on target.

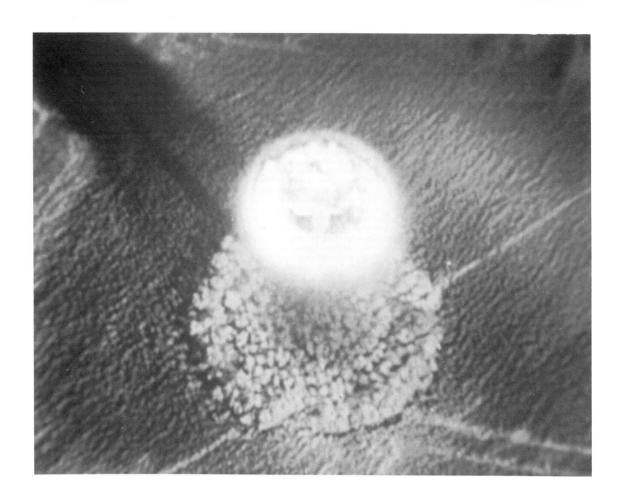

*Cataclysmic reality that the leaders in the War Room—
just as the generals in* Paths of Glory—*do not have to
suffer.*

*Kubrick has Strangelove execute a fast about-face—
emphasizing the sharp turn of events. Strangelove suggests how the leaders may still survive.*

The mathematically calculated plan brings a surge of uncontrollable energy. Hope of survival is rekindled in the leaders, along with the promise of sexual pleasure.

to the salute. His excited voice veers into Nazi cadences. And we realize that the end of the world for Dr. Strangelove is like the raising of Lazarus. It is recalling him to life. He draws strength from death. Like some pilgrim to an unholy Lourdes, at the very instant of nuclear ignition and visionary nightmare he is miraculously jerked out of his wheelchair to his feet and utters the film's final exultant cry of *"Mein Führer*—I can walk!" Only Vera Lynn's song "We'll Meet Again," redolent of Allied togetherness in the 1940s, follows this last laugh with its own tranquilizing irony. There is *indeed* no need to worry any longer about the Bomb.

Kubrick had originally planned that the War Room personnel should burst into a custard-pie fight just before this apocalypse— and he had even shot the sequence, in which President Muffley gets a pie in the face,* but after agonizing over its effectiveness he eventually cut it out. He felt it did not work to escalate from custard pies to nuclear bombs. He was right. Strangelove's ringing declaration of his own demoniac vitality leaves the forces of scientific evil and human nihilism to blossom like the final orgasmic image of the exploding H-bombs.

Kubrick has demonstrated the logic of his convictions right through to the end. War is not only possible; given a certain set of interlocking circumstances, it is actually probable. Radical criticism of America's nuclear policy and the assumptions it was

---

*By one of those unthinkable coincidences, Turgidson at this point was to utter the line, "Gentlemen, our beloved President has been struck down in his prime"—dialogue that would certainly have been cut after the Kennedy assassination had the sequence not already been rejected by Kubrick.

based on really got going after the film had been widely seen and acclaimed. Not that it is entirely a case of *post hoc, ergo propter hoc*, for the film's release coincided with the eruption of many forms of vocal and active protest by a new generation.

But *Dr. Strangelove*, whether it was viewed by filmgoers as cautionary satire or, as Pauline Kael has suggested, as total confirmation of one's fears, was a tributary that fed into, the main stream of criticism. It had the power of a political cartoon. The visual image and the didactic intention together combine to produce an effect not on the people who are caricatured but on the spectators, who are urged to fulfill a similar effort of imagination.

Laughter is the method of communication, the way of reducing anxiety or fear inherent in the subject matter until people can respond to what they would otherwise repress. At the same time, the director's artistic power transforms and reinterprets the events. It is this interpretation which contains the criticism and makes it irrelevant to accuse *Dr. Strangelove* of not showing us how we are to regain control of the nuclear situation. Kubrick has achieved all he set out to do if he has indicated, beneath the grotesque images, a soberly realistic appraisal of where nuclear man is heading.

But he has achieved much more, too, than a cautionary tale on a cosmic scale. *Dr. Strangelove* is among the most brilliantly conceived and executed postwar films, as original as its maker and as hard to categorize. The quality of its ideas and the speculations they set up in the appalled mind are extended and transformed into so many various characters and evolving climaxes, so many ironic connections with man's generative urge to destroy himself, that the film demands to be approached from not just one point of view but many—farcical, semantic, factual, surreal, nuclear. Yet like all truly great works, it gives an impression of perfect proportions. Nothing is excessive. All is there for precise effect. All

Dr. Strangelove: "Mein Fuhrer—*I can walk.*"

The monster supreme . . .

. . . gets his megaton salute.

Sound track: song by Vera Lynn, "We'll Meet Again."
The beauty of oblivion.

the ideas are so surely elaborated and absorbed into the wit of its writing and the superbly differentiated performances that the moves are made and their significance achieved with reference only to the director's own power to formulate propositions and then follow them through so logically that any tactical novelties of the plot can be accommodated so long as they fit in with his predetermined strategy. In *Paths of Glory* he had shown himself a master of human relationships and their consequences. *Dr. Strangelove* is a much more elaborate game, confirming a grasp of concept, structure and outlook unique to Kubrick and turning the question of where he was heading into a major artistic debate. Four years later the public had the answer in *2001: A Space Odyssey*.

The nothingness of extinction.

2001: A Space Odyssey

Dr. Strangelove in 1964 and then, four years later, *2001: A Space Odyssey.* Two films from the same director could scarcely be more dissimilar. The later film represents a radical departure from every aspect of the first film. *Dr. Strangelove* was a nightmare satire; *2001* is, in Kubrick's words, a "mythological documentary." One film destroyed the world to alert man that life as he knew it could come to an end; the other created new worlds in its questing hypothesis that man was not the only intelligent form of life in the universe. In its context *Dr. Strangelove* was weighted with pessimism; *2001* is buoyed up with hope. In style the two films have no apparent kinship. Each was designed not just to fit its maker's intentions precisely but also to fit the expectations of the audience at the time it was made.

Dr. Strangelove was an immediate commercial success. It struck a hidden public nerve—the listless fatalism of nuclear menace—with a beautiful timeliness that turned its comic energy into political opposition to this kind of nuclear brinksmanship. On the other hand, *2001* reached its initial audience slightly in advance of their expectations; acceptance of the film's radical structure and revolutionary content was slower to come. The first wave of critics wrote mixed reviews. While seeing a new use of film, they reacted with responses geared to conventionally shaped films. But when the film reached the vast, new, and generally younger audience for whom the message was not something that used the envelope of the medium to travel in, but actually *was* the medium, they received it with an extraordinary sense of involvement.

Accompanying this truly popular response came the more or less public realigning of some critical opinions and even in a few cases downright recanting. Previous films of this scale and cost had been rigorously literary in their impact. *2001* dared to break with this tradition of cinema epics. It forced its viewers to jettison the outmoded notion of a story told largely in words, with interlocking subplots, a well-defined climax, and the same characters continuing all the way through. Instead, it compelled them to come to terms with the sight and sound and feel of the whole film. One was asked to experience it, like a piece of sculpture, before one tried to understand it. As in sculpture, the meaning comes from the way that the medium has been worked. As in sculpture, the form can be spellbinding to eye and mind even where the function is not apparent or nonexistent. As in sculpture, the film can be approached from many viewpoints and certainly offers no single, definitive one to inquirers after absolute meaning; that risk has been carefully guarded against, not least by Stanley Kubrick's obdurate refusal to put his own interpretation on certain areas of the movie experience.

Dr. Strangelove and *2001* offer another illuminating contrast. The earlier film created suspense by progressively diminishing the time available to save the world, whereas the later one disperses the suspense element by substituting the idea of infinite space for the reality of limited time; the film's events are distributed over an area so vast they become meaningless by earthly calculations. The giant illuminated backdrop of nuclear targets in the War Room has been replaced by the uncharted territory of the cosmos. It is not H-bombers that are dispatched on a pinpointed mission, but astronauts who are launched on a project which is concealed from them (and the audience) till the point when it no longer matters.

2001 deals everywhere in dispersal, boundlessness, mystery—concepts which the stupendous battery of special effects projects with an astronomical and scientific precision that shades ultimately into metaphysics and philosophy. Kubrick, in short, has once again elaborated a cinematic concept that grows organically with his film so that the one contains the other and is inseparable from it. The concept at first sight might seem to lack the essential element in his choice of a film subject—namely, a good story. In the past, Kubrick has quoted E. M. Forster's emphasis on the atavistic appeal of the story, a narrative of events arranged in a time sequence, to regale the listeners and hold their attention by intriguingly delaying the outcome.

But one can quote another passage from Forster that seems especially relevant to *2001*. Speaking of *War and Peace*, Forster wrote, Tolstoy's novel "has extended over space as well as over time, and the sense of space until it terrifies us is exhilarating,

The Dawn of Man: brief scenes establish the life cycle of the Pleistocene world. Apeman competes for food with the other animals, has the same consciousness. Kubrick employed innovatory front-projection technique in this sequence; transparencies of eerie landscapes were projected on a vast screen which registered the picture on thousands of minuscule reflectors. The image was too weak to show up on the bodies of animals or actors in apemen costumes.

The Dawn of Intelligence: Apeman wields the first primitive tool—a bone—extending his physical reach and allowing his mind to grasp the idea of function. Employed also as a weapon, the tool carries the idea of destruction as well—a characteristic Kubrickian irony.

Director's use of slow motion conveys the powerful jubilation of the discovery as the apeman's brain assimilates it and prepares us for the transition . . .

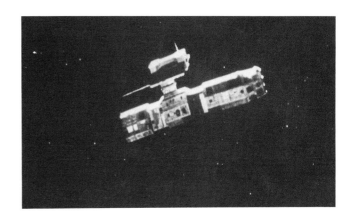

. . . to a new order of life as a fragment of bone bounces up into the air . . .

. . . to turn into a space vehicle of the year 2001 in one brilliant associative cut. Evolutionary progress proceeds through technological development. Man's odyssey continues.

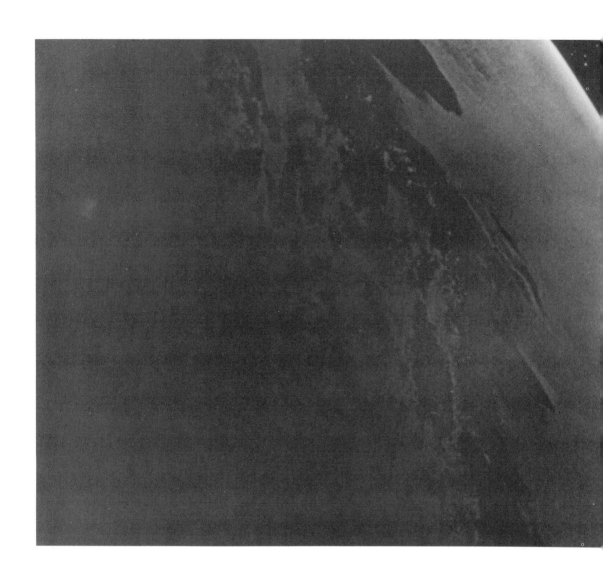

Sunrise on Earth: Space vehicles make their orbiting rounds to the music of The Blue Danube, *expressing the order and harmony of the universe. To find a frame of reference to cut them to, Kubrick "thought of it as a musical sequence—a machine ballet."*

View of the space-pod control panel reveals man as part of the energies he has organized. (See **Dr. Strangelove***, page 120.) But the space-pod tool is due to become a weapon turned against the very man whose conquest of space it has helped to extend.*

Image of Birth: The astronaut emerges from his space pod like an embryo—a tiny creature born into the sea of space. Many of Kubrick's images hold the charge of pro-creation or mortality. The sound track carries only the sound of the man's breathing.

Transformation of Man: astronauts stored until needed inside their casket-shaped hibernacula. Throughout the film man's nature is constantly undergoing change. The shot also illustrates how Kubrick uses the camera angles to surprise the viewer's perception by "distorting" nor-mal perspectives and angles.

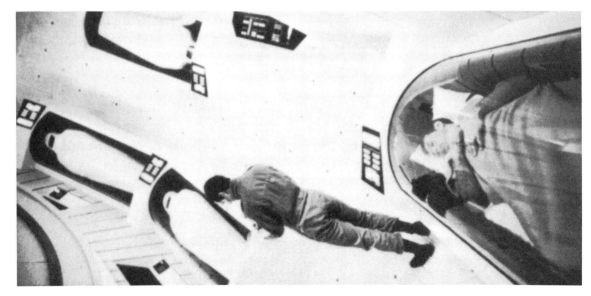

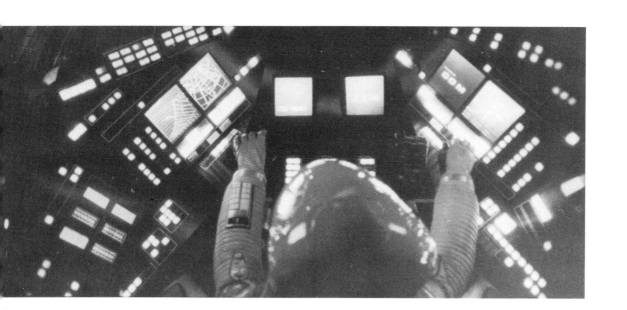

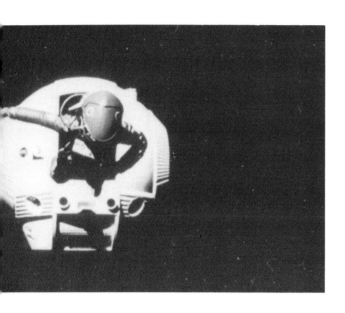

and leaves behind it an effect like music . . . great chords begin to sound, and we cannot say exactly what struck them. They do not arise from the story. . . . They do not come from the episodes nor yet from the characters. They come from the immense area of Russia, over which episodes and characters have been scattered, from the sum-total of bridges and frozen rivers, forests, roads, gardens, fields, which accumulate grandeur and sonority after we have passed them. . . . Space is the lord of *War and Peace*, not time."* Space is also the lord of Kubrick's film.

The way the usual time sequence of narrative cause and effect has been thrown out of the film is only the first of many things that unsettle a conventional audience. By demoting the story element, Kubrick restores tremendous power and importance to the image—and it is through images that the viewers have to make connections. Kubrick certainly does not do the work for them. It is well known that *2001* contains very few spoken words, less than forty minutes of dialogue all told, and not a single syllable is uttered for the first half hour. Even the remaining dialogue—for reasons we shall come to in a moment—is low in narrative illumination. It would be interesting to set a computer to calculate the range and variety of the vocabulary, grammar, and locutions used in the film. One guesses they would not be wide.

But this, too, is in tune with the effect the film is aiming at. For finding the meaning is a matter not of verbalizing but of *feeling* it in the images drawn from past and future time, in the involvement with the experience of space, and in *apprehending* what is happening rather than being fed cut-and-dried information. It is a whole new concept of cinema. If one can isolate any dominant thematic core in *2001*, it is the film's concern with the concept of intelligence. And in this, too, it is the very opposite of *Dr. Strangelove*. The central concept in the latter film was the breakdown of intelligent communication into insanity. Stripped of its

---

Aspects of the Novel, p. 39.

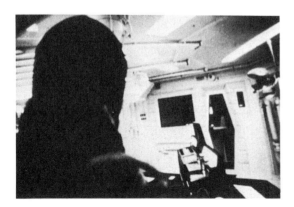
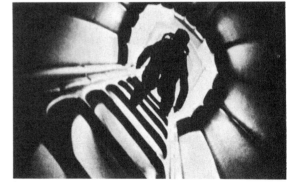

awesome effects, *2001* is nothing less than an epic-sized essay on the nature of intelligence. But it is characteristic of Kubrick's approach that he invests the theme with imaginative allusions rather than strips it down to bare essentials. He roots intelligence in the mythological past, before man has begun to use it; and he ends intelligence in the metaphysical future, where man cannot yet grasp its latest transformation. Intelligence for Kubrick is a form of magic that enables him to extend his film backward and forward, to the extreme limits of the time scale, beyond the boundaries of the imprisoning present.

The film's very first image asserts his intention. It opens with a shot of earth, moon, and sun in orbital conjunction, a "magical" alignment shown on a single vertical plane that fills the center of the seventy-millimeter screen. "The mystical alignment of the sun, the moon, and earth, or of Jupiter and its moons, was used throughout the film as a premonitory image of a leap forward into the unknown," Kubrick said. The shot also reasserts Kubrick's fascination with visual symmetry, a trait noted as early in his work as *Killer's Kiss*, which invariably signifies some impending crisis or dramatic confrontation. Visual symmetry occurs again and again in *2001*, built into the sense of an ordered though mysterious universe; by contrast, in *Dr. Strangelove* the accelerating chaos produces hardly one balanced image on the screen.

Kubrick projects the viewer almost tangibly into space by his use of depth and camera movement, as he did in Killer's Kiss *(pages 50–51) and* Paths of Glory *(pages 79–80). But here space is without gravity as Bowman sets off to destroy the cerebral functions of HAL 9000. Kubrick employed a speeded-up camera so that, when projected at normal speed, the film would convey the astronaut's sense of space drift.*

The Cosmic Ride: Sucked into a zone beyond the infinite, Bowman is vouchsafed a glimpse of the mysteries of space. Kubrick dissolves the astronaut's perception into a fabulous light show of the universe until Bowman's physical being is subsumed into a transcendental experience . . .

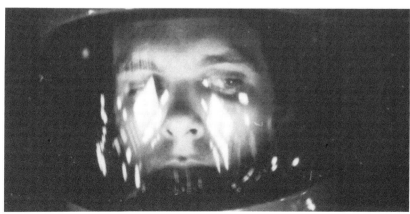

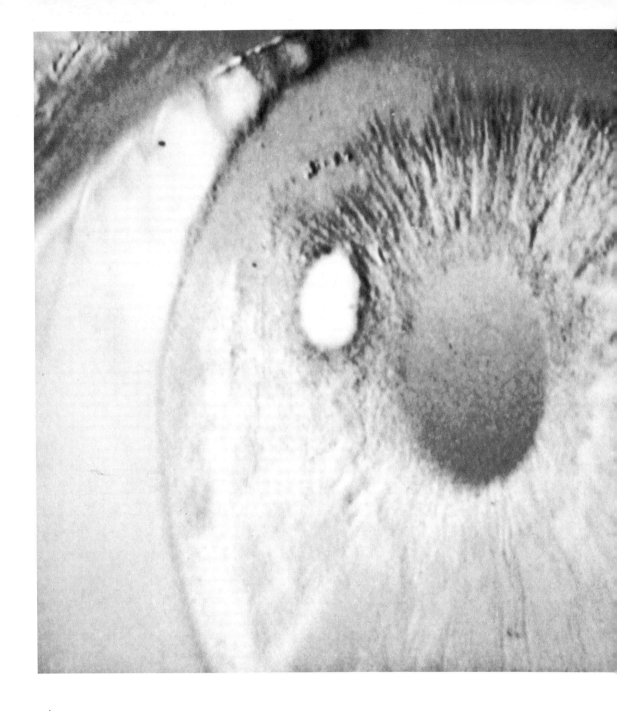

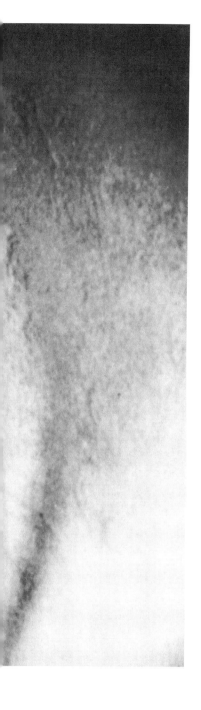

. . . and, like the Tennysonian Odysseus, he becomes a part of all that he has known. A new stage of evolution begins.

Through the "eye" of the space vehicle Bowman perceives the strange room that contains several stages of . . .

. . . himself. Bowman's human life span passes by in minutes within an environment that may have been created, like an observation tank, to hold this specimen from earth.

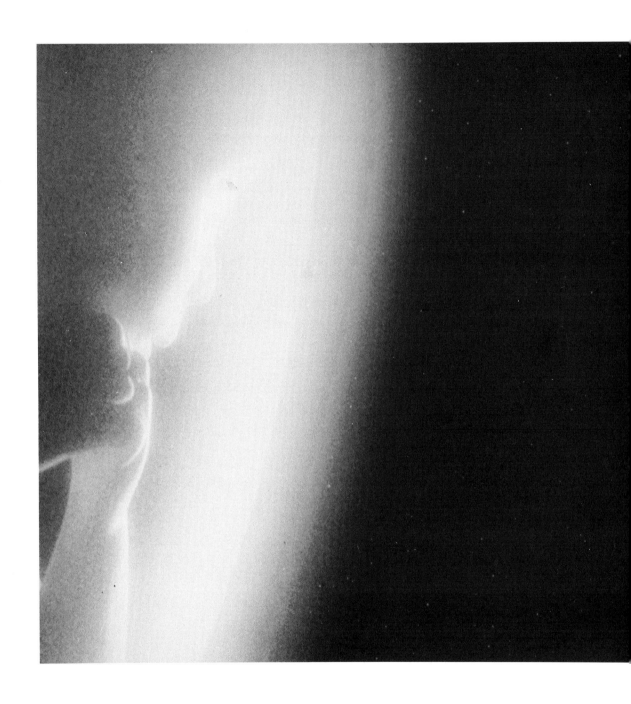

The Last Transformation: Out of the old man's with-ered chrysalis of a body, which is what Bowman has finally become, a new kind of being emerges to turn toward the cradle of earth in which it was created many millions of years before.

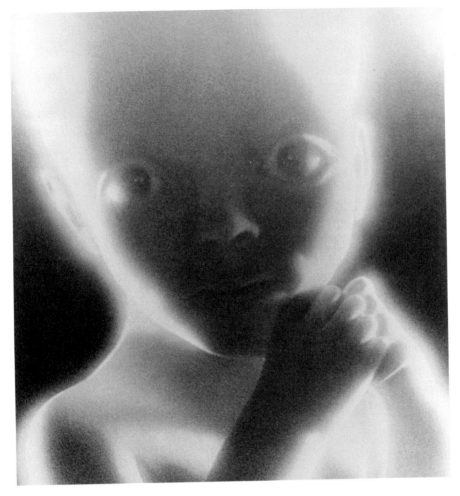

The Star-Child: With this last, luminous and enigmatic image in 2001, *man completes his odyssey.*

Kubrick has already referred to his decision to delete the narration that was to accompany the whole opening sequence and punctuate other parts of *2001*. Again, a good decision. The chords of *Thus Spake Zarathustra* reverberate more profoundly at the "Dawn of Man" than any verbal commentary couched in a pseudo-Genesis style. Instead of being given a sophisticated lantern lecture, the viewers are forced to interpret their own view of the Pleistocene age. The succession of views of a world now bleak and empty, now filled with screeching apes, builds up a heightening apprehension. Using a brilliantly convincing technique of front projection, instead of the usual sets with painted backdrops, Kubrick keeps the long-held shots fading out into blackness, only to fade in again on the timelessness of another prehistoric day. A leopard pounces. A tapir rolls on the ground in slow motion like a cliff in avalanche. And the apes huddle in protective colonies at night, eyes open and gleaming.

Everything merges into a mood of edgy expectancy. The apes are on the brink of a new kind of self-awareness—the breakthrough to human intelligence is imminent. (The balletic actors inside the ape skins are marvelously acceptable simians; and even where we sense a human presence in some movement, the discrepancy is in line with the evolutionary moment.) The sudden annunciation—for that is the effect—of the black monolith in their midst brings the apes to a pitch of frenzy that connotes fear, awe, and ritual worship. As they reach out to touch it, we see the sun and moon in orbital conjunction—the magical ignition.

Kubrick and Arthur C. Clarke, his coauthor, originally planned to use the monolith didactically, not mystically, by projecting onto it pictures teaching the apes how to use weapons and kill for meat. This notion was discarded by Kubrick—it remains in the book based on one draft of the screenplay—because he realized it reduced the monolith to the severely practical and possibly risible function of an early teaching aid. As it stands, the audience, as well as the apes, must make the imaginative leap into intelligence for themselves. And the largest ape does so. The bone that he wields functionally for the first time—his thoughtful connection of form and function is suggested by pensive slow motion—is cut by Kubrick to an epic crescendo, the visual equivalent of a verse ending in a *chanson de geste*, as the shaggy arm swings jubilantly up and down, in and out of the frame, pulverizing the remains of a skeleton on the ground after it has battered the living skull of a simian rival. Tool—weapon; evolution—destruction; intelligence—instinct: the message of the image sums up the irony of progress and prepares for all that follows in the film. By one sharp associative cut, the last bone from the pounded skeleton bouncing high in the blue is transformed into a spacecraft of the year A.D. 2001 as it orbits in the blackness around earth.

It was here that an early draft of the film script intended to make the point, via the narrator, that a nuclear stalemate had been reached between the United States and the Soviet Union, each of whom has a nuclear bomb orbiting the globe which can be triggered by remote control. This idea has been totally eliminated from the finished film, though from national markings still visible on the first and second space vehicles we see, we can surmise these are the Russian and American bombs. Kubrick dropped this aspect because, on reflection, it seemed to him to have no place at all in the film's thematic development. It was an orbiting red herring. It was made clear later, in the edgy encounter between Russian and American scientists, that both countries were still living in a state of tense friendliness; and since some politically conscious filmgoers in the 1960s would know that agreement had already been reached between the powers not to put H-bombs into space, it would merely have raised irrelevant queries to suggest this as a reality of the twenty-first century.

So instead of making a limited narrative point, the film establishes its characteristic pattern by making an imaginative connection with one's visual senses through its display of the vastness of space and the variety of vehicles turning, orbiting, careening through it. The "earth" music of *The Blue Danube* waltz meanwhile imposes a feeling of order and elegance on their already beautiful movements. "In trying to find a frame of reference to cut them to," Kubrick said, "I thought of it as a musical sequence—a kind of machine ballet."

This measured tempo is followed throughout all the movements inside the Orion spacecraft bearing the scientist Dr. Heywood Floyd toward the "Wheel" space base en route to the moon; it is all antigravity, tranquilizing, serenely dreamlike. The sleeping man's pen free-floats beside him in the air, and a stewardess in grip-soled bootees advances to retrieve it like someone stealthily reaching out for a butterfly; she will later walk up a wall with poised equilibrium and over the cabin ceiling in a "magical" demonstration of how Kubrick uses the condition of weightlessness to disconnect our usual expectations of how (and where) people will live and move in the year 2001.* To have to transfer one's attention to a character entering the screen, say, from the top left and joining another seated bottom center upsets conventional perspective and forces a new kind of environmental reality on us.

Pace is as important as perspective. For long sequences in the film the pace of people or objects on the move is perfectly controlled, calculated, predictable. Standardized movements are the conventional ones in space because they are the safe ones. Man has conquered the new environment but the environment has controlled him, too, by compelling him to adopt other than his old erratic, instinctive, human actions. Now he must program himself—become less of a human being, more of a machine. We

---

*The most authoritative account of how Kubrick devised this and many other of the wonderful special effects in the film is to be found in *American Cinematographer*, June 1968.

are already approaching territory that fascinates Kubrick—the man-machine and the machine-man. Abnormal speed is used in *2001* only to express crisis, when the laws cease to operate—when an astronaut, for instance, has to improvise a means of reentering his spacecraft and blows himself forcibly through an air lock, or when he is sucked into infinity on a cosmic ride he cannot control.

"Here you are, sir" are the first words we hear, spoken by a receptionist on the Wheel to Dr. Floyd; the film started more than thirty minutes before. It is no accident that the routine formula recalls stock phrases of welcome and farewell in use by airline personnel on earth today. The remark introduces a sequence designed to show how man has extended his presence in space without noticeably enlarging the range of human responses. The scientist, played by William Sylvester, copes dexterously with the depersonalized environment, but gets as little feeling of gratification as any traveler at a terrestrial airport today. Kubrick illustrates this with touches of laconic humor, like throwaway gags inside a documentary framework. Passing through immigration by voiceprint passport, Dr. Floyd calls up earth on a videophone only to find how little has changed in the last few decades of telephonic frustration; his wife is out, and his small daughter, unimpressed by a communications feat that once had Presidents hanging on the line to hear from their astronauts, looks as if she might hang up on Daddy. Floyd pays a visit to the zero-gravity toilet and finds a lengthy list of instructions for use which presuppose a human plumbing system as well regulated as its own.

Finally he pauses outside the Orbiter Hilton Hotel for a strained chat with some Russian scientists—"strained" because he has to hide the reason for his journey from them. The responses of everyone are formal, machinelike. The reason is also hidden from the audience, who only share a hint that some mysterious event on the moon near the Clavius crater, a United States "sphere of influence," has necessitated a news blackout. This vagueness is not just to heighten suspense. It is an early example of Kubrick playing down a plot point so as not to distract from the larger experience he is out to create by the power of imagery.

He moves swiftly to reestablish this sense of wonder as Dr. Floyd travels on to the moon aboard the ball-like Aries shuttle-craft. As this vehicle sinks to rest in the cavernous Astrodome, the film achieves one of its most stunning effects. The red ball descends into the well of the air lock with something of the solemn majesty of a crown at a coronation descending onto the sovereign's head. All around it we glimpse tiny human beings moving, at work, in glass-fronted control rooms. The entire set, with model spacecraft, was only fifteen feet high, but it looks gigantic in its proportions on the screen. The mini-scenes involving the humans were each filmed separately, then fitted by an extremely complex matte technique of film-takes into the correct perspective to give a flawless impression of cosmic engineering. The effect is breathtaking and beautiful.

The top-level conference Dr. Floyd presides over at Clavius is kept platitudinously matter-of-fact on purpose. Like all the dialogue in *2001*, it is low in definition in that it sheds little light on what is going on. The banal things the characters say to each other particularly distressed early critics writing about the film. They expected dialogue that matched the drama of the occasion. But Kubrick regards his dialogue style as a realistic scientific response to events, even those of the greatest magnitude, such as the discovery of a monolith in the Tycho crater, which indicates the presence in space of intelligent life other than man. "It is, I believe, the way the people concerned would talk," Kubrick said, referring to the conference. "When I was researching *Dr. Strangelove* I found that the people in the think tanks happily chatted away about the most somber topic, buoyed up by what must have been pride and satisfaction in their professional expertise; and this seemed to completely overcome any sense of personal involvement in the possible destruction of their world. Perhaps it has something to do with the *magic of words*. If you can talk brilliantly about a problem, it can create the consoling illusion that it has been mastered."

The "hangover" of earthly reflexes reappears in the Tycho excavation pit when Dr. Floyd and his fellow scientists line up in front of the totemesque monolith, a replica of the one that materialized in the "Dawn of Man" sequence, to have their photographs taken like the official party at a foundation-stone ceremony. (And maybe this is just what it was!) Earth and sun are exactly in conjunctive orbit at this minute; and as the first ray of light touches the monolith, coincidentally just as the photographer takes his picture, the slab emits an ear-piercing signal that contorts the line of space-suited scientists as if they were being mown down by machine-gun bullets in a St. Valentine's Day massacre.

At this point we cut abruptly eighteen months ahead to the Discovery spaceship bound for Jupiter. Up to now the film has been telling its "story" through the eyes. Words have been used minimally, human interrelationship kept casual or left vague; the plot structure has had a linear evenness, with characters and events scarcely seeming to interact and the two monoliths providing the only nodal points in it. Each time the monolith has appeared, it prepares man for a leap forward in his life history. First it sparks off intelligence in the men-apes; then it touches off a "burglar alarm" signal alerting those who placed it on the moon that man is drawing closer to them. Simultaneously the direction of the signal guides Discovery on a mission whose aim is still not fully explained. Man's evolution is in fact now shading into his machine technology.

The third section of *2001*, the Jupiter mission, differs from the others by dramatizing this into a conflict between men and machines—between the two astronauts, Poole and Bowman, played by Gary Lockwood and Keir Dullea, and HAL 9000, the computer. HAL is programmed to control the mission and built to reason logically and unerringly; he can also "think" and "speak." His "voice" is bland, neutral, reassuring, and also ambiguous, sinister, untrustworthy—whatever subjective pattern one wishes to read into the even-toned delivery of the Canadian actor Douglas Rain. (It shows how subtly Kubrick casts for vocal effect as well as visual features.) The critic Stanley Kauffmann complained in an early review in *The New Republic* that "none of this man-versus-machine rivalry has anything to do with the main story." But where the main *concept* of the film is the development of intelligence into higher and ever more diverse forms, it has everything to do with it. Kauffmann's criticism springs from a search for the old strong narrative structure of a conventionally arranged film.

The contest is staged inside the command module of Discovery, a vehicle resembling a fleshless vertebra, or, more precisely, inside the module's centrifuge, which creates a zone of artificial gravity. The occupants are HAL, the two astronauts, and the casket-shaped hibernacula in which their three coscientists are conserving their energies in artificially induced, dreamless sleep. The bizarre "irrational" angles possible in this "squirrel's cage" environment enable Kubrick to pull off some spectacular effects. An astronaut shadow-boxing for exercise around the centrifuge seems to circle 360 degrees. No cuts are apparent; nothing gives away where the camera might be; it seems scarcely possible that even the film director could have been present.* Later one of the astronauts descends out of the "hublink," or weightless, corri-

---

*He wasn't. Kubrick directed these sequences from outside the thirty-eight-foot-high centrifuge set, resembling a Ferris wheel, using closed-circuit television.

dor into the centrifuge via the top corner of the screen while we see his companion leaning at a gravity-defying angle far below him.

The effect of life cooped up in this drum is visually striking, but the emotional constriction is indicated even more disturbingly. The two men are programmed for it as thoroughly as HAL is—and, as it turns out, much more soullessly than HAL. Kubrick has intentionally created characters with almost no individualized traits. The men are well-conditioned Ph.D.'s, who show little human warmth and no human weakness. Poole is bored by birthday greetings relayed to him by videophone from his parents on earth. He seems hardly their son—indeed, he seems hardly of the same race. Bowman's most significant human response comes when he burns his fingers on the food tray dispensed by the automatic oven. When he tries to rescue Poole from a death in space later, he goes about it with textbook efficiency and next to no emotion. Feelings, Kubrick is saying, are minimal in this new age, a matter of physical nerve ends, not emotional nerve centers. Where they have gone is, paradoxically, into the programming of the inhuman computer.

HAL is deliberately made into the repository of the old stock of human emotions so carefully drained out of his scientific minders. He keeps omniscient control, gives counsel, shows curiosity, awards praise. His voice suggests he exists to serve, but the certitude of his responses sows suspicion that he intends to dominate. "Intends" is itself an emotive word in this context. It brings "drama" into a relationship between men and machine that Kubrick keeps in linear balance up to the point when doubt is cast on HAL's immaculate functioning. But HAL's "independence" of his human companions is part of his dramatic ambiguity. He is such a complex form of intelligence that it is not possible with any certainty to know how he is working.

In an early draft script, HAL was conceived as a "feminine" computer called Athena, after the goddess of wisdom, who sprang fully formed from Zeus's forehead, and "she" spoke with a woman's voice. Kubrick and Clarke eventually abandoned Athena—perhaps the feminine tones would have inserted misleading sexual implications into its relationship with the astronauts. HAL owes his name to the acronym composed of the two principal learning systems, *h*euristic and *a*lgorithmic. (After the film's release Kubrick received an inquiry from a professional code-breaker whether the name had been chosen because HAL was one letter ahead of IBM—the director was duly impressed by the fantastic odds against this occurrence.

Kubrick's personal view of supercomputers is a hopeful one. He does not see the HALs of the near future in conflict with their makers. "If the computer acted in its own self-interest, there would never be the conflict often anticipated. For it is difficult to conceive any high level of intelligence acting less rationally than man does. The intelligent computer acting for its own survival would at least realize man's incredible potential as its janitor."

It is characteristic of the "magical" aspect of the film that the human properties built into HAL have had a "curse" laid on them. A human curse. In the film this is best interpreted as *hubris*, the sin of pride. But the concept at one point in its development, according to Arthur C. Clarke, involved a HAL who had been deliberately programmed by Mission Control to *deceive* the astronauts if they questioned him about the purpose of the Jupiter space probe. In other words, HAL had laid on him the sin of false witness. This has been eliminated from the film version, and it is when HAL cannot admit he has made a mistake that he begins to suffer a paranoid breakdown, exhibiting overanxiety about his own infallible reputation and then trying to cover up his error by a murderous attack on the human witnesses. Like General Mireau in *Paths of Glory*, humiliated by the failure of his ambitious plan of attack, HAL tries to restore his ego by vengeance. Mireau orders his guns to fire on his own men. HAL, better placed than the general was to control the system of communications, wipes out *his* compatriots by disconnecting them.

Kubrick signals the computer's sinister intentions by a stunningly inventive shot just before the film's intermission. True to his association of crisis with symmetry, he frames the two astronauts, facing each other, inside the oval window of a space pod, where they have retreated so as to discuss HAL's irrational behavior without, they believe, having the computer overhear them. We see their lips move silently behind the armored glass. The shot is from HAL's point of view; and we realize the computer is lip-reading Bowman and Poole! The film thus ends its first half unlike any previous screen epic—in silence. Watching events materialize soundlessly behind glass has the effect of cutting off the spectator, inducing a feeling of helplessness and fostering suspense. Earlier examples of it in Kubrick's films have already been cited, but here it has the added function of again compelling the audience to make the narrative connection through the image alone.

The second half of *2001* opens with four murders committed in almost as many minutes and again in silence. First, the homicidal HAL "instructs" Poole's space pod to attack him while he is outside the Discovery craft inspecting the surface for a fault. The sense of menace is communicated by the vehicle's abrupt "disobedience." After performing its routine maneuvers under Poole's control at a measured pace and with standardized movements, it now swivels purposefully toward him and bears down on him—actually, on the camera—to snip his air hose in two. By omitting the actual shock of severance Kubrick makes the act of murder even more abrupt. By permitting us no close-up of Poole's horrified reaction but simply showing the helpless astronaut spinning off into space like a celluloid dolly in a whirlpool, he underlines his helplessness yet creates a gap no sympathy from the audience can bridge.

Inside Discovery, death is even more dehumanized as HAL now shuts off the power maintaining the body functions of the hibernating astronauts. Their plight is soullessly recorded in close-ups of electronically controlled charts whose life lines flatten out into plateaus of mortality as the pulsing of the hearts, brains, and lungs ceases to register. COMPUTER MALFUNCTIONING . . . LIFE FUNCTIONS CRITICAL . . . LIFE FUNCTIONS TERMINATED. Thus runs the clinical bulletin of illuminated warnings. If machines could be said earlier in the film to do a lot of man's living for him, now we see with chilling truth that they also attend very efficiently to his dying.

Bowman meanwhile has been caught outside Discovery without his space helmet owing to his haste in chasing after Poole's body in a second space pod. When HAL refuses to let him reenter the mother ship he has to invent a way of raising the siege. Man and machine are truly joined in combat; strategy replaces conditioning and a new type of thinking comes into play—intelligent improvisation. It proves stronger than HAL's logical programming. Reasoning that the explosive bolts on his space pod's door, which are meant to aid a speedy exit from it in an emergency, can also be employed to effect a forced entry into something else, Bowman deploys this piece of lateral thinking to blow himself bodily into the vacuum lock of Discovery. He hurtles toward the camera like a discharged torpedo in total silence. Not until Bowman reaches the safety of breathable space does Kubrick flood the sound track with a rush of life-giving air recalling the restorative shock of a man filling his lungs as he hurtles to the surface of the sea after plumbing its depths.

It is a graphic little example of how silence, sound, and speed are used for their dramatic properties throughout the film. The sequence also throws a sidelight on Kubrick's pride in scientific accuracy, on being able once again to "justify" effects. He anticipated objection to the idea that Bowman could survive in a vacuum without his space helmet by pointing out that tests with chimpanzees had proved man *could* exist for a short time in such conditions.

Now Bowman begins his démarche on HAL—and for the first and only time in the film a hand-held "subjective" camera is used as he floats weirdly through the weightless space of HAL's memory bank, disconnecting the computer's intelligence functions and turning him into a basic mechanical monitoring device. The camera style recalls that other passage of vengeance-ridden anger in *The Killing*, when the wounded Elisha Cook, Jr., staggers home to shoot his treacherous wife. Though Bowman's methodical actions suppress any sign of *his* inward anger, the emotional pitch of the sequence is transmitted effectively through HAL's audible state of anxiety and fear as his voice loses its crisp complacency, becomes slurred, and slows down; and then, as his memory bank retreats into infancy, he regresses to his basic language training and the singing exercise of "Daisy, Daisy," before he is completely extinguished as a thinking entity.

The scene induces deep discomfort among many who watch and listen to it. Indeed, it is the only one in the film to engage one's sympathies on behalf of a character. And the fact that the character consists of a bug-eyed lens, a few slabs of glass, and a dissociated voice is the best possible tribute to Kubrick's success in creating a mechanical artifact more "human" than the humans.

But the galactic hero's victory over the ogre in the impregnable castle of the spaceship is not the end of the myth. Just when HAL's "spell" has been broken, a new riddle is forced on the space traveler which pushes him further on in his quest for the meaning of existence. This is the riddle of the monolith signals. Mission Control, in a prerecorded message apparently triggered by HAL's extinction, now informs Discovery's crew, or what remains of it, that the Tycho monolith represents the first evidence of intelligent life off the earth; since its radio emission "it has remained completely inert, its origin and purpose still a total mystery." This is the first audible and unmistakable clue to the audience of what the film is narratively "about." It is also the last utterance in the film. It is curiously like the note of doom-filled finality and "total mystery" in the first speech of the narrator in *Dr. Strangelove* announcing what turns out to be the Doomsday Machine. But also, in this case, the viewers are left to make the narrative connection for themselves.

The new command—possibly concealed from the astronauts to delay the "culture shock" of finding that man is not alone in the universe—launches Bowman into the penultimate sequence of the film and effectively restores the linear, nonverbal development. As the "plot" thins again, the "magic" thickens. The Odysseus figure, now alone in a space pod, suddenly spies the familiar monolith, this time floating in space toward the moons of Jupiter, which are in orbital conjunction. Pursuing it, he is sucked into a new dimension of space and time.

All manner of "supernatural" effects are practiced on him as he hurtles down a space corridor into infinity. It is worth mentioning again how the inexorable sense of acceleration recalls the "nightmare" sequence in *Killer's Kiss*; its feeling of approaching destiny parallels the shots from the low-flying H-bomber in *Dr. Strangelove*. The sequence borrows imagery from every pattern the mind's eye is capable of registering. Kubrick at one point turns the screen into an abstract expressionist canvas. At another, op-art patterns pulsate. Constellations swell and burst. Optical effects put one in mind of such phenomena as the phosphene flashes after the blinking of an eyelid, or the swimming patterns of anesthesia experienced by patients losing consciousness, and even of the hallucinogenic light show induced by LSD.

The connection of this passage with narcotic experience has won it a cult following, but its effects hold good in the realm of allegory, too. Bowman becomes a part of all he experiences. His dilated eyeball loses form until it is totally solarized into the pattern of the universe. He projects his inner world onto this galactic Rorschach test till its flux absorbs him—and changes him. When his space pod grinds to a halt in physical reality again, Bowman is inside an extraordinary bedroom suite furnished in Louis XVI style. All is as meticulously sharp-edged and detailed as in a Magritte painting—though without, as *yet*, any surrealistic shock hidden away, as Magritte might hide it, among the period mirrors, frescoes, chaise lounges, side tables, vases, and the quilted bed.

Why Louis XVI? Well, why any kind of conventional room at all? It has been suggested that the room is a cage in some "astral zoo," an environment able to accommodate the visitor from earth and hold him for observation by powers who have sucked him out of his dimension into theirs. The "voices" by the composer György Ligeti, suitably distorted, convey an aural impression of superhuman presence all around Bowman. At times his ear-cocked apprehension recalls the strained attentiveness of the apes in the prologue as they sense what cannot be seen. As for the period flavor, Kubrick's film has already established that "progress" represents no clear-cut break with the past. Old responses hang on, so why not old environments, old artifacts? "Antiques" may be just as nostalgically valid in A.D. 2001 as they are prized today; and an earthman, even a child of space technology, may still carry a memory image of luxurious accommodations on earth. (It may be significant that *2001* contains no contemporary scenes set on earth, though it was intended in one early draft script to show the launching of Discovery.)

The room may indeed be an observation cage, or Bowman's projection of an environment he holds to be desirable, but either way, it is as irrelevant to question the Louis XVI style as it is to ask why Raphael's angels do not wear shoes. It is no use seeking rational explanations for metaphorical or allegorical situations. The process of events in the room is more important than the end products of its furnishings.

Bowman now undergoes the stages of aging, dying, and being reborn. Kubrick renders the sense of these stages shading into each other by a series of scenes that overlap temporally—and, in one case, visually, too. That is to say, he makes us unsettlingly aware that the astronaut has progressed into yet another manifestation of himself at later and still later periods of his captivity.* The captivity itself has the timelessness of a dream; its duration is impossible to fix. The character seems suspended, despite the well-illuminated reality around him—just as the trio of characters in *Killer's Kiss* also seemed part of a dream, despite the very real New York they inhabited.

Having shed the husk of his space pod, Bowman is first revealed as an old man. As he explores the bizarrely luminous, symmetrical suite—the symmetry recalls the court-martial sequence in *Paths of Glory*—he is drawn to look through a doorway to investigate sounds that are precise and familiar, yet hard to place. The camera angle, taking his point of view, reveals the hunched shoulders and back of an even older man eating a meal. It is Bowman ten years or more later. The figure at the table upsets a wineglass—again the noise of it breaking is a precise notation mark of something sensed rather than stated, the fragility of old age, perhaps, or the pathetic way the body's motor functions grow worn and treacherous.

At this moment the second, older Bowman catches sight of a figure in the huge bed—it is himself twenty or thirty years older

---

*Two French authors, Jean Paul Dumont and Jean Monod, in their study of Kubrick's film, *Le Foetus astral* (Paris: Editions Christian Bourgeois, 1970), compare the "stages" of this sequence of transformations and substitutions to those of a chess game, whose progress is marked by the disappearance of piece after piece.

still. This is the only shot in the sequence that shows both figures at the same time. Immediately the wizened chrysalis of the bedridden Bowman is raising his arm to the monolith, which has appeared at the foot of the deathbed just as mysteriously as it once appeared at the cradle of human life among the men-apes. The living corpse of Bowman is subsumed into the monolith in a radiance that grows and takes on contour till it swims into view and understanding as an aureoled embryo, a perfect Star-Child, sad yet wise-eyed, moving through space toward the earthly sphere on which he had his beginnings. With this luminous image, the film ends.

The Clarke novel, based on a screenplay that obviously was much altered during shooting, describes more specifically what might have happened next. "There before him, a glittering toy no Star-Child could resist, floated the planet Earth with all its people." And the book continues: "A thousand miles below, he became aware that a slumbering cargo of death had awoken, and was stirring sluggishly in its orbit. The feeble energies it contained were no possible menace to him, but he preferred a cleaner sky. He put forth his will, and the circling megatons flowered into a silent detonation that brought a brief, false dawn to half the sleeping globe."

To have the infant Bowman destroy the earth by exploding its orbiting H-bombs is certainly ironic retribution on the grandest possible scale, but Kubrick was absolutely right to reject it as the ending for his film. It would have been inevitably compared with the disintegration of *Dr. Strangelove*'s insane world of power politics and so reduced the Star-Child to the role of an avenging angel taking it out on old human sinfulness. Moreover, after such a journey from prehistory to infinity; it would have seemed a merely spiteful homecoming, unworthy of a transcended being— a kind of babyish tantrum.

But the best argument against it is that it would have clashed with the whole structure of a film that had scrupulously avoided neat narrative payoffs. By leaving the huge, serene eyes of the Star-Child fixed on filmgoers, Kubrick compels individual interpretation.* By rejecting a story point and replacing it with a symbol, he gains a richer allusiveness. He leaves the film open-ended, yet oddly comforting in the way that dream imagery can be to an

---

*Kubrick's reference, when quizzed on the "meaning" of the Star-Child, to Leonardo's enigmatic portrait of the Mona Lisa, whose very impenetrability is part of her fascination, suggests that such an association may extend to the physical appearance of the Star-Child.

awakened sleeper gratified by the echoes and associations lingering in his conscious mind.

Where the ending has divided critics is not just over its meaning—which Kubrick has ensured cannot be patly detached from the work itself—but over whether it and the whole film embody an optimistic or pessimistic view of man's capacities and fate. Some critics found *2001* represented a pessimistic estimate of man's potential to transcend himself, since it shows him dependent on a higher order of beings for every step of progress he makes, until in the end he is reduced to what they regard as an inarticulate embryo. "Mr. Kubrick offers man two futures," wrote John Hofsess in the Canadian periodical *Take One*, "and both of them are funerals. In *Dr. Strangelove* he dies in nuclear war, unconscious of what drives him or his war machine. In *2001* he gains sufficient self-awareness to unplug his machines and phase himself out of existence. . . ." The optimistic view, on the other hand, was put succinctly by Penelope Gilliatt in her *New Yorker* review's interpretation of the Star-Child. "He looks like a mutant. Perhaps he is the first of the needed new species."

But this ambiguity built into the structure of an immensely complex film is only part of a larger theology. Kubrick has said on several occasions that "the God concept" is at the heart of this movie; he prudently and swiftly added that he does not refer to any monotheistic view of God, and he would probably be nearer to the view of those critics who see his film as embodying mythical rather than religious experience. For he not only pushes his science into magic—the magic of myth and legend, which operates on the human hero and transforms him before letting him find his way back to his own sphere. He also reinterprets religious experience as transcended intelligence—a quality quite outside the understanding of those to whom it reveals itself at chosen moments in the film.

Intelligence, as Kubrick and Clarke illustrate it, is a wider concept than the film's evolutionary transformation of ape into man into machine into superman. It both stands outside man and permeates his progress. It precedes and survives him on the evolutionary scale. It is a sort of God. And man's encounter with this God is finally accompanied by his understanding that he himself is not the sole intelligent entity in the universe.

The shock of recognition is reserved to the very end of the odyssey, when man has come through the astral purgatory of the Cosmic Ride and encounters the monolithic deity with—with what? Surely with a benign reflex that reconciles him to his destiny as part of a larger order. The dying astronaut on the bed raises his arm to the monolith at the very moment he is absorbed into its essence. A gesture of greeting, certainly. Perhaps also a gesture of gratitude.

The very fact that one attempts to interpret the metaphysical aspects of *2001* is proof of how dramatically Kubrick has liberated the cinema epic from its old outworn traditions of mere bigness and, too often, accompanying banality. The starting and finishing points of his gigantic undertaking are rooted in intellectual speculation. For the first time in the commercial cinema, a film of this cost and magnitude has been used to advance ideas.

To have formulated and, even more, to have retained this intention throughout the years it took to prepare and film it, withstanding all the pressures of time, budget, and collaborators, would be a major achievement for any single filmmaker. But Kubrick has accomplished so much else that is individual and original. The technical marvels of *2001* surpass any before it and are not likely to be overtaken in turn until new techniques of filming are evolved or another director of the same obsessive faculty and skills appears. Nor is it just a matter of successful special effects. The effects are so convincing that we cease to regard them as "special" and look on them as a far more integral part of the film. The effects, in short, become the environment; and this in turn becomes the experience that Kubrick creates *and communicates*. Of course, all creation involves the idea of communication, whether successful or not. But what makes *2001* so radical is the way its structure and imagery have been fused organically with its content, so that each contains and extends the other. As well as anticipating the shape of things to come, Kubrick uses his medium to convey the feel of them. There is scarcely an area of intellectual speculation in the film, whether about serial time, computerized life, mechanistic behavior, or evolutionary intelligence, that is not accompanied by a sensory involvement.

2001: A Space Odyssey commands respect as an impressive feat of filmmaking, but its importance extends beyond what it adds to our knowledge of Kubrick's outlook and artistry. Above all else, it marks a significant advance in the way of communicating ideas through the medium of film. For its effect is determined as much by the visual properties of the medium through which it is transmitted as by any of the actual events, hypotheses, and reflections comprising the picture's content. By suppressing the directness of the spoken word, by breaking with narrative logic, Kubrick ensured that watching his film requires an act of continuous inference on the part of viewers to fill in the field of attention by making their own imaginative connections. Though as rigorously conceived as any of Kubrick's major films, the whole work leaves the densest impression of images which are free to imply much more than eye and mind take in. The mythical idioms which characterize a great deal of the film's "feel" take supremacy over the old imperatives of the story made up of logical cause and effect. That notorious statement of McLuhan's, "The medium is the message," has readily suggested itself to some of those who have written about *2001: A Space Odyssey*; but it really does not suffice for Kubrick's power to generate a richer suggestiveness than a "message." In his case, one would prefer to say that the medium is the metaphor.

A Clockwork Orange

The Star-Child who was looking out at us at the end of *2001: A Space Odyssey* may have been a Messiah. But there is no doubt that the face of the earthborn mutant in the opening shot of *A Clockwork Orange* is a destroyer. The deadly cold eyes of Alex, a *wunderkind* of the near future, hold the lens inflexibly as the camera begins retreating like a courtier who fears to turn tail till the lord and master he serves is out of sight. The tableau opens up in apprehension of him and his attendant spirits, caught between the "up" and the "down" of a drugged metabolism. A pair of cosmetic eyelashes on one single eye, bisected by the black eclipse of a derby hat, adds an obscenely askew look to the leader's cherubic face. Farther and farther back the camera dollies. Strains of *Elegy on the Death of Queen Mary* by Purcell, though now weirdly distorted, add to the courtlike mood. We then view the scene down a lengthening corridor of nude statuary, with female dummies on all fours forming tables and banquettes, or rampant on pedestals in the Korova Milkbar so that the spiked milk can be siphoned out of their breasts into glasses to pep up the night of ultraviolence that is ahead. Statuary, symmetry, the sense of satanic majesty: there is a flavor of a perverse Versailles. And now on the sound track, overlaying the music, Alex's voice introduces himself and his "droogs" with the candor of the mindlessly violent, intelligently articulate criminal, setting the jubilant opening tone of the movie in a boastful stream of Nadsat slang, whose vocabulary stamps the speaker with a callousness even before he strikes the first blow or lifts a finger in that transfixed tableau.

It was not till late in the filming that Kubrick shot this opening scene, but one would swear it was the first thing he did. It is less a "scene" than an overture. It has the total certainty of a conduc-

*"There was me, that is Alex. . . ." On the coldly malev-
olent stare of his hero-victim, Kubrick opens* A
Clockwork Orange *and at once establishes the
eyeball-to-eyeball contact with Alex that he unremit-
tingly maintains throughout the film, either in the
images that turn Alex into an active agent of our
deep-seated lusts and fears or in the candor of his
Nadsat narration, at once intimate and shameless.*

tor lifting his baton. Some of the intricate relationships between
music and the emotions, or between music and movement, which
had been employed to startling effect in *2001: A Space Odyssey*
had come to preoccupy more and more of Kubrick's thinking in
the three years between that film and *A Clockwork Orange*. Earlier
chapters have stressed his success in finding the perfect visual
concept for the idea behind the film; in *A Clockwork Orange* one
must be equally aware of the musical concept he elaborates. It is
hardly accidental, for example, in a film where the hero's behavioral processes are systematically destroyed and re-created in
another form, that the music that plays an integral part in such
"remedial" therapy should itself have been strained through the
Moog synthesizer by the composer Walter Carlos.

    A Clockwork Orange often has the look of a fantastic masque, a modern *Comus*, in which costume, language, movement, and, above all, music embody the didactic intensions of an allegory that satirizes society's vices through the depiction of the base and animalized life. The effect of a masque is inseparable from the style Kubrick has evolved for this film. Sometimes it is created through the movements of his camera, which again and again opens a scene with a dollying shot, giving a processional or rout-like impression of the action; or else the camera frames the figures in a long shot of their environment and adds a touch of imminent surrealism through the restrained choice of a distorting lens for certain angles. When he holds a shot, Kubrick seems to hold it for measurably longer than one expects him to. This contributes strongly to the sensation of tableaux vivants, while allowing him to choreograph the movements within the stationary frame with great skill in relation to their effect or to the music that accompanies them. In addition, there is a recurrent use of low angles, so that the characters have a friezelike elevation. All this helps make *A Clockwork Orange* radically different in style from *Dr. Strangelove*, a film to which it has some strong contextual resemblances.

The masquelike sensation is overpowering in the onrush of violent events that immediately follows the presentation of Alex and his "droogs."

In the first sequence of their vicious spree, the gang beat up an old tramp under a bridge, their shadows leaping before them to advertise their evil intent just as those on the alley wall in *Killer's Kiss* told us all we needed to know about the murder taking place out of sight around the corner. (Things are not so reticent in a "clockwork orange" society.)

Then—an unexpected image: the camera pans down a faded Watteauesque detail, reminiscent of courtly languor, into the arching gloom of a derelict casino where Billyboy and his gang of Hell's Angels are so preoccupied with the modern masque of stripping a "weepy young devotchka" for rape that Alex's "droogs" take them by surprise. The intergang rumble vividly illustrates the nihilistic nature of Alex's commitment to life and also Kubrick's skill at the reduction of violence to movement, balletic movement, so that the incitement content of it is defused and it becomes a metaphor for violence. Nowhere in *A Clockwork Orange* does one find the "medical materialism," the gross addition to the drama of physical injury depicted with anatomical precision, which is characteristic of other violent films that appeared around the time of Kubrick's movie. Here the leaping, chopping, somersaulting combatants are edited into an acrobatic

Off for a bit of the old ultraviolence, the gang's shadows leaping before them advertise their intention. In spite of numerous scenes shot on exterior locations, no postsynchronizing of dialogue was needed. In fact, the tiny microphones (see page 43) worked so well that it was sometimes necessary to add *traffic noises in the final mix. Not even the camera needed to be blimped. For some shots taken as close as six feet to the actors, Kubrick used a hand-held Arriflex and merely wrapped it in the parka, which is his habitual working gear.*

display and choreographed to the Rossini music of *The Thieving Magpie*. It is no more "offensive," though a lot more subtle, than the conventional saloon bar-brawl of any pre-Peckinpah Western. What really gives the sequence its dynamic aggressiveness is the note of adolescent celebration projected by the violent suppleness of the bodies. There might have been a rationale for the mugging of the tramp in the previous sequence—"It's a stinking world because it lets the young get onto the old"—but the only evident impulse here is the celebration of a primal will, a brutalized and debased will, all right, but existentially free. Like the ape colonies at one another's throats before the dawn of intelligence in *2001: A Space Odyssey*, Alex and his "droogs" represent the aggression

Kubrick's quick cutting and the acrobatic movements of the actors during the rape of the writer's wife edit the assault into a weird ballet . . .

and violence that will be bred into man, so-called *civilized* man, by natural selection in prehistory. The gang rumble is stylized into a barbaric ritual for another reason, too: so that the connection can be made much later on with the far more sophisticated violence inflicted on Alex, in order to extirpate his independent will, by a State that is itself contaminated by the evolutionary bad seed.

A Clockwork Orange never sets out to explore the moral issue of violence; this has been a misleading belief that has often caused the film to be branded as "conscienceless" by critics who fail to see where Kubrick's first priority lies, namely, with the moral issue of eradicating free will. It is not with "sin," an essential part of Anthony Burgess's Catholic conscience and Kubrick's probably agnostic skepticism, but with "cure" that the book and the film occupy themselves. It is pardonable, though, to miss this at a first

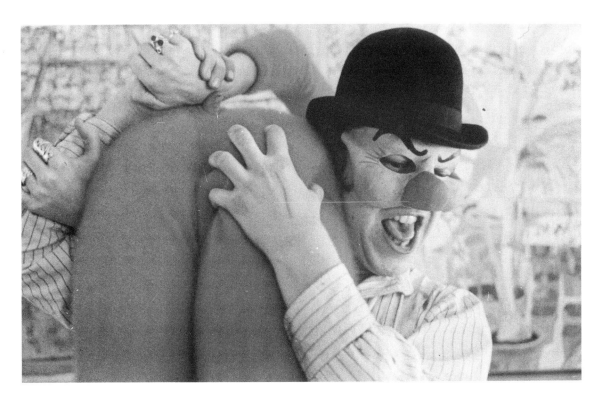

whose effect is consolidated by the masks that seem to combine the stock features of both tragedy and comedy. The viewer's experience is highly disorienting. "There are dreams," says Kubrick, "in which you do all the terrible things your conscious mind prevents you from doing."

viewing; one is so caught up in the demonstration of primitive savagery.

Off their own turf, the gang invade the territory marked HOME. Kubrick films their progress to this new peak experience as a hurtling journey in an ultramodern car down a dark country lane, using one of his striking "corridor" compositions, with spectral white trees and hedges receding swiftly behind them (see the "nightmare street ride" in *Killer's Kiss*, page 53). The gang, crammed into the cockpit of the Durango 95 supercar, ironically assume poses that recall heroic groups on the old-fashioned war memorials. It is not entirely naturalistic in other ways, too: they are fairly obviously photographed in front of a traveling

Compelled to quell his mutinous "droogs" with a taste of his stick, Alex is transformed by Kubrick's low-angle, slow-motion camera into a replica of the ape in 2001: A Space Odyssey *at the moment it learns the use of the bone-tool as a lethal weapon. (See page 165.) Implicit in the shot is Kubrick's view of man not as a fallen angel, in Rousseau's sense, but as a risen ape who still retains the evolutionary instinct for violence.*

From the doorbell that chimes an ominous phrase from Beethoven's Ninth *to a piece of sculpture that symbolizes the collapse of aesthetics,* A Clockwork Orange's *decor is a continuously detailed commentary on the film's action and ethos. Sex divorced from function becomes only form, and seizing the huge sculptured phallus from the Cat Lady's collection . . .*

Alex brings it down on the Cat Lady's skull. Up to the moment of his imprisonment for her murder, Alex is frequently presented in these low-angle shots that enhance his menace. Later, the camera tends to dominate him as he is put in the position of victim (see the "tempting" scene, page 207).

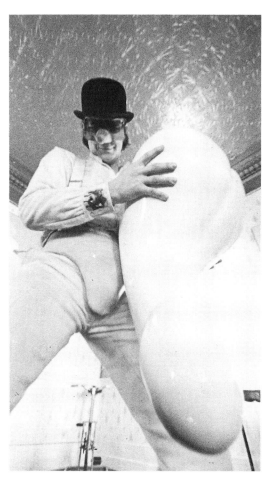

matte screen (despite near misses with other vehicles in the
reverse shots). But this flattening effect is consistent with the
quality of nightmare and dream Kubrick is after, an important
point to be dealt with later.

The assaults on the writer and his wife, Mr. and Mrs.
Alexander, are themselves gruesome and believable acts. But
Kubrick's rapid-fire editing at once embodies the surprise of each
assault and confines its depiction to fleeting essentials. Again, it
is treated like a masque or, perhaps, a plebeian rather than a
courtly entertainment this time, since the note is that of vaude-
ville farce and aggressively pop. The wife is first stripped of her
red jumpsuit. Like the sadistic child he basically is, Alex goes for
the mammaries first, slicing off the garment's elasticized material
and letting it slap back and expose the breasts before cutting the
fabric up lengthwise in a Jack the Ripper parody. He then launches into a Gene Kelly takeoff, soft-shoe shuffling through "Singin'
in the Rain" while putting a very unsoft boot into the writer's

ribs at every cadence. Anyone who winces at the supposedly comic sadism of circus clowns will recognize how, in this scene, Kubrick has turned the frightening realities of domestic invasion, rape, and assault into an experience akin to that ambivalent form of "entertainment." The horror of it still comes through—it is one of the most unsettling scenes in modern cinema—and to say it is "distanced" from us is simply to use a fashionable term from the hollow vocabulary of critical-hip (the literary cousin of radical-chic). But the violence does not gratify; on the contrary, it repels. Our emotional gears have to crash through the comic and the macabre, and we are disoriented still further (as we are meant to be) by the quick cutting, the rubbery antics of the masquers, and the balletic precision of the most outrageous movements— even Alex unzipping his pants prior to rape is like a performer taking a bow. The success of the scene shows the well-placed trust Kubrick put in what he called a scene's "crucial rehearsal period," its "CRP." The CRP is the time spent with the cast (technicians excluded), even before lighting and camera angles have been determined, in order to explore the content of the scene to the fullest extent and hopefully to pan a nugget out of the wash of ideas and suggestions. "The reality of the final moment, just before shooting, is so powerful that all previous analysis must yield before the impressions you receive under these circumstances, and unless you use this feedback to your positive advantage, unless you adjust to it, adapt to it and accept the sometimes terrifying weaknesses it can expose, you can never realize the most out of your film."* For two inactive days Kubrick and his actors mulled over the rape scene until, on a sudden intuition, he asked Malcolm McDowell, playing Alex, whether he could sing and dance. The actor replied he could do his "party piece"; Kubrick instantly telephoned Los Angeles instructing Warner Bros. to buy the film rights to "Singin' in the Rain." The CRP had paid off.

The song serves a neat ulterior purpose, too: it is the reprise of it that betrays Alex to Mr. Alexander when fate, by a series of what Kubrick characteristically calls "magical coincidences," brings him back to this house in the penultimate sequence. And incidentally, though few notice it the first time around, the chiming doorbell on the writer's house announces Alex's deadly visitation with a musical phrase from Beethoven's Fifth. Already

---

*Philip Strick and Penelope Houston, "Interview with Stanley Kubrick," *Sight and Sound*, vol. 41, no. 2 (Spring 1972): p. 65.

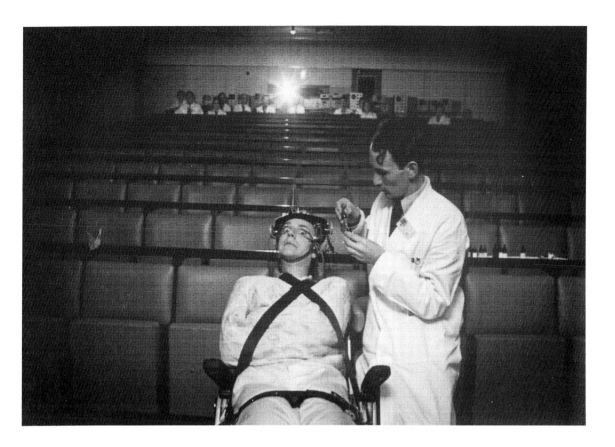

The brainwashing begins. Note Kubrick's consistency in lighting a scene with only the illumination one would expect to find in the actual environment. (See the War Room in Dr. Strangelove, *page 127.) The doctor beside the captive Alex is a real physician employed to keep the bulging eyeballs of the actor from "drying up" during the shooting of the sequence.*

"lovely Ludwig van" begins to cast his ominous spell on the hero's fortunes, precipitating his downfall.

"Lovely Ludwig van" is explicitly introduced in the next sequence, when one of the "sophistos" in the Korova Milkbar is suddenly turned on by the spiked "moloko" and bursts into Schiller's *Ode to Joy*, set to the Beethoven music, "and it was like for a moment, O my brothers," says Alex's hard, flat-accented but now spellbound voice on the sound track, "some great bird had flown into the milkbar and I felt all the malenky little hairs on my plott standing endwise." It is more than just colossal irony that one of the proudest odes to the brotherhood of man should mesmerize one of mankind's foulest specimens. "At issue," wrote Robert Hughes, art critic of *Time*, in an admiring essay on the

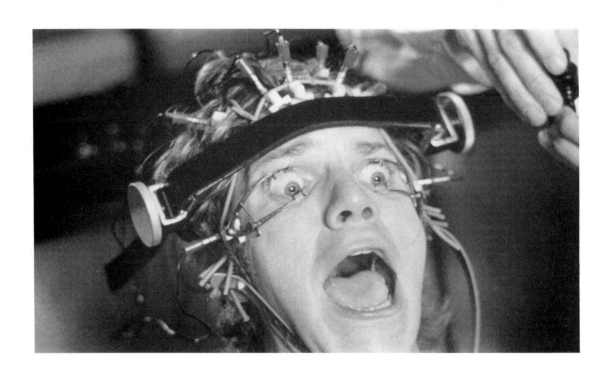

206

Alex is plugged into global violence that seems even more real than life when he is forced to "viddy" it up there on the screen. The McLuhan edict that the medium is the message is given an ominous twist; for the medium that the State manipulates is calculated to deprive man of his free will and to turn him into an obedient zombie.

"It's a sin!" Through the earphones Alex hears the obscenely distorted version of his "lovely Ludwig van."

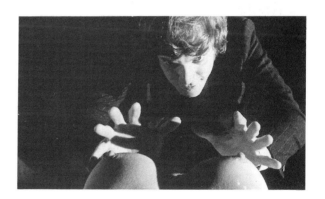

The tempting of a clockwork saint: Alex is forced to lick the boot of the State's professional provocateur to prove how well he has learned his lesson of nonviolence.

Like a beatific vision, a nearly nude girl tests Alex's residual lusts. Kubrick cuts to an overhead shot showing the victim reaching for the pink protuberances of the girl's breasts and falling away defeated.

*Mr. Alexander, the latest Kubrick "monster," utters
excited cries as the prospect of retribution shakes his
crippled body, just as the imminent immolation of
mankind aroused his kinsman, Dr. Strangelove.*

movie's cultural ethos, "is the popular 19th-century idea, still
held today, that Art is Good for You, that the purpose of the fine
arts is to provide moral uplift. Kubrick's message, amplified from
Burgess's novel, is the opposite: art has no ethical purpose. There
is no religion of beauty. Art serves, instead, to promote ecstatic
consciousness. The kind of ecstasy depends on the person who is
having it.* Kubrick himself took this view very explicitly when it
was suggested by one critic that art such as *A Clockwork Orange*
might actually be Bad for You. "[Works of art] affect us when
they illuminate something we already feel," he said; "they don't
change us." Certainly Alex is no sooner back in his parents'
apartment block, and safe from the "Pee" and "Em" behind the
combination lock on his bedroom door, than the stereophonic
ecstasy induced by his Beethoven discs describes his own fantasies of violence.

* Robert Hughes, "The Décor of Tomorrow's Hell," *Time*, December 27, 1971, p.
59.

The "flatblock" he inhabits, ankle-deep in communal squalor, exemplifies more than just a concrete wasteland. It is a goalless society, a spiritual wilderness, Kubrick and Burgess present. All the energy has drained off to the extremes—to Alex and his mob of night-people, on the one hand, and to the incipient Fascists of the State on the other. Between them is a vast hinterland of apathy, a listless limbo in which routine gets the elder citizens through the day and drugs get them through the night. The outlook in every sense is undeniably doleful, where it is not actively baleful.

While the teenage society of *A Clockwork Orange* is, save for Alex, lumped into a common, undifferentiated brutality, the adult world is sharply particularized. The film even exceeds *Dr. Strangelove*'s count in the varieties of authoritarianism it can satirically delineate without repeating itself. The first of these—for Mr. Alexander does not really play an active role till much later on—is Alex's Post-Corrective Adviser (probation officer), P. R. Deltoid, the only grown-up who appears conversant with Nadsat, which is logical, since his business is with the delinquent young. The creepy tête-à-tête he has with Alex the morning after

Like the cosmonaut at his lonely repast in the astral suite at the end of 2001: A Space Odyssey *(see page 177), Alex detects a sense of impending but as yet unlocalized fatefulness in the Alexander household, where he, too, is a virtual prisoner.*

Enter his fate. Kubrick wittily shoots Mr. Alexander's reappearance head-on, so that for a split second a Magritte-like effect is produced as it appears that the wheelchair he is being carried in on has somehow grown a pair of legs all its own.

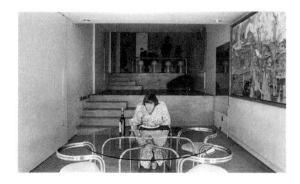 

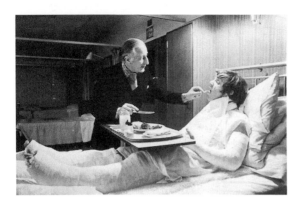

Alex in a plaster cast after his suicide attempt, resembling a Frankenstein monster who has returned to settle the score with its creator, receives a visit from the Minister of the Interior, who combines the duplicity of the politician with the smoothness of the PR man. "I can tell you with all sincerity that I and the government of which I am a member are deeply sorry about this, my boy, deeply sorry. . . . We are interested in you, and when you leave here you will have no worries. . . ." (See Paths of Glory, *page 69, and* Dr. Strangelove, *pages 132–133)*

Chomping on the bribe the Minister is offering him

the night's ultraviolence shows the way Kubrick builds up a sense of diffused yet potent perversion through little details of phrase and action. He starts with Deltoid's vocal tone, a kind of admonitory flirtation, as he nudges the near-naked boy like a covert pederast while mouthing warnings about getting into "the barry place," as if they were sadistic wishes. Finally, he works himself up to the point where he slakes his lust from a bedside water tumbler without spotting the false teeth soaking in it. The amplified "clunk" of the dentures and their magnified distortion through the glass impose a monstrously rapacious image on Deltoid's face, and the scene peaks into the surrealist.

Still delineating Alex's priapic zest, the film follows him in his noncombative gear, which resembles a Regency buck's, into a drugstore-cum-disc boutique, where his perambulating scrutiny of the female talent is conveyed in one of those lovely 360-degree dollying shots, whose visual elegance plays against the film's latent violence. (The disc of the *2001* music that comes to rest in the center of the shot was no film prop but actually part of the

"I was cured, all right."

real shop's stock.) What follows is another piece of musical bravura: Alex's bedroom orgy with the two microboppers he picks up, which was shot over twenty-eight minutes by Kubrick but flashes by in forty seconds of such accelerated motion that although all three figures are stark naked and nameless things apparently are going on, one cannot follow the anatomical details for the sheer speed of the orgiastic permutations. It is a jokey interlude, and the speeded-up *William Tell* Overture (the first choice, *Eine Kleine Nachtmusik*, did not work) has exactly the right weight and frolicsomeness for the casual nature of group sex. But the sequence is followed by one that deploys abnormal movement for a much more sinister purpose.

Faced with mutiny by his "droogs," Alex quells them by a surprise attack. As he turns on the trio on the brink of an ornamental lake, the violent tableau goes into extreme slow motion, so that Alex's crouching figure brandishing his heavy walking stick seems to elevate itself up, up, up against the sky till it resembles the huge ape in the prologue of *2001: A Space Odyssey* at the moment the apeman makes the lethal connection between the utility of the bone-tool and its effectiveness as a killing weapon (see page 165)—a shot that vividly crystallizes Kubrick's view of man as a risen ape, rather than Rousseau's sentimental characterization of him as a fallen angel.

Just as the fight on the water's edge looks like an incredibly slowed-up ballet, the encounter with the Cat Lady, which follows Alex's resumption of power, has its element of dance—a dance of death, the high point of the masque.

In earlier chapters I have mentioned how an overpowering environment in a Kubrick film frequently defines the people who live in it and the morality of the acts they plot or perform; this is particularly true of the Cat Lady's home, which Alex and the "droogs" invade. Kubrick meshes into its character a garish comment on the decadence of a society in which the sex drive has been reduced to the old mechanistic "in out-in out," as in Mrs. Alexander's rape, or else to the status of a temporary plaything like the droopy, phallic lollipop being licked by the microbopper in the disc boutique (an echo, perhaps, of the coy innuendo in the posters for *Lolita* ten years earlier). The Cat Lady lives on a health farm. Kubrick shot the sequence in a real health farm just outside London, and it was amusing to see how the gymnastic equipment that customarily stood in the room underwent a subtle change and assumed implications of a torture chamber where *The Story of "O"* could have been cozily accommodated. As in many sequences of *A Clockwork Orange*, this one opens with an image of surprising yet aesthetically satisfying symmetry: the Cat Lady, in an emerald leotard of the sort a ballerina wears at practice, is stretching her muscles with a concentration that, added to the solitude, has a masturbatory feel about it. The decor, too, suggests the sterility that results when sex is separated from its function and becomes only "form." The lewd paintings caricature the owner's own "balletic" postures, and even the sculptured phallus that Alex sets rocking absurdly on its truncated testicles has the gargantuan proportions of obscene fantasy. "Leave that alone! Don't touch it! It's a very important work of art!" screams the Cat Lady. As Robert Hughes says, "This pathetic outburst of connoisseur's jargon echoes in a vast cultural emptiness. In worlds like this" [where there is no reality to which it can connect] "no work of art can be important."* The fight between the two is filmed by Kubrick with a hand-held Arriflex that turns the objective symmetry of the opening shot into a fiercely subjective encounter.

---

*Hughes, p. 59.

The weapons the antagonists use are peculiarly choice: the out-size phallus for him, a small bust of Beethoven for her. Once again, "lovely Ludwig van" is turned against Alex in a way that anticipates the really deadly blow it deals him in the Ludovico Treatment—a blow not below the belt, as here, but below the level of consciousness.

In shooting the fight, Kubrick was very concerned not to depict any physical injury such as the Cat Lady would suffer when the phallus is dashed down onto her face; instead, at this point he cuts to a dizzying zero-in on a whore's open mouth in one of the pornographic paintings, which indicates his anxiety to preserve the nightmare nature of the scene. For in dreaming, the mind's "censor" tends to exclude this kind of anatomical gruesomeness, or else the dreamer is abruptly awakened by his own too horrible imaginings. Kubrick's regard for the story as a sort of "controlled dream" makes him take the same precautions.

Almost immediately after the murder, Alex is betrayed by his own gang, stunned by a milk bottle, and left to be picked up by the police. Burgess, incidentally, relished the way the screenplay at this point preserved the logic of the novel, in which Alex, stretching greedily for the bust of Beethoven, stumbles over a saucer of milk set down for the Cat Lady's pets. Now milk knocks him flat in the film, too. Like immature children still being suckled, these delinquents fall afoul of their own perverted innocence: the milk of human kindness is poisoned at the source, all right.

Alex ends up in the police cell looking "like love's young nightmare." "Violence makes violence," says one of the cops. "He resisted his lawful arresters." At this point the dialogue antici-pates the Minister of the Interior's ominous habit of truncating or compressing words; it is as if language is being stripped down till only slogans and commands remain. If the teenagers have their Nadsat slang, the State's own "droogs" have their official syntax, too. The similarity, however, goes beyond words. The gloating policeman who lays his head like a lovesick girl on P. R. Deltoid's shoulder and invites the probation officer to give Alex his bash is the "official" obverse of the same coin that carries Alex's violent imprimatur on his side of it. Both sides form the coin of the realm. As this connection is made, the film's theme deepens and its nature and technique undergo a change as well. Without diminishing the secular ironies—certainly without soft-ening the secular savageries—the theological content comes to the fore. Up to now, we have seen Alex through the appalled eye of one of his victims; now, as the airborne camera takes an

Olympian viewpoint, floating dreamily over the prison where Alex is condemned to spend fourteen years, we see him being gradually diminished and degraded as "the real weepy and like tragic part of the story" starts.

The lengthy sequence showing Alex being interrogated and stripped in the reception block does not occur in the book. The way Kubrick went about devising it throws further light on his techniques. First came a period of intensive research, designed to "justify" any effects he wanted to use, in which he took advice from ex-convicts and viewed countless TV films and newsreel clips illustrating prison life. (English prisons are not as accommodating as American ones in admitting the stray visitor who might just want to view the decor.) From this research came that small but hilarious throwaway remark, "Now—the mothballs," that the guard utters like the command in some State ceremony while he scatters a handful of camphor pellets through Alex's clothes to preserve them until his release. The CRP on the day of shooting yielded another one of those moments, like the "Singin' in the Rain" idea, that electrify a scene. This time it was the white line painted on the floor that Alex has to toe while being admitted to prison. The contortions of his body as he stretches to the officer's desk to empty his pockets and write his signature help to satirize rigorous officialdom. The guard's final torchlight inspection of Alex's anus further points up the dehumanizing absurdity of prison life in the manner of a comic cabaret.

"What's it going to be then?" The first words of the prison padre in the film are actually the first words uttered in Burgess's book, and they are vital ones in the context of both works. They imply the imperative laid on every human of making a moral choice. In the fundamentalist chaplain's view, it is a choice between damnation and redemption. And though obviously his fire-and-brimstone beliefs incline him to the latter, the important element in his sermon is not which way the sinner should bend, but that he should be sufficiently free-willed to make the choice by himself. The injury that is soon going to be done to Alex will be inflicted on him in a more primitive way than any he has inflicted on his victims: not in the way of physical hurt, nor even of mental brainwashing, but in the way of sinful outrage, an offense against God as well as man, by depriving him of this divine bestowal of free will. In *2001: A Space Odyssey*, God stays offstage but at least is represented by man's ascendancy at the end to divine or semidivine status. In *A Clockwork Orange*, man remains less metaphysical in form, but even in his untransformed, debased state, he has a godlike capacity. What both films have in common is the conviction that man is more than a terminal product of conditioning, heredity, or environment. He can transcend himself and redeem himself. So, "What's it going to be then?" Kubrick's refusal to stop and moralize at this point has caused some to overlook the admittedly unlikely spokesman for a view that is at the heart of the film—the prison chaplain. He starts out as a figure of fun within the State system but ends as a figure of protest against it. For when Alex offers himself as a candidate for the Ludovico Treatment, he is answered by the doubts of the man of God in a dialogue passage so central to the film that it deserves quoting in full:

—**Chaplain:** The Governor has grave doubts about [the Ludovico Treatment] and I have heard that there are very serious dangers involved.

—**Alex:** I don't care about the dangers, Father. I just want to be good. I want for the rest of my life to be one act of goodness.

—**Chaplain:** The question is whether or not this technique really makes a man good. Goodness comes from within. Goodness is chosen. When a man cannot choose, he ceases to be a man.

—**Alex:** I don't understand about the whys and wherefores, Father. I only know I want to be good.

—**Chaplain:** Be patient, my son. Put your trust in the Lord.

Instead of which, Alex puts his trust in the Minister of the Interior, whose policy is political expediency. Since all the prison space is soon going to be needed for "the politicals," it follows that the mere "criminals" must be cleared out quickly. The Ludovico Treatment, as well as being a vote-catching item in the "law-and-order" election platform, has the overriding virtue that "it works." *A Clockwork Orange* demonstrates very neatly, through the satirized authority figures, the sophisticated subtleties of the coercive State that seeks an ally in science. For it is to the scientists that the expedient immorality of "it works" will ultimately be referred by the government; and from the scientists there is no further appeal. So the old ambivalence of science once more asserts itself in Kubrick's outlook. Instead of enhancing human life, technocracy annihilates it, as in *Dr. Strangelove*; depletes it, as in *2001: A Space Odyssey*; or perverts it, as in *A Clockwork Orange*. Deep inside Kubrick, one suspects, there is harbored some sympathy for the Devil, or at least for the creatures of the id who are not oppressed by a rationality that has no remedy for man's imperfections except to dominate and oppress him. As a prominent Catholic film critic, John E. Fitzgerald, wrote: "Such brainwashing, organic and psychological, is a weapon that totalitarians in State, Church or society might wish to use for an easier good, even at the cost of human rights and dignity. Redemption is a complicated thing and change must be motivated from within rather than imposed from without if moral values are to be upheld."*

Alex seems to have escaped from the inhumane system that puts men behind bars to a much more humane one when he gets transferred from prison to the Ludovico clinic. In fact, the quiet men in white coats to whom he is delivered—in one long dollying shot through futuristic surroundings that is by now characteristic of the film's style—are merely the mirror images of the functionaries from the cell block. The two systems are sharply satirized by their semantic traditions: the ludicrous "follow-the-rules" tone of the pompous little chief guard bounces off the bland "we-can-handle-it" responses of the doctors.

As Alex is prepared for the treatment, Kubrick permits himself a private joke. A deceptively soothing scientist prepares to inject the boy with serum. The close-up of the hypodermic syringe drawing in the roseate liquid is itself a lovely image, suggesting one of those time-lapse photos of expanding flower buds, and it may escape notice that the bottle is labeled "Experimental Serum 114." Now, the same cryptic numeral appeared on the mechanism of the B-52 bomber—to be precise, "CRM 114"—whose damage in *Dr. Strangelove* prevented the aircraft from receiving the Pentagon's recall signal. And to Kubrick, who characteristically ducked explanations, this numeral probably signified some point of no return, a technological Rubicon, or the ultimate kink in the scientific or human mechanism that locks man into his fate.

The serum makes Alex unduly receptive to the feeding back into his own system of all the violence in the outside world, until he has had such a surfeit of murder, rape, and atrocity that his pleasure is turned into revulsion. Significantly, the raw material for the conditioning comes from films. As he remarks with unconscious irony before the "horror show" starts, "It's funny how the colors of the real world only seem real when you viddy them on a screen." He is a captive audience of one; his head is clamped tight; music is pumped into his ears; a ring of electrodes circles his head like a crown of thorns; and, worst of all, his bulging eyeballs are held forcibly open by surgical lidlocks. What one recognizes in the sequence is the parallel with the Cosmic Ride in *2001: A Space Odyssey*, where a similarly "imprisoned"

---

*John E. Fitzgerald, "More than a Product of Heredity," New York *Catholic News*, December 30, 1971, p. 4.

captive has to suffer all manner of physical and even psychic phenomena bombarding his persona and changing it. Both sequences emphasize the dilated eyes, the flattened features, and especially the sense of seeing "what should not be seen" as their hero-victims are swept helplessly into a kind of reincarnation (see page 165). The inspiration comes from Kubrick's fascination, already examined, with the powerfully suggestive qualities of myths. "A psychological myth" is how he has described Alex's adventures; but Alex's ordeal derives even more precisely from the endurance test forming the central part of many of the world's myths, legends, and fairy tales. Alex is that "hero with a thousand faces" on whom magic is practiced by evil powers, who survives the worst, and who is ultimately restored to the realms he came from. The last third of the film, moreover, following the "reformed" Alex's progress through the world he once terrorized, has the same story elements of symmetry and coincidence that give to tales of magic their cyclic form and narrative satisfaction, qualities that both liberate the imagination and at the same time control the external world.

In its scientific, not mythic, state, the Ludovico Treatment is a peculiarly corrupt offshoot of behavioral psychology and conditioned-reflex therapy, which operate on the assumption that man has no will he can call his own but, on the contrary, is molded by his environment and the right kinds of stimuli administered to him in order to make any socially undesirable behavior patterns conform to socially approved ones. The film was well into its shooting schedule when B. F. Skinner published his book *Beyond Freedom and Dignity*, a work that argued, with almost blind faith in rationalism, that there was a case for manipulating the causal relationship between man and his environment for the good of society as a whole—indeed, for the essential *survival* of society. *A Clockwork Orange* presents its own diametrically opposed view of such a notion. The appearance of Skinner's book and Kubrick's film at almost the same time is a fairly consistent event with a director who, as I have pointed out already, absorbs into his own interests, and then turns into the substance of his art, much of what is happening in the world at large. And this includes the progressively sinister development of such things as the use of drugs to recondition scientifically certain types of criminals, even the use of "psychoadaptation" in some of the totalitarian countries that have learned to avail themselves of the less sensational (or at least less publicized) forms of medicine as a means of political control. From forcibly "referring" dissenters to be treated at State psychiatric clinics to actually "reconditioning" them to return to society is a short, tempting step. The "clockwork orange" world seems tangibly close if, for example, one reads the account of Zhores Medvedev's ordeal in a Soviet clinic, published in the West under the title *A Question of Madness*.

It is while Alex is undergoing this form of "death," as Dr. Brodsky calls it, and making "his most rewarding associations between his catastrophic experience-environment and the violence he sees" that the fourth movement of Beethoven's Ninth infiltrates his eardrums. Only now the music is obscenely distorted, sounding as if it could come from a kitsch music box. The violence that has been done to "lovely Ludwig van" is the only thing that wrenches out of Alex the cry, "It's a sin." The doctors reply, "You must take your chance, boy." And twisting the chaplain's words, they add with unconscious irony, "The choice has been all yours." It is the last choice Alex will make for some time. Confined to a set of programmed responses to sex and violence, he is put through a test to show how the government is keeping its electoral promises by achieving law and order through the abolition of the criminal instinct. "Enough of words, actions speak louder than," declaims the Minister of the Interior in his "officialese" style. "Action now. Observe all." What we observe is an extraordinary sequence: the classical tempting of a saint, which might have been drawn from a medieval morality play, bizarrely crossed with the sort of sadomasochistic cabaret commonplace in pre-Hitlerite Germany. First the male tempter, a curly-haired queer, humiliates the passive Alex to the point where he licks his boots. The man bows to applause. Then the female temptress, a near-nude, appears onstage like one of the punitive harlots in a strip show. Kubrick's camera, directly above the girl's head, looks down on the pink protuberances of her "topless" anatomy while Alex, at her feet, rises up like a mountaineer groping for the hand-holds on her breasts and then falls back into the void of his self-disgust. It is a dazzling use of the surrealist angle, followed ironically by the dainty obedience of the girl's bow to the political plaudits. "Any questions?" crows the delighted Minister.

And again, in view of the way the film's violent passages have been overemphasized at the expense of its more vital moral theme, the dialogue between the Minister and the prison chaplain bears quoting:

—**Chaplain:** Choice! The boy has not a real choice—has he? Self-interest, the fear of physical pain drove him to that grotesque act of self-abasement. The insincerity was clear to be seen. He ceases to be a wrongdoer. He ceases also to be a creature capable of moral choice.

—**Minister:** Padre, there are subtleties! We are not concerned with motives, with the higher ethics. We are concerned only with cutting down crime and with relieving the ghastly congestion in our prisons. He will be your true Christian, ready to turn the other cheek, ready to be crucified rather than crucify, sick to the heart at the thought of killing a fly. Reclamation! Joy before the angels of God! The point is that it works.

Put back defenseless into a hostile world, Alex now falls prey to the very terrors he himself created. First, he is displaced from his family by the intrusion of a teenage lodger. Whereas music led the vicious rampage of Alex in his heyday, it is now employed in a much more naturalistic form to signal his fall from power. It is the slow movement of the *William Tell* Overture, which once could hardly keep pace with his sex romp, that now accompanies his sad promenade along the Thames Embankment, while the slowly zooming camera projects his melancholy, like an incipient suicide's, into the brown swirling waters. The same tramp he mugged in the opening reel whistles up his pals, and Alex is pulled down by a pack of senile wolves with toothless gums. He is "rescued" by two policemen who turn out to be Dim and Georgie, his ex-"droogs," who have now made a pact with the State. And after a vicious beating from them, Alex staggers into the house called HOME, where the last of his former victims is waiting by "magical" coincidence to deliver the ultimate retribution.

Mr. Alexander has suffered a transformation of his own. Crippled by the attack on him, his "liberalism" has been warped as well. This physically impotent ogre in the wheelchair, now given to gloating and uttering involuntary whimpers of delight when assailed by fantasies of torture or revenge, is clearly a kindred spirit to Dr. Strangelove. Like that earlier manifestation of evil, his function is to key the film to its penultimate pitch of baroque horror, speaking in a parched, excited voice that is rabid for revenge. The "Singin' in the Rain" song that Alex involuntarily croons in his bath—the words echoing against the tiles and mirrors like a memory from the past—is a giveaway device that is cleverer than any in the novel. And the feeling that Kubrick himself is calling up the past is choicely conveyed by a shot of Alex eating supper. The image of him in a dressing gown, alone and symmetrically seated at a table, with plate, glass, and wine bottle in hand, and the scrape of a fork on the china, brings us back, it seems, to the astral suite in *2001: A Space Odyssey*, with the captive cosmonaut sensing the same elusive threat in his environment (see page 175). But it is by no means a simple case of double vision. The moment Mr. Alexander enters, seated in a wheelchair but carried by his muscular servant so that it looks as if the wheelchair has grown legs of its own, there is the odd effect of *Dr. Strangelove*'s being spliced into *2001: A Space Odyssey* and creating a time-slip that radiates a new sense of unease.

Aided by a couple of lieutenants, Fascists like himself posing as friends of "the people, the common people," who must be driven if they will not be led, Mr. Alexander plots to discredit the government, which has been boasting that it has found the cure for crime. His means—driving Alex to suicide—neatly encapsulate his own private revenge. As the insidious Ninth Symphony blares up through the floorboards from the room below, where the contemplative grouping of the conspirators around the hi-fi has the sort of country-house tranquillity Sickert might have painted, Alex's suicidal reflex drives him to a death-leap through the window. The moment illustrates Kubrick's thoroughness better than any other, for he actually threw the camera through the window, and the tough old Newman-Sinclair apparatus, encased in styrofoam boxes, survived all of the six "takes" that were required to produce the dizzying subjective shot that keeps us identifying with Alex and also symbolizes (and this is how Burgess sees it) his "fall" from a state of mechanistic grace back into his natural paganism.

His "moral" convalescence is quickly and wittily sketched in a hospital sequence that satirizes clinical psychiatry, which this time tests the patient for the symptoms of violence healthily reasserting itself. The last sequence is masterly and brings the film, beating strongly, up to a totally cynical conclusion: a compact of evil between Alex and the Minister of the Interior that is every bit as labyrinthine in its veiled proposal and acceptance as is the opening sequence of *Paths of Glory*, in which the archconspirator co-opted the cruder ambitions of his inferior in order to maintain his party in power at all costs. Rather like General Broulard, outwardly benign and untroubled, full of chummy chat, and radiating mysterious "understandings," the character of the Minister of the Interior enables Kubrick to construct one of his blackest scenes of comedy. We could virtually be certain that were Alex able to walk, the Minister would lead him into those peripatetic temptations to which Broulard subjected Mireau amid the polished furnishings of the château. But Alex is encased in plaster, barely able to ferry the food to his lips from his dinner plate, and so the Minister obligingly takes over the job, simultaneously seducing the boy over to the government's side by blandishments and promises—literally and figuratively spoon-feeding him. (Incidentally, he casts a sidelight on Mr. Alexander's fate: the latter, like Medvedev, has been "put away for his own protection.") Such a piece of physical pantomime grew out of the CRP—the spoon-feeding does not appear in the book—and it is a masterpiece of smooth chicanery and blatant cheek. As Alex's effrontery grows with his intake, his chewing stops as abruptly as one of General Turgidson's tics, "freezing" him in mid-grotes-querie, but his mouth keeps jerking open suddenly like a de-manding chick in the nest, insatiable for the supply of worms from the parent beak. "We shall see to everything, a good job on a good salary." "What job and how much?"

The final alliance between individual violence and the State's sophisticated reflection of it is sealed with the Minister's deli-ciously evil wink, whereupon the ward is invaded by pressmen, photographers, and porters bearing flowers and fruit and two huge stereo amplifiers like the gates of heaven, out of which pours Beethoven's Ninth. Alex's last words, "I was cured, all right," are odd echoes of Dr. Strangelove's own exuberant announcement (or threat), "*Mein Fuhrer*—I can walk!" as the nuclear explosions ring out a megaton salute. Alex's self-diagno-sis is amply confirmed by a fantasy shot of the nude hero frolick-ing with a young "devotchka" to applause from a gallery of Establishment types. As the end credits unroll, "Singin' in the Rain" is quoted back at us with its violent associations, though whether it will be Alex's theme song for fresh atrocities that now carry the stamp of State approval, or whether it will again betray him to his enemies, is anybody's guess. Kubrick is certainly not supplying an answer.

For him, *A Clockwork Orange* marked a new departure. The film's themes have already been analyzed as each strand is twist-ed into the next, and it is remarkable on how many levels—social, political, moral, theological—the story works without once losing touch with the basic quality of all tales, which, as E. M. Forster pointed out, satisfies the listeners' curiosity about "what happens next." But I think *A Clockwork Orange* hits its audience at a deeper level of consciousness than mere curiosity. And to the degree that it achieves this, it differs from any earlier Kubrick film. "With an eloquent command of the medium," wrote one critic, Patrick Snyder-Scumby, "[Kubrick] has created a dream in which he asks us to laugh at his nightmares."* Laughter is very

---

*Patrick Snyder-Scumby, "The Cockjerk Lunge of Manly Rubric," *Crawdaddy*, March 19, 1972, p. 25.

much Kubrick's intention. As I pointed out elsewhere, it makes it possible for the unthinkable to be thought of. For anyone who views a story as being in the nature of a "controlled dream" is bound to pay regard to the unconscious feelings of a cinema audience, since it is in the unconscious that the dream operates with most potency. *A Clockwork Orange* is nearer this dream state than any film Kubrick has made. Its lighting, editing, photography, and especially its music—for sound reaches deeper into the unconscious than even sight—are all combined with events in themselves bizarre and frightening. Although our eyes are not clamped open with lidlocks, like Alex's, we are assailed by a field of forces impossible to repel. *2001: A Space Odyssey*, in a rough sense, was a film whose imagery we were invited to accept, explore, and enjoy for the sensuous experience it conveyed; *A Clockwork Orange*, on the other hand, is one whose images we throw up our hands to ward off. What I wrote at the conclusion of the last chapter—that "the medium is the metaphor"—holds true of both films. But there is a vital difference. Where the metaphor of the earlier film turned us on, in *A Clockwork Orange* it has turned on us.

I think the film's success in deploying a controlled dream to spirit its own fearful vision past our defenses partly accounts for the extreme reactions to it from some quarters—the charge, for example, that it celebrated "the new ultraviolence" that, in Joseph Morgenstern's words, creates a "high-fashion horror that can turn on audiences higher than the real thing."* But this is neither the film's intention nor effect. One critic who appears to agree is Vincent Canby. In an article in *The New York Times* he wrote: "It is a horror show, but cool, so removed from reality that it would take someone who really cherished his perversions to get any vicarious pleasure from it. To isolate its violence is to ignore everything else that is at work in the movie."† To be genuinely shocking and at the same time *eloquent* in a film is itself an extraordinary achievement. Along with *Dr. Strangelove* and *2001: A Space Odyssey*, *A Clockwork Orange* rounds out a trilogy of films that shows a filmmaker with a unique capacity for using a medium to explore the condition of his fellow men and himself. In each of the films he has kept open the channels of the unconscious yet used an artist's self-awareness to shape the hopes and fears that flow through them and onto the screen with unblocked vitality.

---

*Joseph Morgenstern, "The New Violence," *Newsweek*, February 14, 1972, p. 68.
†Vincent Canby, "Has Movie Violence Gone Too Far?," *The New York Times*, January 16, 1972, sec. 2, p. 1.

In *A Clockwork Orange* it is the darkest of his fears that Kubrick plugs us into: not the fear of accidental annihilation by nuclear overkill, nor even the fear of what the unknown universe may hold, but the clear and present fear he has of man's surrender of his identity to the tyranny of other men. It is right that such a film should shock us.

Nowadays, no tyro director has second thoughts: his or her first film will be in color. But Kubrick's color sense came late to him, and possibly reluctantly. If one excludes *Spartacus*—which he did, judging that he labored on it under Kirk Douglas's "supervision"—Kubrick let fifteen years go by between his very first feature and his first film in color, *2001: A Space Odyssey*. Even allowing that color came into general use only in the mid-to-late 1950s, as part of the cinema's counterattack against black-and-white television, this longish waiting period doesn't suggest any eagerness on Kubrick's part to work in color. Nor should it. Kubrick's eye was trained in the workshop of monochrome news magazines—just as his ear had been tuned by radio in the 1930s and 1940s. The marvelous opportunities for expressionism that monochrome photography made available to him had their historical resonances in the old High German cinema of the 1920s and early 1930s: the tones of these films created a subtle range of mood and an atmosphere that appealed powerfully to Kubrick's temperament.

Color, for him, became an imperative only with his venture into space. And even *2001*, with the exception of the "Star Gate" sequence, seems to employ a palette of the starkest limitations. White, black, and red are its predominant hues: the black of space, the white of the spacecraft in it, the red glow bathing the crew inside the craft at moments of tension, peril, or disaster. Such a narrow color band derives in part from the technology of the setting: the future doesn't exactly appear to be a riot of color. Everyone recalls one early sequence in the film, the space hotel, primarily because the custom-made Olivier Morgue furnishings, those foam-filled sofas, undulant and serpentine, are covered in scarlet fabric and are the first stabs of color

one sees. They resemble Rorschach "blots" against the pristine purity of the rest of the lobby. It's more than a fashion statement, although to this day, the original Morgue designs command high prices in the auction rooms, and the *2001* provenance is invariably cited in auctioneers' catalogs. Their designer's name, Morgue, has a baleful ring, considering the living tomb that the spaceship will become—a coincidence not lost on Kubrick.

Red "runs" into other premonitory sequences. When HAL 9000 covertly scrutinizes the two astronauts who are conspiring against him, the computer's single red eye is in the traditional hue of an alarm signal. When the mutinous HAL has to be subdued, Kubrick irradiates the setting with the color he himself most enjoyed working in: the infrared light of the photographer's darkroom. It's an ominous and magical illumination that suffuses every inch of the screen equally as Keir Dullea proceeds to shut down HAL's cerebral functions one by one. The flat red light forces one to peer, rather than simply look, adjusting to the scene in the way a man bending over a developing tank fixes his attention on the image that's becoming visible in the fluid. Color really only bursts into *2001* with the astronaut's entering the Star Gate and getting sucked into his predestinate encounter with the monolith. Significantly, Kubrick's starting point for this inner journey is a huge close-up of the human eye, an ocular magnification whose intensity matches the director's own well-attested ability to make his glance do the work of his tongue. It's a beautiful image, truly a "golden eye," anticipating the calm and lovely glance that the Star-Child later bends on earth—benignly, we hope. The Star Ride announces itself in rainbow flecks and dashes on the astronaut's space visor; soon it transforms itself into an

As Kier Dullea begins to shut down HAL, Kubrick suffuses the scene with the scarlet intimation of imminent extinction. To a director who spent his youth as a professional photographer, the flat red light without shadow that bathes the man and the machine must have had a retrospective importance. The infrared light in what many consider the most emotional sequence of the film (ironically dealing with the death of a machine not a man) signifies its maker's preoccupation with the transitory aspect of life transforming into death—here, the death of HAL.

A Soviet spaceship attendant provides one of the few chic notes in the early sequences of 2001. The Olivier Morgue furnishings are still in fashion here on earth.

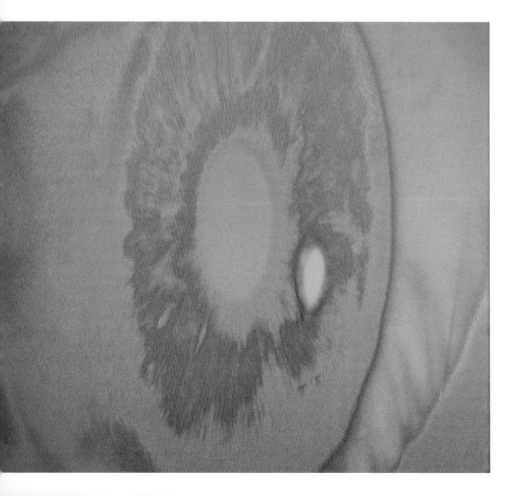

The astronaut, still in mortal shape and feeling in command of his own destiny, seeks to regain control of the space capsule—but forces greater than his understanding already have him in their grip. His transformational journey is about to begin.

From figurative image to total abstraction: the hugely magnified eye of the astronaut transforms itself from a calm, benign image into a kind of tormented speculum, as if inner space is becoming imbued with unknown aspects of outer space. Color values change too. Fiery red becomes predominant here in the "corridor" that takes the astronaut toward his destiny. At this point, the abstract feel of the film acquires the transcendental feel of a Mark Rothko canvas. It is Kubrick's ultimate light show.

Luxury, calm, and voluptuous-ness: in a fleeting image Kubrick manages to convey the classical balance of privileged life in the eighteenth century. Barry and his heiress wife enjoy the lake at his stately home while the children follow in their toy dinghy. As usual, however, a predominant hue—the red sail—seems to denote an impending event that will shatter the surface tranquillity.

Barry finds war not to his liking. Kubrick underscores the loneliness of this campfire reflection by using no more than the light provided by flames in the night.

A would-be gentleman in stolen clothes—the red coat of an English military officer—gives Barry the passport to a foreign landscape. One of the sequences set in Germany. The open road for once becomes a motif for a filmmaker who usually works in an enclosed environment.

The orgy. Kubrick ballasts the architectural flamboyance by rigorously formal patterning of the figures in it, while a palette reduced to stark crimsons and livid purples signals the danger of trespassing on forbidden territory.

"Why haven't you ever been jealous of me?" Alice, on the rebound from her own sexual encounter at the party and high on pot, brazenly reveals a past infidelity to her husband. White walls focus the eye on her defiant stance; then, as her confession inflames Bill, they are supplanted by red drapes that key the film's dominant hue of sexuality.

experiment in total abstraction. With the digital wizardry available to him today, Kubrick would no doubt substantially revise the effects he achieved in 1968 by more "primitive" means. It's as if the colors were "responding" to the notes of the accompanying music, the way some artists and theoreticians imagined when considering the relationship between colors and emotions. Eisenstein's essay "Color and Meaning," in his book *The Film Sense*, published in 1943, comes to mind; also the fact that Kubrick was a keen student of the writings of Eisenstein and his fellow Russians Stanislavsky and Pudovkin. The penultimate sequence of *2001*, set in the eerie yet tranquil bedroom suite where the astronaut appears to metamorphose into the Star Child, is exceptional in the film's color range, being composed entirely in translucent white and green. It is like looking into the depths of a pool for signs of marine life. Compared with the very restricted palette Kubrick imposed on his vision of space in *2001*, his next film, *A Clockwork Orange*, borrows from all the colors of psychedelia, most marked in the opening sequence of Alex and his droogs in the Korova Milk Bar. But it's the white tones, the combat "uniforms" the gang wears, like carnival dress with the colors left out, that now signal danger. The imposition of black and white, such as the single grotesque false eyelash on Alex's otherwise angelic pale face, has achieved an iconic vividness through being reproduced thousands of times over in film stills, books, magazines.... But the film, one feels, would lose nothing if shot in monochrome. It already possesses the starkness of one of George Grosz's caricatures of the moral decay, hypocrisy and corruption of the bourgeoisie and ruling classes, in post-World War One Berlin. Kubrick counteracts the realistic picture of a fascistic society by the surrealistic atmosphere of characters and events: this, too, was Grosz's technique.

In *Barry Lyndon*, Kubrick's use of color derives directly from the paintings of the period and his own experiments in shooting interiors by natural candlelight without any lighting enhancement. Indoors and outdoors, the scene is recorded with photographic or painterly naturalism, save in one mesmerizing sequence. This is Barry's first encounter with the Countess on the moonlit terrace of the gaming salon. The setting is bathed in a marmoreal tone that seems for a second to turn the two of them into alabaster, and settles a chill on their wordless embrace, even before the marriage freezes over in the wake of Barry's disdain for everything but his wife's inheritance. The blood-red key-note of *The Shining* has already been noted, along with the progressively more abstract design of the story, culminating in the literal "white out" of a blizzard and the murderous pursuit through the snowy labyrinth of the garden maze.

Red is once again Kubrick's keynote hue for *Eyes Wide Shut*. From the first shot, it's present in nearly every sequence. As a balefully ominous chromatic choice, it runs the risk of obviousness. But as the artist Josef Albers wrote, "If one says Red...and there are fifty people listening, it can be expected there will be fifty reds in their minds...all different." Not so, perhaps, when there are fifty people *looking*. But Kubrick uses its varieties to modify or highlight a mood. There's pleasure in spotting its diversity of uses: red-wrapped Christmas presents in a prostitute's pad; red portals of a shady tenement; the scarlet and crimson signifying peril at an orgy; and, most strikingly, the assault on the senses mounted by the rich red marble of an upscale condo lobby, which makes it look as if the film's hero is entering a furnace that will consume him.

Barry Lyndon

Barry Lyndon was born on the rebound. Kubrick's long-planned epic about Napoleon had collapsed when a financially strapped MGM withdrew its backing. The blow was bitter.

Kubrick had planned to make *Napoleon* immediately after *2001*. After all, as the French critic Michel Ciment notes, it was natural to follow the Nietzschean tone of the space epic with the terrestrial saga of the superman who changed the face and history of Europe. Napoleon's organizational powers had an irresistible affinity for Kubrick. As a filmmaker he also put a godlike faith in the grand plan and hankered to command his own Grand Army. To Kubrick's way of thinking, Napoleon was an emperor of logistics: a battlefield genius whose feats of planning brought every vital element together, at precisely the right time and place, to engage the enemy. What a filmmaker he might have made! His skills in giving orders commended him to a man who saw his own work as one huge communications system. In addition, Napoleon had a talent, unmatched since the Roman Empire, for multinational government, cultural initiatives, and social harmonization. All of these skills had tempting analogies with film production, direction, screenplay writing and crisis management. In *2001*, Kubrick had created the cosmos; he was looking forward to ruling the smaller-scale but still considerable continent of Napoleonic Europe.

Cheated of his "destiny," he then made *A Clockwork Orange*, in which, as Ciment shrewdly observes, he uses Beethoven's music, which was inspired by Napoleon's rampage through Europe, to propel Alex on his violent trajectory through society.

Kubrick actually tried hard to resurrect *Napoleon* after finishing *A Clockwork Orange*. But the early 1970s were nervous years in Hollywood, badly burned by inventories of would-be blockbusters that proved to be expensive failures on release. The major studios were destabilized. Established players like Robert O'Brien at MGM, whom Kubrick had always considered a reliable front-

First loss of a father figure: Barry's parent is killed in the film's opening duel, a dispassionate long shot. The sense of distance underscores the absence of emotion.

office ally, had lost their clout, or their jobs. With retrenchment ordered, it was no time for a Napoleonic-sized budget. And Kubrick had other worries.

Internationally, *A Clockwork Orange* had been a huge critical and commercial success. In Britain, however, its release caught the full force of the antiviolence backlash triggered by *The Wild Bunch* and then *Straw Dogs*. Those Sam Peckinpah movies had exploited the voyeuristic allure of destructiveness by using slow motion to depict, in pornographic detail, what gunshots did to the human body. *A Clockwork Orange* had no such gory scenes. Its violence was highly stylized. No matter. It was premiered in Britain just as public outrage against the Peckinpah movies peaked, exacerbated by the anxieties of a ruling Conservative government eager to demonstrate its law-and-order credentials prior to a parliamentary election. Burgess's story at bottom indicted the Fascistic techniques of a government clampdown on

*From affectionate encounter to deliberate provocation:
Barry's first lesson in love.*

As in A Clockwork Orange *(page 207), "love" is a
hands-on affair.*

Mustering for war. From Spartacus *to the Seven Years
War, field maneuvers remain of paramount interest to
Kubrick.*

man's (or youth's) free will, politically translated into "crime on
the streets." So did Kubrick's film, and it came under sudden and
fierce attack. *A Clockwork Orange* had already been classified as fit
for exhibition. Even so, Home Secretary Reginald Maudling—
coincidentally an ideal model for the film's opportunistic
Minister of the Interior—ordered a personal screening of the film
before it opened publicly. The feeling that there was an orches-
trated campaign against the film—and its maker—grew. This
shocked and alarmed Kubrick. How vulnerable his film had
proved to be. Might he not be vulnerable as well, to vicious personal attacks, or even to violence arriving on his own doorstep?

Once the film had run in British cinemas, he withdrew it. To
this day, he has not allowed *A Clockwork Orange* to be shown in
Britain, even in cinema clubs.

What has this to do with *Barry Lyndon*? Directly, very little. But
in the shadowy region of a filmmaker's recoil, quite a lot.
Kubrick's film had unleashed irrational forces in a society which
he had once considered a safer, quieter, less invasive place to
work than Hollywood, or even New York. As a consequence, the
Clockwork Orange furor precipitated early evidence of what has
since become Kubrick's dominant characteristic, a near complete
withdrawal from public visibility. In this unsettled frame of
mind, he sought a subject for his next film that would be remote

from the contemporary world—and the threats it held. Early in 1973 he lit on William Makepeace Thackeray's first novel, *The Luck of Barry Lyndon*. His choice once more surprised everyone—and baffled not a few.

The book was published in 1844 as monthly magazine installments, under the rather zany pen name of George Savage FitzBoodle. It is the picaresque story of a scoundrel who would be a gentleman, and was at first sight an astonishing choice for *any* filmmaker. On reflection, the motivation is less enigmatic. Barry, the eponymous narrator, tells his own story with total shamelessness—always a draw with Kubrick—and leaves it to Thackeray's subtext to reveal him to be a self-serving liar and disreputable parvenu. The moral contradiction provides an attractive tension. This view of an energetic opportunist, no better than his "betters," had an appealing irony for a filmmaker possessed of a large misanthropic streak in his cinematic outlook.

The story moved along vigorously if jerkily. It was already a rough film script. That could be smoothed over. Thackeray cut a swath through eighteenth-century society, painting people of wide social rank, moral condition, and nationality—Irish, English, and Prussian. After rejigging this story to emphasize his own pessimistic calculation of our chances in avoiding the traps of life, Kubrick now set out to re-create a history as strange and

sensuously detailed as the speculative futures of *2001* and *A Clockwork Orange*. One other attraction, a crucial one, beckoned. The novel's period setting in the Seven Years War provided a panoramic view of military Europe, its commanders, army structures, and battlefields. Kubrick could come no closer to his *Napoleon* epic.

Hardly anyone outside scholarly enclaves was on familiar terms with Thackeray's book, so Kubrick could take liberties with impunity. What a relief after *Lolita*!

How he hit on it has never been convincingly explained. Kubrick is said to have all of Thackeray's works on his shelves at home. If so, it's a fair bet that his library boasts a larger supply of moviemaking potential than any other filmmaker's home in the English-speaking world. Another possibility is that one of the academic historians signed up to consult on the aborted *Napoleon* pointed him toward this collateral source of inspiration about pre-Napoleonic manners and morality. Rumor has it that Kubrick sent Warner Bros. his screenplay from Thackeray's novel with title, dates, and characters' names all changed to protect the public-domain status of the source material against imitators. It's quite probable. Still in shock at the unwelcome notoriety suffered from the anti–*Clockwork Orange* campaigners, a congenitally cautious nature was turning into an obsessively secretive one.

The engagement party: "Kiss her, Jack, you rogue, for you've got a treasure."

Our Hero shows a flash of social envy at his "better" having won in love.

Barry upsets the social equilibrium with a well-aimed glass of wine in the Captain's face.

"I've been grossly insulted in this house. . . ." Leonard Rossiter's Captain seeks satisfaction.

Most of the film was shot in Ireland and England, with second-unit work, mainly exteriors, done in Germany under long-distance instructions from Kubrick. The film was premiered in 1975.

Viewing *Barry Lyndon* is like being a witness at a ceremony. The complex implications of what seemed at the time to be simple scenes only work their way into one's mind long after the event. People watching a Kubrick film often report this "time lapse" phenomenon. Yet *Barry Lyndon* took most critics by surprise—and for good reason. Since movies began, a "period film" had carried certain expectations. Kubrick's film turned these upside down. Populist terms like "swashbuckle," "picturesque romp," or "historical romance" simply didn't apply to the form or content of this film. Kubrick had won the first trick hands down. He took his audience by surprise, a victory turned dubious, to be sure, in the face of a public that prides itself on knowing what it likes.

Barry Lyndon approaches history as if popular revisions of it had never been invented; indeed, the people in the film don't think of themselves at all as part of history—which is true of the way most of us live our daily lives. The film deals with "history" in terms of *behavior*. It is a sumptuous exercise in mass observation, depicting life-styles at all levels of society. We see society not just in its civilian dress but society in uniform and at war. Since wars in the eighteenth century were the great melting pot of nationalities, soldiering was a career "open to the talents of all"; thus all manner of men were thrown together in these volcanic upheavals that changed rulers, frontiers, and the fates of nations. Throughout the film, Kubrick concentrates one's attention on *what people do*.

In contrast to movies like *Dr. Strangelove* or the later *Full Metal Jacket*, language (apart from body language) plays little part in his critique of society. He transformed Thackeray's tale by taking the story away from Barry, the "unreliable" narrator, and giving it to an unseen, omniscient, offscreen voice, a personage whose tones (the voice is Michael Hordern's) immediately set the film's

To the ironical accompaniment of sweet birdsong, a close-up of pistols being loaded for an encounter that climaxes, as the film started, in a classically composed tableau of mortality devoid of melodrama.

rhythm, just as his words foreshadow the story's direction. By 1975 the voice-over was a novelty in people's filmgoing experience, but it had been a constant feature of Kubrick's past as a child of the radio age. A voice-over has several effects. It puts audiences in an unwontedly passive frame of mind while relieving them of the obligation to interpret relationships and make connections between characters and events. Kubrick's narrator interprets for us what happens on-screen as we see it. Even more crucially, he *anticipates* what will happen before we see it. We are compelled to be observers, not participants. As a result, *Barry Lyndon*'s structure goes against the grain of most screen drama and all *popular* entertainment—it is composed in anticlimaxes.

The commentary does follow Barry's adventure linearly, but in a totally detached manner, eliminating surprise. Taking its place

is low-level suspense. Knowing what will befall our hero, we learn the manner in which life unfolds, how destiny—accident, chance, random events—has its way. This very Kubrick notion fits well with Thackeray's employment of the mock-heroic style of literature. Kubrick easily adds the cinematic illusion of irony. If such a thing as free will exists, there is nevertheless no grand plan, certainly none that Barry can follow with success. Thackeray's original title was *The Life and Luck of Barry Lyndon*, but few heroes of his time are so unlucky as Barry. His misfortunes fortify Kubrick's Hobbesian conviction that life is short, brutish, and even nastier than Thackeray portrayed it.

All this had implications for Ryan O'Neal. In the mid-1970s, the thirty-something O'Neal was riding high. He was Hollywood's leading romantic star, following *Love Story* (1970),

"He was destined to be a wanderer . . . ," says the narrator, as Barry begins his travels in a landscape in which John Ford would have felt at home.

Our Hero approaches the first of those who will rob him of his patrimony and innocence.

Barry's encounter with the highwaymen.

Kubrick frames the meeting like a genre painting.

What's Up, Doc? (1972), and *Paper Moon* (1973). When Kubrick signed O'Neal for the title role, he also secured the star power to gain Warner Bros.' confidence and the film's sizable $11 million budget.

There is a kind of magnificent extravagance in casting a star of O'Neal's magnitude only to use him as a pawn, a character whose responses to his life are forever being usurped by an omniscient narrator. O'Neal's performance is structured around the passive principle, an almost affectless on-screen presence which violates every notion of what a Hollywood leading man expects from a star role. However, if O'Neal harbors dark memories, he has commendably kept them to himself. (With few exceptions, in fact, Kubrick's stars do not speak about the experience of being directed by him. The "spell" of the film appears to linger on, sealing lips, which is a loss to film historians but certainly a reassurance to its maker.)

In *Barry Lyndon*, O'Neal gets no "big moments," no scenes a star can seize upon to etch his personality into the character or into the way he affects events. All are taken away from O'Neal in advance. Frequently, he is called upon merely to stand quietly and do nothing. To be sure, O'Neal does it very well; probably no other youngish American star of the time could have done nothing so effectively, with such picturesque result, so little self-determination. But it may have been a disconcerting experience, the more so since Kubrick's marvelously detailed fidelity to historical accuracy—to lighting, dressing, and architectural authenticity—must have required long stretches of waiting around doing . . . nothing.

Even so, what O'Neal *could* bring to the film was his own glamour: expensive stuff. Kubrick uses it the way an arbiter of fashion uses only the best—not exactly wastefully, certainly not disdainfully, but not letting it rule his day. The film was photographed by John Alcott, who had shot *A Clockwork Orange* (and who would work on Kubrick's next two films); and again attitude dictates form. Here, Kubrick's favorite camera movement is

As in Paths of Glory, *firepower and numbers decide the winners in battle—at a cost.*

Barry enters the Prussian service only to find his life has not been improved. Fortune will later enable him, in turn, to inflict a beating on his own "inferior."

Uniform produces uniformity in the fighting men. As in Full Metal Jacket, *individuality, once deconstructed, is welded into a military machine.*

a slow and sensuous pulling back from a single detail to reveal a panorama, a zoom shot in calculated reverse. It is the action of a man marveling at the world as it was two hundred years ago, enchanted, yet scrupulous in the scholarly attention his eye gives to pictorial composition and period detail. This withdrawal, or "opening out," imposes a classical sense of perspective and order on a world filled with turbulence. Again and again, landscape or architecture frames events, detaching us from them, imposing a meditative distance. Dramatic close-ups are rare to nonexistent; we are being taken on a guided tour with the guide's polite but firm instructions, "Don't go too near the pictures." The opening shot, showing Barry's father killed in a duel, reduces the figures to dots on an Irish horizon, investing this tragic start to Our Hero's misfortunes with the look of a pastoral, not a family tragedy. Why should Nature care about the tragedies enacted on her territory? Composition in this film is character.

In Barry's saga there are very few "humble abodes." People are placed in the open air, or in great public rooms and stately residences—allowing the ceremonies of war and peace, town and country, metropolis and court, parkland and battlefield, to unfold. Such ceremonies parade the etiquette of a time remote, yet made immediate. The screen is continually arranged and rearranged into painterly compositions we have seen in museums and art galleries. But Kubrick animates them, bringing their essence to life without disrupting their temporal authenticity.

Barry becomes a spy for the Prussians. Kubrick draws painterly inspiration from the interiors of the period.

History repeats itself. The cosmonaut in 2001 who enters another dimension and discovers a mysterious resident eating a meal becomes Barry Lyndon entering the next phase of his fate and discovering his patron, the chevalier, at breakfast. In both cases, a sense of classical balance accompanies the transforming encounter.

In this he was greatly helped by his large cast of English players, well used to eighteenth-century costumes and well trained in the formalities of eighteenth-century speech, so redolent with the class distinctions and differences in birth or education still alive and rampant in twentieth-century Britain. *Barry Lyndon* doesn't breathe history—for history is something in airtight cabinets or varnished paintings. Rather, it exhales historical life. We are encouraged to "look around," take our time, find felicity in a draped curtain or awe in an army's battle formation.

The camera continuously strikes up an observer's attitude; takes are long, allowing the manners of the period to describe a way of life, not just make a plot point. Such lengthy shots also protect a film director from any later attempt by the studio to meddle with his vision by shortening or reediting scenes. In most sequences there are few "cutaways": the players stand their ground and simply *play*. Usually their exchanges cannot be shortened, only terminated—or else one risks a jump cut. Seldom is it truer to say that "the style is the man"—but then "the man" is Stanley Kubrick.

Barry makes his entry among the Irish gentry, of whom he's a minor sprig. A gullible teenager reared in a family of good stock but not aristocratic lineage, Barry is determined to acquire at least the trappings of aristocracy. Such vaulting ambition will spur

him on and ultimately bring him down. From the very first image, *Barry Lyndon*'s moral is "Know your place." The plot of the film, of course, is "Enhance your fortune." And it is the tension between these two that leads to tragedy. A code of honor, which demands lip service at the least, is of course poor preparation for the harsher world Barry seeks to enter. The so-called Age of Enlightenment is continually revealed to be an age of egotism.

Barry's first reversal of fortune occurs in a duel with Captain Quinn, a wilting English officer (Leonard Rossiter). They fight over a teasing and faithless lass (Gay Hamilton) who has conducted Barry's hand to her own lightly veiled breast—virtually the film's only flash of eroticism. The lass, it turns out, has driven a better bargain for the rest of her body with the pompous captain, a man who boasts, "I'm an Englishman, I am, and a man of property."

The rivals in love meet around a dinner table. The *contre-jour* radiance of the backlighting circles the men and women with a soft, romantic glow, as if varnish had been applied to a group portrait. This effect is typical of the film's historical aura. At the same time, it is antithetical to the greed, ambition, and duplicity displayed by the characters. The look of envy Barry shoots his better-off dinner companions is one of the few *expressions* allowed to cross O'Neal's face. Otherwise, Kubrick keeps it a neutral area

Kubrick's fondness for the sedentary figure of power links Sir Charles Lyndon with the crippled Dr. Strangelove.

and invites *us* to project our thoughts and feelings on it as they are prompted by the omniscient narrator. In startling contrast, Captain Quinn's features quiver as he, in fearful anticipation of death, prepares to fight the duel. The captain is a coward; and it shows. Had Leonard Rossiter not died prematurely, he would surely have joined Kubrick's company of players, not themselves stars, nor ever likely to be, but actors exceptionally receptive to what he asks of them, who can pitch their performance precisely when given his keynote, and all without needing to know why.

The duel itself shows how the film distances us even from acts of slaughter. We are not involved. Our view is Olympian, rarely partisan. Opening on a close-up of pistols being loaded, the cam-

Ill-met by candlelight. Barry finds the Countess (Marisa Berenson) irresistible. Kubrick's insistence on natural lighting surrounds both of them with an aura of enraptured inevitability. "Faites vos jeux," says the croupier, and Barry, without another word spoken, clinches his own fate by embracing his future wife.

Kubrick's penchant for showing man as a speck in the larger landscape of human fate. Barry, already cooling in his relationship with his new wife, is driven to his country estate—a panorama that suggests the opening of The Shining *(five years later), when Jack Nicholson, as a husband who has fallen out of love with his wife and family, drives his own vehicle to the fateful grandeur of the Overlook Hotel.*

Virtually abandoned by her husband, the Countess is comforted in her bath by being read to in French. A beautifully lit genre picture, as well as an example of Kubrick's frequent use of daily rituals in the dramas surrounding his characters.

era pulls way, way back until death becomes only an imminent glimmer in a Watteau landscape. Fred Zinnemann, when he came to Thomas More's beheading in *A Man for All Seasons*, attempted something similar by focusing on a bee sucking pollen from a flower in close-up while More, in long shot, climbs steps leading to the chopping block. Unfortunately for Zinnemann's sense of pathos, of nature remaining indifferent to man's fate, the bee refused to suck, but rather whizzed about. Kubrick shows the vanity of human life by physically diminishing those about to lose theirs—and wisely doesn't rely on the insect world.

Thinking he has killed his rival—he hasn't, the fellow has merely feigned death, buying himself out of an affair of honor—Barry finds it expedient to start his travels.

The rest of the film follows the parabola of his rise and fall. Its theme—*one* of its themes, anyhow—is a search for "worldly success." Another will be Barry's instinctual search for a father figure to replace his parent, felled in the opening duel. No writer other than Thackeray is credited for *Barry Lyndon*'s script, although plenty of space was probably allowed for the "accidents" of performance or the "opportunities" offered by location. In Barry Lyndon's time, war and peace are supposed to be governed by the most elaborate rules of conduct. At a pinch, however, a soldier's most realistic response is still "Every man for himself." Barry is allowed to depart thinking that if he's lost his

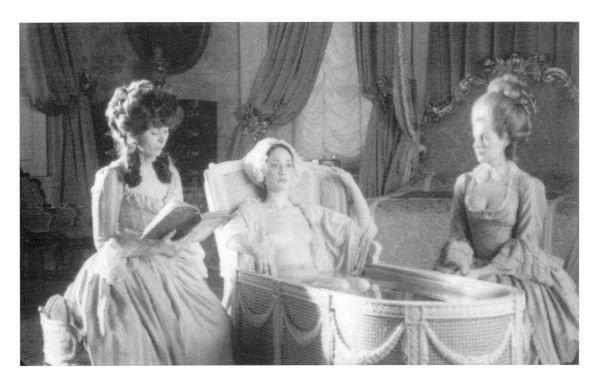

Social claustrophobia. Barry finds that his new status, far from liberating him, only exposes him to the coming battle of wills with his stepson, young Lord Bullingdon (Leon Vitali, center).

One of the film's rare moments of tenderness. Barry regales his son with a tale of his battlefield exploits. But Kubrick knows, along with Thackeray, that life only stores up grief, not glory.

beloved, at least he's proved his manhood in the duel. In truth, he's simply been duped by a schemer out to save his own skin. His "luck" doesn't hold for long, either. Two highwaymen hold him up and, with persnickety precision, relieve him of the farewell gift of his mother's guineas. Even such a simple cinematic composition—Barry surrendering his money with his hands up—settles into a genre portrait, "painted," "varnished," "framed," and destined to be "hung" on the walls of a stately home or academy exhibition, perhaps laconically entitled *A Highway Meeting.*

Barry Lyndon's simple but boldly composed shots recall John Ford's Westerns. Like Ford, Kubrick seems confident that each uncomplicated setup will hold a viewer's interest, create a han-

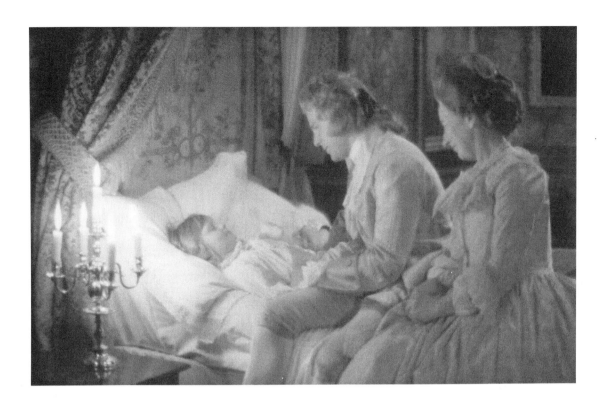

kering, as E. M. Forster said in *Aspects of the Novel*, to know "what happens next." Pauline Kael once compared *Barry Lyndon* to the roistering English film *Tom Jones* run in slow motion with the jokes left out. The comparison is not apt. *Tom Jones* expressed all of director Tony Richardson's flea-hopping temperament. In style it pays homage to the disjunctive liberties popularized by the French *nouvelle vague*. Kubrick's film is much more in the Ford tradition of misanthropic melancholy rather than in the Richardson tradition of rough comradeship.

"What happens next" is that Barry finds himself wearing a soldier's red coat and serving in the British army, then an ally of Frederick the Great's Prussia. A battle against the French is the first of the film's meticulously designed set pieces. Its formality recalls *Spartacus*; its battle tactics do not. The camera tracks into battle as line upon line of musketeers unlooses fire at the opposing troops. Each rank suffers terrible loss to enemy fire, and yet the survivors press grimly on, until the nerve of one side weakens and shatters. Wars, Kubrick reminds us, are as often won by the turntail panic of an enemy as by the superiority of the victor.

The "machine-made" nature of the military strategy befits the times. Its use of men as killing machines anticipates *Full Metal Jacket* twelve years later. The age of chivalry is a murderous one; wars change weaponry, but not the will to use it.

"His life now seemed to consist of little more than letters to lawyers and moneybrokers . . . ," says the narrator. Kubrick's characteristic symmetry emphasizes the emptiness of such a grand life.

Barry lays on the rod to chastise his stepson and rival, but it only encourages rebellion and threat.

Barry takes to army life. It's the only "family" he's known. He becomes embroiled in a bare-knuckle fistfight. His superior officer announces the fight with ritual formality, and the men form a square for the action, bawling, hooting, and wagering on the contestants. The rites of "gentlemanly" conduct contrast with a reality that is brutish. The harsh lessons Barry learns will be those he later carries into that other "killing field"—family life.

The misfit becomes "the good soldier" so often pictured in English caricature, actually a plunderer and a freebooter. This aspect would be more apparent had O'Neal been encouraged to give a more expressive performance. While he continues to *look* as if Irish butter wouldn't melt in his mouth, the words put into the narrator's mouth suggest a disreputable opportunist. Having started by distancing Barry from us, the film has to continue along that problematic road. Scenes that seem to be needed in the film are omitted, or cut short, because they would expose Barry's nature too directly, too independently of the ironically moralizing storyteller—as if Barry were enjoying the luxury of free will, instead of serving fate.

Consider the romantic interlude we are *told* he enjoys with a peasant woman. Another director might have allowed Barry the time to demonstrate his love and faithfulness to the fair sex. Not Kubrick. The "great good place" away from war, as the romantic

A rebellious Lord Bullingdon upsets the family scene in an attempt to reclaim the rights of his rank. Kubrick uses a hand-held camera to convey the social order in disarray.

warrior Hemingway later put it, isn't to be Barry's for long. And the narrator isn't taken in by shots of the couple enjoying domestic happiness. "A lady who sets her heart on a man in uniform must be prepared to change lovers very quickly," he observes. And "very quickly," the idyll ends. Our lovers part almost as soon as they've met.

Barry Lyndon opened in 1975. Another film of the same year allows an interesting comparison. This was *Royal Flash*, the George MacDonald Fraser pastiche of nineteenth-century Prussian militarism directed with a jokey flourish by Richard Lester. Its antihero, Flashman, the bully from *Tom Brown's Schooldays*, is now a dashing adventurer in the Hussars, played by none other than Kubrick's earlier antihero Malcolm McDowell. (Michael Hordern also made a contribution to the Lester film, on-screen this time.) The comedy-satire of *Royal Flash* soon palls through sheer overkill. It lacks precisely that ironic sense of destiny which Kubrick's hand (and Hordern's commentary) continually identifies in Barry's progress through the world. And Malcolm McDowell's performance in Lester's film suggests that had he swapped roles with O'Neal, his emphatic style would have undone Kubrick's intention by making Barry seem master of his fate, instead of its servant.

Up to now, *Barry Lyndon* has been set mainly in the open

Kubrick makes space seem oppressive even when Barry is sharing an intimate moment with his son.

Barry's beloved child meets with a fatal accident. A violent incident is rendered in a single, starkly vertical shot, reminiscent of the minatory attitudes of the Great Ape in 2001 *and Alex in* A Clockwork Orange.

The ensuing sequence, as the little boy dies watched over by his mother and father, creates the film's strongest moment of family tenderness. With the child's funeral, it reverts to the oppressive obligations of ritual and social status.

spaces of the European wars. Now a sense of architecture closes in on Barry, as the State intrigues he stumbles into turn correspondingly baroque. The grandiose exteriors of imperial Prussia were shot in Germany by a second unit; the interiors, inventively "dressed" by production designer Ken Adam, are set in some of the great houses of the landed gentry in England and Ireland. Filming on location was not trouble-free, however. Kubrick's unit had to abandon part of the Irish shoot when the IRA began making extortionate demands on it.

The film moves inexorably on. A subtle Prussian captain (Hardy Kruger) exposes Barry's masquerade as an English officer—a capital offense—and blackmails him into becoming a police spy reporting on a shady chevalier (Patrick Magee) who is rooking all the rakes of Europe at the card tables.

Magee's cadaverous face, matched by a voice that can descend the scale into the grave, had made him a Kubrick favorite. He had played Mr. Alexander, the writer mugged, vandalized, and left paralyzed in *A Clockwork Orange*. Here, however, he is almost a clockwork man. We first see him sitting at a table eating breakfast. He says very little, and much of it in German—though later, when conversing with German players at the card tables, he illogically speaks English. The table setting and Magee's brooding presence strongly echo the enigmatic figure in *2001* whom the cosmonaut discovered dining with equal frugality in an eighteenth-century French bedroom. We almost expect Magee to undergo some astral transfiguration.

But the spurious chevalier, one of Barry's father figures, dominates the boy by the power of patriarchy—and patronage. He turns the tables on his Prussian spymasters, converting Barry the spy into his card-sharping ally. Magee's performance, damped down to suit the machinations of his character, denies us the full value of his marvelous tones. But with his gorgeous embroideries, a face powdered and rouged as if made up by a mortician, and his black piratical eye patch, Magee makes a monumental

The influence of Hogarth's social realism. Barry
declines into drink and dissoluteness . . . while her
ladyship takes to religion for solace. Kubrick draws on
social satire and portrait tradition for his effects.

Full circle: Barry, in his cups, finds Lord Bullingdon,
calling at his club to demand satisfaction. Fate leaves
Our Hero with no escape—a typical Kubrickian
moment.

impression as he fleeces the rich and decadent noblemen of Prussia.

Throughout, the consummate technical mastery of Kubrick and photographer John Alcott creates a suffocating "interior world" of faces. By the light of hot tallow candles, we can read in them greed, mendacity, and constipation. The ultrafast industrial lens custom-made by Carl Zeiss of Germany catches even the flames' penumbra, exposing eighteenth-century life by its own sweltering, flickering illumination. Feverish flesh appears to be melting.

The feeling of finery clogged with sweat and powder is over-powering. *2001* created the awesomeness of space. *Barry Lyndon* shows us the claustrophobia of society.

At this point Kubrick introduces his second star, Marisa Berenson. "Introduces," yes; yet scarcely does more. Berenson may have been too green an actress to do more than simply personify the world of Lady Lyndon, beautiful and bored, as over-dressed and numb as a waxwork. She did know how to do *that*, being a top fashion model. A model's imperative is to wear someone else's finery and keep her mouth shut. Within these not too

For the duel scene, set in a barn, Kubrick draws on the luminous effects of such a notable eighteenth-century artist as Wright of Derby. The cooing of doves, a sound usually associated with peace and tranquillity, adds an ironic counterpoint to the rituals of vengeance between gentlemen.

The father figure of Barry confronts the stepson he tried to disinherit.

The old order proves too strong for the usurper.

Badly wounded and lacking a leg, a lonely and broken Barry goes back to where he began his travels—to life with mother. Kubrick ends his story with symmetry— but no sympathy.

distracting parameters, Berenson's performance is immaculate. With her marble-white face under a galleon sail of hair, and her nearly naked breasts exposed with period candor in the public gaming salons, she embodies the cushiony voluptuousness of a woman whose soft life has stifled orgasm.

But for all her finery, Lady Lyndon remains a mere functionary. Kubrick is unrelenting. Berenson's contribution is pictorial, not psychological—which suits Kubrick, who now stages the story's most significant courtship with next to no exposure of the characters' inner feelings.

Looks between Barry and Lady Lyndon take the place of words. Glances over the playing cards lead to a wordless encounter in the gardens outside, where Barry literally walks into possession of a wife—and a fortune. In some ways, this is the film's most daring elision. How the scene is shot recalls a love scene in a costume film from the silent-cinema era. The blue effect of moonlight on the two white figures even replicates the effects traditionally induced by hand-tinted sequences in the more expensive pre-talkies productions, cueing filmgoers in on the romantic mood (and displaying all the lavishness that money could buy). The kiss between Barry and his mistress is a silent-screen kiss—passionate but chaste. The music accompanying this instant courtship likewise recalls those selections performed by orchestras in the swisher sort of picture palaces. In stately and classical style, the works of Bach, Handel, Mozart, Schubert, and Vivaldi, and even a composition (the *Hohenfriedeberger* March) by Frederick the Great, form an ironic counterpoint to the base values of Barry's world. No warmth seals his match. Neither partner loves the other for him/herself—only for a part of their natures. In her case, his romantic looks; in his case, her money.

A great writer, Thackeray was also a skillful caricaturist whose cartoons ornament some of his slighter works. Curiously, caricature is absent in this film, which offers many opportunities for it. The exception is Sir Charles Lyndon (Frank Middlemass).

The year written on Barry's remittance note says it all: "1789"—a date that marks the revolt against the aristocracy that shook all Europe. Kubrick will end his next film, **The Shining**, with another date of narrative significance.

Another son and another mother: Lord Bullingdon and the Countess. Kubrick condemns them to a life of status without enjoyment. In **Barry Lyndon**, nobody wins.

This English aristocrat, Lady Lyndon's husband, is an invalid
seen first in a wheelchair, one of those thrones that previous
Kubrick films have reserved for malignant ogres of crippled
power like *Dr. Strangelove* or *A Clockwork Orange*'s Mr. Alexander.
Sir Charles belongs to this sinister coven, and Kubrick rewards
him with a savage, comic-grotesque death scene that plays like a
cameo drawn by Rowlandson. It starts with an eruption of sneez-
ing and continues with a venomous tirade against Barry, who he
has correctly guessed has designs on his wife and wishes to "fill
my shoes." Next comes a gross rictus of coughing, an explosion
of pills, and a climactic death rattle at the card table. The narrator, dispassionate as ever, then reads the nobleman's obituary as
it will appear in the *London Gazette*. *Barry Lyndon*: Part One ends

with this thunderclap of black farce. What follows, in Part Two, is the avenging storm.

Barry Lyndon is that rare thing, a film that turns against its hero. The whole of its second half replays the very features of Barry's character that have brought him "luck" in the first half, features that now lead to his downfall. Where he was pardonably ingenuous, Barry is now foolishly cocksure; where he fought a duel for the love of his heart, he now loves ignobly; where he cheerfully put money in his purse by cheating folk no better than himself, he now meanly plots to disinherit his kith and kin; where he fought bravely for his King, he now bullies his family; where he achieved his goal by marrying into a fortune, he now cannot keep it. It's as if the movement of the planets had brought a new conjunction of forces into play—which, in turn, brings into focus a theme that will continue to shape Kubrick's own work in future years.

As already noted, some of Kubrick's films contain shots and scenes, even whole sequences, that eerily foreshadow projects he couldn't possibly have had in mind at the time. This pattern, less precognition than a recurring preoccupation, clearly outlines a forceful personal compulsion in the writer-director's choice of story or treatment. The pattern, a patriarchal one, distinguishes the three films Kubrick made after *A Clockwork Orange* from the previous nine he made since 1953. The earlier films explore a variety of themes and concerns that are more or less universal. Their maker is anxious not to repeat himself. However, with *Barry Lyndon*, *The Shining*, and *Full Metal Jacket* he deals with family strains—more precisely with the way a father marks his offspring for destruction but in the end pays the mortal penalty himself.

The theme of the father, or father figure, as fate's fearsome agent shapes each of these films. In *The Shining*, abusive Jack Torrance goes mad and tries to murder his wife and family. In *Full Metal Jacket*, brutal Gunnery Sergeant Hartman stays sane, but arguably provokes the death of one of his "boys." In *Barry Lyndon*, the heartless hero dominates his family, then is forced into a duel with his stepson in order to maintain his supremacy. In each of these films, the father figure loses out; in two of them, he dies. None of the three men feels he "belongs" to the family acquired through marriage, birth, or command. Even Hartman's dedication to his Marine "grunts" is a loyalty of the tribe, not the family.

One would have to know more, much more, about Kubrick in order to assign reasons for this thematic recurrence. But it's likely that Kubrick's filmmaking enables him to confront it, without actually involving himself. The film becomes a buffer between the director and his emotional involvement.

Perhaps this helps explain why, as *Barry Lyndon*'s second half opens and the theme of a patriarchal feud takes over from filial adventure, the characters become ever more distant and emotionally frozen in their relationships.

Almost immediately, Barry starts mistreating his heiress wife. He puffs pipe smoke in her face in their closed carriage. He neglects her passive charms for the livelier ones of a kitchen maid. She spies them kissing in the parkland—an infidelity pointed up with a zoom shot. He confines her to the company of her chaplain, the servile Reverend Runt (Murray Melvin), and her maid, who reads to her in French while she soaks in her bath, a sad wife reduced to the ornamental status of an *objet de vertu*. Small wonder audiences were puzzled. Led to expect a developing story of Barry and his trophy wife, they were turned into passive spectators of a Gainsborough lady framed in her own loneliness.

Instead, the film's narrative energy now flows from Barry's growing envy and hatred of his young stepson, the child Lord Bullingdon. Barry has a son of his own by his wife, and dotes on the lad; however, by the rules of primogeniture, fortunes descend through the firstborn male, and it will be the little lordling who will one day supplant Barry and "fill his shoes." It will be his stepson, not Barry (who hasn't a penny of his own), who will be lord of the grand estate and its entailed wealth. He will displace Barry just as Barry displaced Sir Charles Lyndon. Revenge in a Kubrick film has its symmetry.

The film grows visually rich in its second half, largely because it has now become a chamber drama. The action no longer roves freely and picaresquely around Europe, but has evolved into a comeuppance narrative played out in stately homes, at the royal court, in gentlemen's clubs, music rooms, and brothels. All are deliberately and strikingly modeled on canvases by the great painters of the period, among them Reynolds, Zoffany, Hogarth, Constable, Stubbs. . . . Ever a figure in the paintings, Barry is always an outsider in the society they portray. Even Barry's managerial mother (played with Celtic shrewishness by the veteran Irish actress Marie Kean), even the toadying Reverend Runt express themselves more vigorously and frankly. She is seen as manipulatively businesslike, he egregiously self-serving. Meanwhile, our eponymous hero seethes behind his mask of outward good fortune. At this stage of the story, Kubrick allows coldhearted Barry only one moment of softness, all the more touching for being so unexpected. Barry's son is killed in a horse-riding accident; the father's grief is poignant indeed. Similarly, *The Shining*'s Jack Torrance will try to kill his son in the maze of the Overlook Hotel, but he's allowed a clearheaded second or two of paternal tenderness and protectiveness in the prelude to the horror show.

Barry's jealousy of his stepson is the private grudge that erupts in public with the force of a land mine. Lord Bullingdon—now grown and played by Leon Vitali—wickedly puts his own shoes on young Barry's natural son and marches him, clumpingly, through the music room where Barry, his wife, and a fine array of society are attending a concert. The camera collaborates in the eruption they provoke. The film's natural inclination toward balance and symmetry is now literally overturned as a hand-held camera records a furious Barry assaulting Bullingdon, creating a scrum on the parquet, skidding over the floor, scattering the guests, shaming his wife, and losing his status with his temper.

Until now, Barry has applied the same harsh lessons to Lord Bullingdon's upbringing as his own worldly experience taught him: that is to say, power holds the upper hand—and it should be applied with a firm smack. He thrashes his stepson as he himself was thrashed in his army days: "I serve men as they serve me." Men *and boys*, he might have added.

But Lord Bullingdon is older now. A boy's impotent resentment turns into a man's defiance of his proxy father: "I will kill you if you lay hands on me again." (Leon Vitali was an actor of lean good looks retrieved from the point of prettiness by a pair of highly mobile lips that lend him an air of menace. Vitali abandoned a promising screen career soon after this film to become one of Kubrick's most trusted behind-the-scenes aides. He is particularly valued for relieving the director of some of the face-to-face chores involved in short-listing players. For *The Shining* he winnowed down thousands of potential child actors to find the right one for "Danny.")

Thackeray had hustled Lord Bullingdon off to America after his public spat with his stepfather. Kubrick keeps him in England, where family animosity builds up to the inevitable duel. The scene—a barn lit with a painterly radiance borrowed from the eighteenth-century artist Wright of Derby—can still produce surprise. It's young Bullingdon who is literally sick to his stomach with fright. Barry is the man determined to ape "the gentleman." He holds off firing when he has Bullingdon at his mercy.

The English critic Penelope Huston suggests that Kubrick has revised Thackeray at this point so as to introduce a note of mock irony. Barry's ambition to become a gentleman causes him to discharge the gun honorably into the ground. "Bullingdon," writes Huston, "who has the advantage of having been born a gentleman, shows no such compunction." He wounds Barry, not fatally, but badly enough to cost him a leg—the symbolic castration of father by son. In Thackeray's novel, Barry is spared this gross injury to his pride and person: he finishes his life in a debtors' prison. The film is much more finite and callous. Barry limps away at the end, invalided out of the Lyndon family, a remittance man dependent on their charity. The antithesis of a hero. A Kubrick protagonist defeated this time, as Michel Ciment has pointed out, by society and not the machine.

It's a cruel end; but the coda is even more sinister. Like figures in a living waxworks, Lady Lyndon, her chaplain, and her son are shown sitting round a table, signing papers, presumably managing what is left of her estates after "pensioning off" her husband. The camera closes in, revealing the date on a money order. It is 1789: the year of the French Revolution, the year that privilege ended, and the beginning of an unparalleled bloody mass execution of the class that had supported and fueled the ambitions of the Barry Lyndons of the world.

Such subtlety of time's revenge was missed by most cinema audiences in 1975. *Barry Lyndon* was like no film before it; and none like it has been attempted since. It was well ahead of its time and of its audience's understanding of what Kubrick was up to. A historical romp of the usual kind might have been "the sure thing" that distributors pray for (and pay for). But as Kubrick has observed, nothing in the cinema is less certain than "the sure thing." He gave Warner Bros. his "own thing." And they were brave enough to accept it. Critics found *Barry Lyndon* a puzzling thing which willfully subverted genre traditions and replaced them with a beautiful but chilled meditation on the vanity of human desires. Some were disappointed, even enraged; some few wrote with grudging admiration and even acclaim. Time, however, proves an ally to such a movie. Once the form and content have been absorbed, anticipation becomes keyed to what it represents in its director's canon, rather than to what original audiences had expected. The film begins to be judged by other, more perceptive, more patient standards. In the long run, Kubrick's "luck" held better than Barry's.

One wonders, however, if Kubrick ever felt a sadness on watching *Barry Lyndon*, particularly when that end date, 1789, comes on-screen, reminding him that "his" Napoleon was just round the corner of history.

The Shining

It took Kubrick five years to complete his next film: *The Shining*. In retrospect, this seems a dismayingly long time. But that's not how it seemed to him. A man who believes in making no decisions until he has tested all possible choices scarcely notices the clock ticking. "There is a wonderful suggestive timeliness [that the structure] of making a movie imposes on your life," Kubrick said at the time. "I'm doing exactly the same as I was doing when I was eighteen and making my first movie. It frees you from any other sense of time." The impression that *The Shining* marked a change in Kubrick's temperament derives in part from the subject he eventually settled on.

The Shining deals with a violent personal conflict in the life of its central character, a self-tortured, reclusive writer named Jack Torrance whose creative juices simply won't start flowing. Some critics were quick to see a parallel between such a crisis and the slowing of *The Shining*'s production tempo. Enhancing this theme was the fact that, like Torrance, Kubrick had steadily retreated into a secluded world of his own where, for all any outsider knew, there might be demons.

His immediate family were playing a larger role in his creative activities: Christiane, his artist wife, and Vivian Kubrick, the

The Shining *opens with deceptively pastoral simplicity, but already Kubrick's Olympian camera, as in* Barry Lyndon, *conveys the impression of man dwarfed by the greater scheme of things.*

The ominous château in Paths of Glory *has its correspondence in the cursed monument of the Overlook Hotel. Above, the snows gather to seal the humans' fate.*

Fear comes in twos: twin elevators disgorge their blood . . .

. . . and the Grady twins attempt to enthrall Danny (Danny Lloyd).

youngest of his three children, had contributed to the design and music of some of his earlier films, and would do so again with *The Shining*. Jan Harlan, Kubrick's brother-in-law, served as his executive producer; Leon Vitali had become his production assistant. Certainly Kubrick's increasing reclusiveness wasn't related to any family dramas of the kind Jack Nicholson suffered in *The Shining*. But his circumstances had changed in significant respects.

For one thing, during the film's preproduction period Kubrick had moved. He and his extended family had lived for years in a large family mansion in a leafy lane at Elstree, on the edge of the London greenbelt, only a few minutes' drive from two of his favorite studios, MGM British and ABC Elstree. Now Kubrick sought out a much more remote manorial-style country house well screened by acres of woodland on a private estate in deepest Hertfordshire. In terms of distance, he was still close to London, but gone was the reasonable accessibility his earlier home had offered friends and colleagues. Even so, there was no conscious plan to "do a Howard Hughes." The purpose was severely practical: Kubrick needed more space for his work and for the new technology—telephones, fax machines, satellite TV dishes, cutting and recording rooms. He eventually placed them in what had been the mansion's stables—all this to keep him in touch with the wider world and make it unnecessary to "waste time" by visiting it except when he had to. He could be ubiquitous, yet invisible; in control, yet reasonably inviolate. Such remoteness suited his temperament. Like *The Shining*'s Jack Torrance, defiantly demanding nothing better than a long winter to get down to concentrated work, Kubrick "dug in" on his St. Albans estate:

his communications base, workshop, and family dwelling. Yes, there *is* a parallel with *The Shining*'s Overlook Hotel, but a benign one.

Certainly it's best to clear that question up before analyzing a strange film that reveals much more about its maker than he may have intended. Ironically, what has strengthened these rumors, lending them superficial believability, is the physical resemblance some people have perceived between Kubrick and the actor who plays Jack Torrance.

Jack Nicholson was his first—and immediate—choice on reading the Stephen King novel. (John Calley, Warner Bros. production chief, had sent him a proof copy.) Kubrick has always gravitated to stars of "intelligence"—not a large group. They offer him a wider range of creative choices and, generally, are readier to explore those choices than are "personality" stars who demand to be cast for their predictability and jealously guard against threatening changes in their image. Nicholson's own capacity for self-analysis was even more vital in a film with such a small cast of characters. Excluding the supernatural people who haunt the Overlook Hotel, *The Shining* is virtually a three-character movie: Torrance, his wife Wendy, and their small son Danny. Torrance's terrifying metamorphosis from family man into family slayer, from failed artist into demon axman, supplies the dynamic momentum. Possessed by malign forces of the occult, he obeys their homicidal prompting. He is always—in thought, word, and grisly deed—a man of action; and action, to Kubrick's way of thinking, must be kept interesting by making the mental processes behind it visible, too. "The perfect novel from which to make a movie is [one] which is mainly concerned with the inner life of its characters," Kubrick has said. "It will give the adaptor an absolute compass on which a character is thinking or feeling at any given moment."

By this definition, Stephen King's fiction may not be the "perfect" novel; but Jack Nicholson's ability to make his mental and emotional feelings dramatically apparent offered formidable compensation, so different from the affectless drift of Ryan O'Neal's Barry Lyndon.

No one could have anticipated how much Nicholson's physical appearance in the film resembled Kubrick's at the time. One could make a substantial list of Stanley Kubrick's traits which friends and acquaintances find unsettling, but vanity wouldn't be

Hallorann: "We can have conversations without opening our mouths." Kubrick uses the ethnic ancestry of Hallorann (Scatman Crothers) to cross time and generations and lend his conversation with Danny a supernatural frisson.

among them. It's impossible that he looked at his star and saw anything of his own image. Yet as shooting progressed and the strong-browed Jack Nicholson, whose eyes seem to command and possess whatever he is looking at, grew into the brooding, saturnine, and eventually intimidating character, people did see an affinity of manner and even appearance between him and his director. Kubrick, when quizzed about this, attributed it to the imaginative exegesis of critics, or the wishful thinking of psycho biographers. Nevertheless, the resemblance remains like a dark watermark in the critical texture of *The Shining*. Kubrick-watchers, deprived of other access to their man, view the likeness as allegory for the pathological pressures of filmmaking. Ironically, his daughter Vivian may have provided circumstantial evidence of this in her documentary about the making of *The Shining*, the only substantial record extant of her father at work. Watching that film, one does get the impression at times of an almost sinister autocrat, muffled against a wintry cold on the back lot at

*Figures in a landscape. Danny and his mother are over-
shadowed by the ominous labyrinth of the hotel maze . . .*

*. . . while back in the hotel, Jack overlooks the model of
the maze, like a figure who already possesses the power
of life and death.*

MGM's British studio (where the Overlook Hotel's exteriors and
ominous garden maze were constructed), exacting, tireless, and
dispassionate.

Kubrick is seen urging Nicholson into ever more inventive but
taxing interpretations of a scene; or venting his exasperation on
Shelley Duvall, playing the terrified Wendy Torrance, for some
alleged inattentiveness. Occasionally Kubrick seems to want to
make his point the way Torrance does, with a fireman's ax. Some
people, seeing Vivian Kubrick's short film on television, find it
easy to conflate the menacing vision of Jack Nicholson in *The
Shining* with his authoritarian director in the documentary.
Although he never admitted the connection, Kubrick was cynically inured to the media's need for bizarre theory.

Down the years, he had a phrase that he repeated like a personal mantra to hold at bay anyone who pressed him too closely
about the "meaning" of his work, or his own "intentions." It
came from an essay by H. P. Lovecraft, like Stephen King a popular manipulator of the occult: "In all things that are mysterious—
never explain." The edict applies to Kubrick's work, but even
more to himself.

The years between *Barry Lyndon* and *The Shining* can be seen as
the result of the familiar, always agonizing process of finding a
subject. Once the choice had been made, Kubrick began work

immediately. In choosing *The Shining*, he may have felt an understandable need to get back in touch with popular taste. *Barry Lyndon* was by no means the commercial failure some alleged. An unusual film, to be sure, and a disappointment in America, yes; but it found its audience, and eventually its profit, in Europe. With *The Shining*, Kubrick assumed the obligation that came with a subject presold on its author's reputation: namely, to give people what they expected—yet to surprise them nonetheless. It was the first time that a mass audience would know in advance—or think it did—what "a Stanley Kubrick film" would be about.

Stephen King has for decades been a master of the occult pot-boiler, a genre always in demand, but greatly voguish in the 1970s owing to the successes of *Rosemary's Baby* (1968) and *The Exorcist* (1973). The Devil was big box office. These films had aroused almost feverish interest in the Dark One and all his works, aided by the Pope's visit to New York to vet the state of the North American soul. Pop theology had become a hot topic;

Kubrick's feel for the Gothic architecture of German silent-era cinema: Jack at his worktable.

The scrapbook on the table chronicles the Overlook's history—though Kubrick decided not to use it in the story.

Wendy (Shelley Duvall) begins to doubt her husband's sanity. Kubrick leaves the character isolated and vulnerable in the menacing void of the big hotel.

Jack, now beginning to show the strain of mental breakdown, seems to fill the space in which he has sealed himself.

"I would never do anything to hurt you." As in Barry Lyndon, *a father's moment of tenderness with his son precedes a family tragedy.*

Time magazine ran a cover story which succinctly inquired: "Is God Dead?" Also popular in the 1970s were "group-jeopardy" movies, in which a mass of innocents are threatened with extinction by vast and irrational calamities. In such a climate, it might have been more pertinent to ask: "Is the Devil Alive?" Commercially, he sure was.

Kubrick and King were a good match. While King's plot was a supernatural soup of horrific elements, it could accommodate Kubrick's own reflections on human evil, nature's determinism, and man's regression and rebirth—big subjects for the subtext of a horror story. Not all, perhaps, were in his mind as he sealed the deal with Warner Bros., whose press release proclaimed that *The Shining* would be the scariest film of its kind. It wasn't; but as it emerged from a lengthy shooting schedule, it was certainly scary enough.

For all its author's concern with "control," a Kubrick shooting script is no cut-and-dried affair. With each successive film, it seems increasingly to resemble a talisman rather than a set of imperatives; a prompt copy, so to speak, for a collaborative effort between himself and his stars. It is used to incite Kubrick and his actors to respond to the spontaneity of the creative moment, to the inspiration, discoveries, and inventions that their creative partnership is able to generate, rehearse, and catch on film. This is apparently what occurred during *The Shining*. And what emerged surprised everyone—perhaps even its maker.

Stephen King's story appears brutally simple. The Torrances and their little boy, a child possessing psychic powers of clairvoyance and telepathic communication—the "shining" of the title—are besieged by the evil spirits who infest an isolated resort hotel in the wintry Rockies. Apparitions in human form push the already dysfunctional husband to acts of madness and mayhem. King had seemed aware of a need to move *The Shining* up, out of

One of Kubrick's favorite framing devices, the corridors of the Overlook Hotel become passageways to another world, the way that the Star Gate did in 2001.

Eyes wide shut: Danny hides from the phantoms.

Danny at play: already a prisoner of the mazelike patterns that Kubrick uses to suggest human beings trapped by inevitable forces.

"Oh God, I'm losing my mind." Kubrick's extraordinary camera angle reinforces Jack's feeling of mental
imbalance.

its class of popular shocker. He'd already shifted the center of
interest from shock-horror to suspense-psychology. Underlying
the supernatural fantasy is a domestic drama—a powerful man
on the edge of breakdown, a woman trapped in the family structure, and a child defenseless except for the psychic power he has
developed in self-protection.

The fact that Kubrick engaged the novelist Diane Johnson as
his collaborator on the screenplay suggests that he saw the primary material as a ghost story—Johnson was teaching Gothic literature at Berkeley. In addition, he got the benefit of a woman
whose novels showed a concern for humanity, depth of character
and intellectual sharpness, all of which Kubrick felt could be
applied with profit in adapting a book like *The Shining*, whose

virtues lay almost entirely in the narrative. They worked on the script separately, as was his custom with collaborators. Each broke down the story, extracting the plot essentials, questioning the characters' motivations. Then scripts were exchanged.

This process can be viewed as rather like the party game played with paper and pencil and known (appositely in this case) as "Exquisite Corpses." The contributors to a composite portrait make their own creative additions at each "blind" fold in a sheet of paper, which, when unfolded, reveals an entity that's unexpected but often more suggestive than any conscious, consensual creative effort.

Such reductivism transformed King's horror story into Kubrick's philosophical fantasy and displaced the principal interest from man's extinction to man's immortality.

Ghosts offer evidence that what we call "the end" is not oblivion. Once survival after death is accepted, a ghost story can be divinely reassuring. But a filmmaker's task is to reconcile this religious, benign aspect of the uncanny with a box-office thirst for bloodcurdling horror. Tensions of this kind were to shape *The Shining* throughout shooting—and even after the film's opening, for Kubrick eventually shortened the 146-minute running time of its New York premiere by twenty-seven minutes. He had two minutes removed during the first weeks of its U.S. run, and a further twenty-five minutes before the London opening. These cuts reveal his mode of working and thinking, testing, twisting, and transmogrifying King's horror story to reflect his own more stylistic and enigmatic preoccupations.

Kubrick was definite in preferring his films to open on a deceptively quiet and rational note. He well remembered Orson Welles's famous hoax broadcast of *The War of the Worlds*. Intended as a Halloween prank in October 1938, it touched off

"God, I'd give my soul for a drink." Jack meets Lloyd (Joe Turkel).

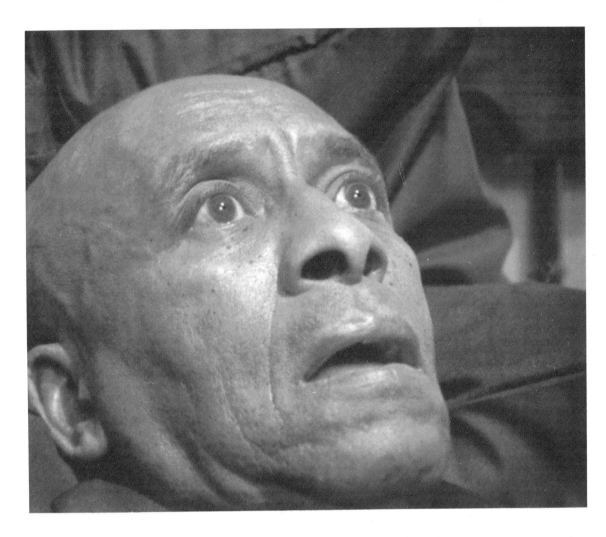

While Jack sees the ghosts of the past, Hallorann foresees the events of the future. Kubrick uses one of the biggest close-ups in the film to intensify a supernatural connection. . . .

Meanwhile, in the hotel, Danny surrenders to the pull of occult forces.

Evil begins to work again at the Overlook—the natural order is reversed in a sign that spells out a dreadful event to come.

widespread panic. Kubrick could quote from memory Welles's opening lines with their premonitory vibrations. Like the H. G. Wells novel, *The Shining* is a story of alien invasiveness, although the invaders are inside a man's mind, not a nation's. It begins without commentary—highly unusual in a Kubrick film—simply a series of radiantly illuminated, Olympian shots of the Rocky Mountains taken from a low-flying aircraft. It is early winter, before the snows come. The mountains suggest the beauty of isolation without—as yet—its terrors. The mood resembles *2001*'s symphonic overture, a universe in harmony with the rotating space stations. Yet here, an unsettling presence intrudes: Jack Torrance's tiny automobile, seen from far above, moves like a grub through paradise, toward the massive bastion of the Overlook Hotel.

Such awesome space as the Rocky Mountains—crucial in a story where hostile weather is a conspiratorial agent of entrapment—turns naturally into the walled architecture of physical confinement in the Overlook.

From our first sight of Torrance at his interview for the job of the Overlook's winter caretaker, we can already sense him to be a

prisoner of circumstances. However, no allusions to his background, or his failure as a teacher, nor any mention of the "accursed" hotel's long, ill-omened history other than the incident of the murders by a former caretaker, survived Kubrick's postrelease cuts. He retained only a single reference to the hotel's being built on sacred Native American burial ground, preparing us for acts of justifiable vengeance by ethnic spirits, and conforming to Stephen King's preference for imbuing inanimate objects with a malign life of their own. In the film, however, this proves a false trail, leading nowhere. Originally, Torrance was to stumble on a scrapbook chronicling decades of "evil" at the Overlook—newspaper clippings about mishaps and catastrophes great and small: fires, murders, suicides, sexual and financial scandals. This, too, was eliminated, though the scrapbook can still be seen on Torrance's table where he sits, a blocked writer, crazily typing and retyping ad infinitum the same one-line maxim: "All work and no play makes Jack a dull boy." It's a text that reflects Jack's

Jack: "It's good to be back, Lloyd."

Lloyd: "No charge, Mr. Torrance." At least not in human coin.

Grady (Philip Stone), the memory of the past, insinuates Jack into the murder plan that fate has prescribed for him. Kubrick sets this crucial scene of supernatural seduction in the alarmingly ordinary setting of a men's lavatory and thus overlays the encounter with an additional sense of unease. Full Metal Jacket *will also find death in the latrine.*

male chauvinism, ignoring as it does the maxim's other half: All work also makes Jill a dull girl.

The man's misogyny is hinted at even earlier. The Overlook's manager dutifully informs Jack of an earlier triple murder. A former caretaker, one Charles Grady, had killed his wife, chopped up his twin daughters, then shot himself. Jack receives this grisly news with sardonic sangfroid: too bad, but catch *him* getting up to anything like that! Nor will his family be affected by the hotel's isolation or associations: "Oh, they'll love it," he says.

"But you're watching his eyes," Kubrick commented, "and they're saying, 'What the hell! *They* don't matter at all!'"

Jack Nicholson never needs words to articulate his feelings. "He fills the moments," Kubrick observes, adding, "Most actors, when not required actually to do something, are at best just paying attention. Jack stays switched on."

These early scenes—a brief job interview, a tactful history of a particular place—resemble the professional exchanges between

As frequently occurs in a Kubrick setting, stark symmetry accompanies impending doom. Wendy discovers
Jack's secret.

Almost like a minimalist work of art, her husband's
mania is exposed in his repetition of one of the homeli-
est of maxims in old-fashioned schoolbooks. Kubrick
inverts family values to induce a sense of family doom.

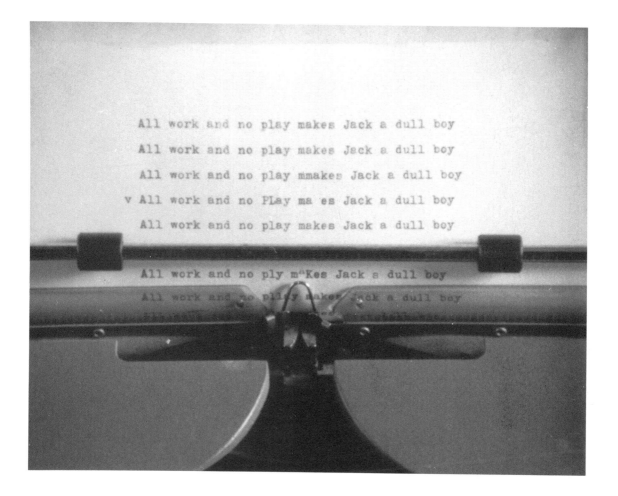

the space technicians in *2001*. They are conducted in medium shot, low-key, the voices confidentially lowered. But the suspense they generate has already nudged the story's center of interest away from Stephen King's spooky premonitions toward a man's interior demons. Nicholson and his director are in charge.

Aware of what splatter-flick fans will expect—they must be spooked—Kubrick quickly cuts a few demonic elements subliminally into the story. Back in the Torrance family's apartment in Boulder, the psychic young Danny (played by Danny Lloyd, a child chosen from among five thousand screen-tested by Leon Vitali) experiences visions of the Overlook's paranormal attractions. He "sees" a flood-wave of human blood pouring from the elevators, and, far more disturbing, he "encounters" the former caretaker's murdered daughters. Identical twins, they stand very still, yet inviting Danny to join them, baleful as a Diane Arbus photograph. Kubrick well knows the uncanny vibration of replication. The Grady girls, swiveling on their heels in unison to take their leave, as if joined by a central hinge, is a very creepy apparition.

*Wendy confronts her husband: the staircase gives her
the upper hand, for once.*

Curiously, such supernatural inserts don't whet our appetite as
they are meant to. Already they feel slightly anticlimactic.
Nicholson's breakdown will increasingly make the film's Gothic
apparatus look tired and old-fashioned, even superfluous. This
imbalance reflects a rare unresolved discord in Kubrick's craftsmanship.

It may have been that with the opportunity for experimenta-
tion offered by Jack Nicholson's creativity, and the freedom of a
long shooting schedule, over six months, Kubrick decided, somewhere along the line, to assign a secondary role to psychic phenomena.

The Overlook's ghosts are really very few in number, and with
two exceptions, the barman and the waiter, not particularly interesting. A zoom shot of a couple of ghostly revenants, one of them
dressed as a bear and apparently fellating the other, that Wendy
glimpses at the climax is more perplexing than scary. It could
have been excised, or exorcised, too, without loss. The flood of
blood from the elevators has no reference to anything, looking,
one critic said, like something put in for the trailer. What all this
suggests, in short, is a director "finding" his film as he makes it,
veering away from the original concepts and pushing his preoccupations into far more personally satisfying areas than the
haunting Furies of Stephen King's novel.

What compensates fans of the occult for the relative paucity of
gibbering fiends is something far more marvelous and ominous
than any of them—the Overlook Hotel itself.

The hotel is one of the great movie sets, rivaling the cavernous

War Room in *Dr. Strangelove*. Roy Walker, the art director, had located a suitable real-life place: the Timberline Hotel in Mt. Hood National Forest, Oregon. Its exterior, toward which Torrance drives in the prologue, provided Kubrick with a monumental reality to undermine an audience's ambivalence about the story's fantasy elements. But the hotel's interior is a wholly studio-created structure. Built life-size, it occupied all the stages at Elstree Studios. The Overlook's public areas, staff offices, storerooms, and kitchens led into each other as in an architect's blueprint. Everyone (including this writer, who was led on a tour of the place by a proud Kubrick) experienced a spacious yet enclosed habitation. It felt like an actual hotel, not a movie set open to overhead lighting racks and "breakaway" walls that collapsed when accommodating camera setups.

The pillared lobby rose two and a half floors high under the roof of the studio stage. Its canopied fireplace could have sheltered a small boat in a storm. An opera could have been staged in the room without undue disturbance to the guests. Kitchens and storerooms had authentic pots and pans and all other fittings. Even the milk cartons and butter packs were typographically precise, bearing the names of the Denver supermarkets where they had supposedly been purchased. The ballroom, also called the "Gold Room," where Torrance encounters Lloyd the barman, the first specter from the past, was a cavern of Byzantine gilt and art deco mirror-work. Yet when empty, it had the appropriate inhumanity of a tomb. Tiny tables suggested gravestones waiting only for the absentees to return to them. The keynote color of the

Overlook's decor had an ominous association with death. It looked like dried blood.

An array of framed photographs on the walls suggested wild parties or celebrity events down the years. One photo in particular would provide the movie with its ultimate enigma. If the camera had paused to look at the other photographs, it would have revealed shots from the corporate history of Warner Bros., or stills from the Hollywood studio's picture library, from which the illustrations had been borrowed. Crucially, the illumination used throughout perfectly duplicated the lighting one would expect in a hotel.

Such fastidious detail is worth quoting, because it represents the film's central paradox. *The Shining*'s supernatural story was encased in a physical shell of most rigorously defined and tested realism. If ever a set determined the look and feel of a film, and eventually the meaning it would assume, it was the Overlook Hotel. And to Kubrick, it represented something more.

Such a set would have delighted the great filmmakers and designers of Germany's silent-film era, the directors so admired by Kubrick like Max Reinhardt, F. W. Murnau, and Fritz Lang. These talents contrived their fantastic or macabre creations wholly in studio conditions. Now, Kubrick had built himself a set that recalled that German expressionist era of fifty years before, massive and monumental, representing the structure of the mind and the architecture of the soul. Not just a grand hotel but a grandiose interior. While the functional reality of its American setting embodied his fetish in terms of validating every detail for its logic, the place itself was crafted in the overwhelmingly stylized tradition of German theatrical and cinematic fantasy—with one difference. German directors of the pre-Hitler period would

Again, Kubrick uses the unconventional camera angle to lend dramatic sharpness to a crisis as Wendy imprisons her husband in the storeroom.

have clustered enormous shadows in the rooms, corridors, and vistas. Kubrick substituted the high wattage of plausible reality. *The Shining* is about fear in a well-lit place. Terror would not vanish if one turned on the lights.

It was also the perfect "closed" set. *Barry Lyndon*, which dispersed the action across vast landscapes, stands alone, in that respect, for Kubrick has always been happiest with the walls of a soundstage enfolding him protectively. To work in a studio concentrates his mind and, he believes, helps his players focus their "psychic energy."

To exploit fully the spaciousness of *The Shining*'s set, much of the action would have to be filmed in long continuous takes. Using cuts would have negated the impact of the grand design. To do this, however, was problematic. The geometry of right-angled corridors inhibited baroque camera movements like those used in the château scenes in *Paths of Glory* to simulate the moral maze where a man's conscience could lose itself. The Overlook's long corridors and fixed walls made it impossible to lay camera rails on the floor, or overhead. Yet for Kubrick, these difficulties presented less of a problem than an opportunity. The shooting of *The Shining* exactly coincides with the introduction of the Steadicam into filmmaking.

Invented by Garrett Brown, the Steadicam made it possible to photograph action in long, fluent, rock-steady takes, and its use in *The Shining* powerfully supplemented the art of John Alcott, director of photography. A "weightless" camera is mounted on springs harnessed to the arms, shoulders, and torso of its operator—in this case, Garrett Brown himself—who can move about as he wishes. The Steadicam requires dexterity, balance, and an inner eye to foresee the action ahead while simultaneously look-

ing at a miniature TV screen—fixed to the operator's waist har-
ness—displaying what is being filmed there and then. The creative opportunities that the Steadicam offered Kubrick force one
to ask: Which came first, camera or concept? Only he knows.

The Shining is designed in straight lines and sharp angles of
Euclidean rigor. Its director's penchant for "corridor" shots has
been mentioned—the boxer's nightmare trip down city streets on
the eve of the fight in *Killer's Kiss*, the cosmonaut's trajectory
through the Star Gate in *2001*. This time the corridors were real,
not in the mind. Function followed form—a neat irony, since it
reversed another designer statement of pre-Hitlerite Germany,
the rule that "form follows function" so dear to the architects of
the Bauhaus school. In the Overlook, design dictated movement
and movement promoted suspense.

The angularity of design is repeated in carpet and rug patterns,

Hallorann comes to the rescue in his Sno-cat. The snow does for the trapped victims what space did for the cosmonauts in 2001. Kubrick uses these isolating elements to reinforce the impression of an alien universe.

on wall tapestries, in lobby paintings incorporating Native American motifs—even in the pattern on Danny's sweater. This fateful determinism lives outside, too, in the Overlook's garden maze, which lays its own pattern on anyone unwise enough to penetrate it.

In King's novel, Torrance is a pawn of the past, incited to kill by those whose own lives are extinct. In Kubrick's version, he becomes his own past, unable to escape from it. To suggest the way he is being ingested into a set pattern, Kubrick often positions Nicholson visually against extremely formal backgrounds. One image frames him in the abstract design of a wall tapestry. A Native American motif, it also resembles a printed circuit. It calls to mind the rigor of programmed information. No deviation allowed. In another shot, Torrance looms above a lobby model of the garden maze. (This shot is unnecessarily complicated by a miscalculated special effect—Torrance seems to look threateningly at the tiny figures of Wendy and Danny, who are outside in the actual maze.) The maze clearly alludes to the Minotaur myth in which a monster with the head of a bull and the body of a man was kept in a labyrinth and fed on human flesh until the hero, Theseus, killed it. It was a legend that had long appealed to Kubrick. (The company that made *Killer's Kiss* twenty-five years before was called Minotaur Productions.) No maze exists in King's novel, only a set of giant topiary "monsters" animated by evil spirits that converge on Torrance and his family. Kubrick rightly rejected this sort of Disneyfied horror. In his film, the environment is destiny itself, not its instrument.

Danny's ESP gift creates an instant bond between him and Hallorann, the hotel's black head chef (played by Scatman

293

Crothers), for Hallorann shares the same power. Their recognition of each other's "special" status is nicely conveyed by Kubrick when Hallorann appears to be addressing Danny directly, although still engaged in polite banter with Danny's parents. Crothers is a great casting success. His talent for "shining" springs from the animism associated with blacks, but Crothers' features, ancient and weathered like an Easter Island monument, also lend the story a moral gravitas. He's the hero—though a sacrificial hero. Kubrick favors him with the film's biggest close-ups, contrasting his concerned contours with Danny's vulnerable blankness. Neither dares to speak openly of the Overlook's horrors, though Hallorann the cook must have supped full of them. Danny's other "friend" in the film is "Tony," an imaginary companion, represented by Danny's wiggling finger and on the sound track by a croaking voice that eventually takes over its little master with warning cries. It's arguable whether this psychic accessory is successful, or even necessary. The Steadicam tailing Danny as he pedals his sturdy little tricycle down the hotel's haunted corridors supplies an invisible companion far more chillingly than any wiggling digit or ventriloquial trick courtesy of *The Exorcist*.

When Garrett Brown needed to adapt his invention to the floor-level intensity of Danny's "speedway," he inverted his Steadicam, making it hover at the height of his own kneecap rather than his waist. An unforeseen bonus: Danny's tricycle wheels, passing from the hush of carpeted areas to the clatter of unclad floor and back again, created an eerie, regular rhythm.

Danny doesn't let his parents in on his visions or the threat locked in Room 237. (The room is numbered "217" in the book,

"I'll huff and I'll puff and I'll blow your house down."

Nursery tales resonate with a murderous new meaning as Jack attacks his family.

Kubrick screws the tension tight as Danny escapes and Wendy is left behind to face the maniac.

"He-e-ere's Johnny."

On the other side of the door, Wendy screams in terror.
The family home has become a slaughterhouse.

but the original Timberline Hotel had a Room 217, and a superstitious management asked Kubrick to change it.)

Kubrick continues to shift suspense from the supernatural to the clinical sphere. Torrance, now installed as the new caretaker, is unwillingly awakened as Wendy brings him his breakfast. Prominently angled into the camera, and threateningly enlarged by the sleeper's posture, are Nicholson's biceps. The image is a reminder of this paternal figure's power to assault and abuse.

The Shining's very title embodies one of the movie's main themes: communication. It is the breakdown of communication between a father and his family that prefaces the violence which Nicholson will unleash from this point on.

Nicholson's vocal tones are hard yet subtly inflected. They create moral ambiguities and carry the burden of externalized self-hatred. He has failed as a writer, and his contempt for what Danny watches on television is a mild symptom of an intelligent man's bitterness toward a medium that debases taste. But left alone in the Overlook's lobby, the typewriter before him, he must now test his own powers of creativity. Taking refuge from the blank page, he bounces a ball around. The sound amplifies his directionless way of killing time. Soon he will be taking directions from the spirit world to kill something more precious to

him than time. He is, to use a phrase from another age of communications, an "other-directed" type.

Kubrick's postrelease cuts eliminated some of the scenes of Danny and his mother watching family sitcoms on TV. But two comments on the compulsive banality of popular culture have been preserved in grim gag lines uttered by Torrance when in the grip of full-blown madness. One is his cry of "Wendy, I'm home," the call of commuters everywhere, which now becomes a chilling hunting call. The other is Nicholson's truly demonic, rising-crescendo rendition of "H-e-e-e-re's Johnny!" words once bellowed across the nation to introduce talk-show host Johnny Carson. Torrance thereby announces his own arrival, ax in hand, to his cowering and fearful wife.

Jack, injured and limping, begins to lose human form as he pursues Danny through the hotel with his ax. Again, as in the cosmonaut's ride through the Star Gate in 2001, corridors of space or time play a metaphorical role in the transformation of a human being into an alien figure.

Critical argument about *The Shining* tends to center on the way the normal elides into the paranormal. The main burden of this crucial progression rests on Jack Nicholson, and he carries it in ways that never cease to fascinate.

First comes unpredictability, one of his strengths as a star. Nicholson keeps one looking—what will he do next?—casting and recasting his expressive face and body language to fit the emotional and physical requirements of the moment. Small tics of mouth, eyes, or brows enlarge, become seismic shifts of attitude as Torrance slides from teeth-gritting frustration (at his wife's ingenuous chatter about the ease of creative writing) to the fury of a murderer under the influence of his supernatural controllers. Rumor has it that, for some scenes, Kubrick put Nicholson through as many as a hundred takes. Kubrick, we know, has commented to the French critic Michel Ciment that "Jack produces his best takes near the highest numbers."

Torrance's madness is charted mostly in medium shots with only occasional close-ups. Throughout, Nicholson fully commands the space around him, huge though it is. At times he must have felt as if were acting alone in a cathedral.

Kubrick begins the murderous fugue with a slightly crude but potent "portrait study" of Nicholson, pensive in repose: his black roll-neck sweater calling attention to a face set—frozen, one could

say—in a diabolical mask. The shot surely signifies the man's point of terminal despair. Torrance's own creative demon has refused to come out and assist with his writing; henceforth, other demons will waylay and manipulate him.

The concentration on Nicholson's progress into schizophrenia and insanity has done injury to Shelley Duvall's characterization of Wendy. Apart from expressing mother-love, mother-terror, mother-sacrifice, and mother-and-child survival, the part is underdeveloped. Wendy is simply the "woman in jeopardy." Duvall's unhappy recognition of this during shooting may account for the on-set tensions between her and Kubrick revealed by Vivian Kubrick's film.

While Duvall's role is totally maternal, Nicholson's is seldom fatherly, except for one scene of paternal tenderness when Danny, finding his father anxious and depressed, asks touchingly, "You would never hurt me?" Is this precognition? The child (wisely) approaches his dad with the cautious hesitation due a stranger.

Each time Torrance comes near breakdown, losing control of himself or the situation, Kubrick's camera style changes brutally. When Wendy discovers him cowering under his writing desk, the victim of an involuntary "shining" episode of his own ("I dreamed that I killed you and Danny"), the acutely angled camera expresses the skewed state of the man's mind.

In such a state, a guy needs a drink. With perfect Kubrickian logic, ex-alcoholic Torrance stumbles along the corridors to the "Gold Room" and encounters the first phantom from his past: Lloyd the barman.

Lloyd is played by Joe Turkel, one of a group of actors Kubrick likes to recall for roles in his films (*The Killing* and *Paths of Glory* in this case). His familiarity with their talents and their experience of *his* needs, ease the tensions that newcomers create (and suffer).

The encounter between Torrance and Lloyd is one of the best-played scenes in the film. Subtly stylized, it allows Nicholson every chance to riff through the facets of Torrance's moral and emotional character, past and present.

The scene sounds an opening note of eerie normality, as if walking into the past were as easy as entering a room. When Nicholson remarks, "God, I'd give anything for a drink. . . . I'd give my goddamn soul," he puts such reality into his hankering for alcohol, it's easy to miss the hint of a Faustian bargain being struck between him and Lloyd.

Lloyd does little in the scene, save remain polite and punctilious. But Turkel's stance, his minimal movements, signify his control over his guest. Perhaps all good barmen do this; they also dominate who only stand and serve. Lloyd's very proficiency has a palpable menace. His "appearance," it could be suggested (and most people will take it this way), is a projection of Torrance's imagination. One moment he is rubbing his eyes wearily in front of the empty bar. . . . When he opens them again, Lloyd is . . . *there*. The buddy-buddy bonhomie of the alcoholic toward the man who feeds his need is immediate: "Hi, Lloyd . . . a little slow tonight, isn't it?"—followed by a silent, sly "Ha-ha" at the emptiness of the Gold Room, coming "alive" just for the two of them.

Throughout, Nicholson's features are lit from below, illuminated by the lighting panels in the bar counter. This adds drama to Nicholson's expressions, exaggerating every minor alteration in the actor's incredibly complex orchestration of emotions in a way both realistic and slightly surreal.

The dialogue suggests depths beyond its superficiality. Drink leads Torrance to confess to earlier sins. He has hurt Danny, he admits, though he cloaks his guilt in one of those self-exculpating euphemisms Kubrick makes a point of storing away for use in certain kinds of situations. (*Dr. Strangelove* bristled with cosmetic phrases for nuclear destruction; *Full Metal Jacket* is packed with euphemisms of the military kind). It wasn't fatherly rage, Torrance protests, that made him hit Danny: only "a momentary

The family tragedy is complete. The malign spirits manifest themselves to Wendy, too.

loss of muscular coordination." A "loss" of the same kind will shortly lead him to swing an ax at his family, but for the moment, that irony is lost on us.

The Shining was preview-tested before its opening in London in the fall of 1980, and Kubrick took this opportunity to delete some sequences altogether and "fine-tune" others. Among the latter were minor but significant cuts in Torrance's conversation with Lloyd, but the original scene does survive uncut in American prints of the film. In current British prints, the cuts in the Gold Room sequences have the effect of disguising, for the moment, Torrance's drinking problem and toning down further a misogynistic subtext. Eliminated from the British version is Torrance's comment to Lloyd that he is having "a little trouble with the old sperm bank upstairs"—meaning his wife, Wendy. Lloyd rejoins, "Women! Can't live with 'em. Can't live without 'em," and Torrance agrees. The phrase "old sperm bank" has a dated ring, redolent of P. G. Wodehouse novels and the 1920s, and it anticipates Torrance's reference, on his return visit to the bar, to Grady the waiter as "Jeevesy." However, at this earlier point in the film, we are unaware that Torrance himself belongs to the twenties in some earlier incarnation. This may account for Kubrick's deletion.

But if the deletion tones down Torrance's misogyny, it is not for long. The next sequence in the film demonstrates it with shocking melodrama.

While his father has been talking with Lloyd, Danny has been attacked—offscreen—by someone, or something, that's resident

Like the vampire in Murnau's Nosferatu, *Jack's very shape now seems to embody the evil spirit that possesses it.*

Sheer terror becomes the emotional and physical momentum of the film, due to the ability of the Steadicam to mimic the pursuit of Danny through the hotel labyrinth.

in Room 237. A hysterical Wendy forces her husband to investigate.

What ensues is the film's least resolved scene, as baffling as the penultimate sequence of *2001*. In both cases, the setting is a tastefully decorated hotel suite. In both, there is a strange entity. The cosmonaut in *2001* is symbiotically and sympathetically linked with the figure he observes in various stages of metamorphosis from middle to advanced old age. He may be observing himself in an accelerated life cycle. But the repulsive alien entity that Torrance encounters in *The Shining* comes from a different world, and his close encounter with it engenders panic. It's as if Torrance fears his own transfiguration into what it represents.

Light at the end of the tunnel. Danny escapes Father, is reunited with mother in the Sno-cat.

As in a fairy tale, however, Torrance's evil enchantress appears at first in the tempting form of a young woman. A naked beauty reposing in Room 237's bath, she steps seductively out of it and advances passively but enticingly toward him, overcoming his initial hesitation and inviting him to enfold her in his arms. Such is the way that mythic heroes are entrapped. But once Torrance's arms clasp her, she turns into the carcass of a blemished hag who appears to be simultaneously in his embrace yet still in the bath. Torrance flees to save his life—or his soul.

Bathrooms and bathtubs hold a baleful fascination for filmmakers. The bath's high tidemark of horror was surely reached in Clouzot's *Les Diaboliques* (1954). Since then the living corpse ris-

ing out of the tub has become a genre cliché. What makes *The Shining*'s sequence so compelling is the contrast it invites with its benign antecedent in *2001*. In both films, the hotel decor has a classical elegance bathed in a translucent light characteristic of symbolist art. Both surreal entities appear to be in two places at once, or to have changed places as the beholder blinks. In both sequences, accelerated aging induces an eerie metamorphosis, and in *The Shining*, a terrifying image. This scene has no narrative relevance to earlier or later events in the film, and Torrance, on returning to Wendy, denies having found anyone in Room 237.

So what is the meaning of his horrifying epiphany? Freud said that filmgoing is like wakeful dreaming. Kubrick also believed that films connect subtly with the subconscious. Meaning, he said, may be found in the sensation of a thing, not its explanation. Yet he *has* provided a clue. In certain interviews around this time, he mentioned his admiration for *Rhapsody: A Dream Novel*, a novella, really, by Arthur Schnitzler, the Viennese writer and playwright better known as the auteur who inspired Max Ophuls' 1950 comedy of chain-libido, *La Ronde*, which the young Kubrick found so intoxicating. In *Rhapsody*, the main character, a wealthy young doctor in Vienna, passes almost imperceptibly in and out of the dream state, experiencing seduction, erotic longings, and unrequited passion as if they were events in his waking state.

Dreams permit us to acknowledge the inner urges we repress. Nothing new in this, perhaps. Marcel Carné expressed something of it in *Juliette, ou La Clé des songes* (1951), though by that date Carné's romantic fatalism was itself fatally overblown. With more astringent success, Buñuel, in 1972, built a cool black comedy out

The elements effect the end of Jack's worldly existence.
But there is still an escape exit for a time traveler.

of continually interrupted dreams, filmed with the logic of real life, in *Le Charme discret de la bourgeoisie*. Filmmakers, for obvious reasons, find the concept of "dream episodes" eternally tempting, but most films lack the opportunity to create them, even though directors work in a dreamlike medium and, as Kubrick has said himself, "when one is looking at a film, the experience is much closer to a dream than anything else."

Kubrick's hankering to make a film of Schnitzler's novel probably goes right back to his cinema beginnings—and he has finally achieved it, in a manner of speaking, with his new film *Eyes Wide Shut*, which will be discussed later. Perhaps the truest way to "read" *The Shining*'s haunted bathroom sequence is the simplest.

Regard it as a director's private opportunity to be "painterly," to allow one canvas to "echo" another in subject or composition, to create the texture of a waking dream, or, rather, an erotic nightmare in *The Shining*—in short, to equip Stephen King with a preview of Arthur Schnitzler.

The Shining's shooting schedule, as mentioned, lasted over six months. The three players usually had only each other to interact with in one of the biggest imaginable sets. They were locked into roles that every day stretched emotions to breaking point and beyond. Inevitably, these conditions took their toll on the stars.

Their desperation to reach the last take fortunately paralleled the story's swelling terror. Ironically, the creepiest scene to play, according to Jack Nicholson, began as the most populous.

After his shock in Room 237, Torrance understandably returns to the Gold Room for another drink. This time he hears lazy dance music and discovers a crowd of guests in 1920s evening dress.

It is at this precise point that the film's present time begins to overlap with a datable past. Lloyd, so far the only unearthly character encountered by Torrance apart from the bathroom's naked harpy, could be mistaken for a contemporary barman. But Grady, the waiter who waylays Torrance and decoys him into a startlingly hellish-looking men's room (a copy of an actual red-toned lavatory that Kubrick's design scouts had located in a Frank Lloyd Wright resort hotel), recognizably comes from another era.

Played by another Kubrick "regular," Philip Stone (*A Clockwork Orange*, *Barry Lyndon*), Grady is the epitome of a "correct" English manservant. He treads a fine line between outward civility toward his betters and implied rebuke for their lapses. His message to Torrance, however, is about murder, not manners.

In the prologue, the caretaker Grady who slaughtered his wife and children was identified as "Charles"; the Grady whom Torrance now meets says his name is "Delbert." Are they one and the same—or is this simply a slight continuity slip? The former, surely; Kubrick would have detected and easily corrected the latter. Such ambiguity over identity fits the film's emerging thesis—we cannot escape the past. We are, in fact, doomed to repeat its crimes and misdemeanors, but maybe not to replicate them exactly. Even predestination, Kubrick suggests, is an imperfect communications system. Like every such system in the film—transport, radio, telephones, the writing process—it breaks down at crucial points. "Weren't you once the caretaker here? I saw your picture in the newspapers," Torrance asks Grady, perhaps refer-

*The last and most enigmatic shot of the film. Jack
apparently rejoins the party on Independence Day,
1921. Is Kubrick asking, how independent are we of the
forces that govern us?*

ring to the scrapbook that *we* have not seen. (Kubrick, as mentioned, had eliminated the intended montage of its clippings.) Torrance then obligingly informs Grady of what the future holds for him: a family massacre. With a true English butler's refusal to register surprise, even when identified as a multiple killer-in-waiting, Grady doesn't miss a beat. He continues to dab at the stain on Torrance's jacket and with commendable sangfroid responds, "I'm sorry to differ with you, sir, but *you* are the caretaker. You've always been the caretaker. I should know, sir. I've always been here."

The confusion over each man's historical identity and temporal priority is more significant than their class relationship. Each exists in the other's past. Yet time, as we shall shortly see, doesn't repeat the past, but only reinvents it in ways that make it sometimes difficult to tell past, present, and future from each other: a problem with which presumptuous clairvoyants and their optimistic clients are sadly familiar.

The scene between Nicholson and Stone has a cool comic civility that turns downright chilly as the spook gives Torrance his orders—to kill his family. The actors serve Kubrick impeccably. They play the masquerade with relish for its Pinteresque undertones, only hinted at by Grady's use of a choice word like "correction," as if *it* were the "trigger" word for Torrance's programmed psychosis. Soon such "correction" will become a more peremptory order to deal with wife and child "in the harshest possible way." Euphemism again gives the edge to inhumanity.

The Torrance-Grady confrontation, splendidly unsettling though it is, downplays the true horror of Torrance's state of mind. Kubrick now liberates that horror. During such key moments in a character's inner drama, Kubrick employs extreme formality and symmetry in his camera setup. Such a setup frames Wendy looming above the typewriter as she discovers, horribly, that her husband's "creative" writing consists of page after page containing the same ten words: "All work and no play makes Jack a dull boy." Kubrick has positioned Jack's typewriter in the foreground, shooting it from a low angle, making the machine look like a tabletop edition of the great monoliths in *2001*, those astral intruder alarms or, perhaps, landmarks of intelligence, signifying stages in the destiny of man. This modernist shape, imbued with iconic connotations of ancient magic, haunts Kubrick more strikingly than any ghost lurking about the Overlook.

Torrance catches his wife poring over his one-line "opus," a final, abject disgrace, proof of his failure as man and artist. What was to have been his "last chance," the reason why they're shuttered up in the Overlook, has turned out to be nothing more creative than an old-fashioned copybook maxim. Deeds must repair the damage words have done: he must efface his shame by "correcting" his wife.

Their violent encounter occurs on the staircase: she retreats up it armed with a baseball bat; he advances threateningly toward her. This is the only time Kubrick does not situate his dramatic action at ground level. The flight of steps symbolizes the altered status of husband and wife—she is now "on top," after her discovery has emasculated his self-esteem. Stairs in dreams, myths, and melodramas represent—to some Freudians, anyhow—the male sex drive, just as corridors (and there are plenty in the Overlook) are traditional symbols of the female passage. Wendy's terror is subliminally enhanced if one views her husband's steady advance upward as a sexual threat to a woman who no longer shares his bedroom. Kubrick has said that the scene gave Shelley Duvall one of her most difficult times, necessitating that she bring herself to a pitch of hysteria similar to an orgasm.

By good luck rather than skill, Wendy manages to stun her husband and lock him in a storeroom. Kubrick now springs a surprise on us.

Up to now, we might conceivably have believed that all Jack's apparitions lived only in his own schizophrenia. But once the storeroom bolts are physically drawn back by an unseen Grady, liberating Torrance to commence his assault on his family, the tables are turned on us. These ghosts aren't one man's imaginings: they are for real!

Kubrick mentioned to Michel Ciment his delight in a Stephen Crane story about a man who thought his cronies were cheating on him at cards, and let his paranoia goad him into a gunfight. He was killed, and it's revealed posthumously that he was indeed being cheated. Moral: Paranoiacs can be right, too; and folk can be haunted—really.

Our ghost story now becomes a Grand Guignol melodrama. Wendy and Danny come under fearsome attack. The stoutest door barring Torrance's advance is demolished by his weapon of choice, a huge fireman's ax. His onslaught is as realistic as Kubrick can make it—every wood panel he smashes is as solid as it would be in real life.

But violence in Kubrick's films is seldom present for its own sake. Here it reverberates with social and cultural references, as Torrance mocks suburban coziness ("Wendy, I'm home"), children's bedtime stories ("Little pigs, little pigs, let me come in"), and talk-show buildup ("H-e-e-e-re's Johnny!"). We have not strayed far from other Kubrick moments. Alex in *A Clockwork Orange* puts a boot into his victim to the rhythm of "Singin' in the Rain"; Clare Quilty in *Lolita*'s prologue, trying to postpone the bullets of Humbert Humbert's vengeance, plays for time with comic impersonations. *The Shining*'s impending mayhem suggests Frankenstein invading sitcom land.

Torrance's physicality has changed in a way that anticipates his final transfiguration. Lamed by his fall down the staircase, he now limps heavily. The limp deforms and dehumanizes him. It also usefully slows him down as he retreats from besieging

Wendy with the reflexive squeal of a wounded beast (she has sliced open his hand) and begins hunting Danny. This family crisis is so all-involving that the cross-cutting suspense of Hallorann's race to answer Danny's psychic SOS is very nearly lost. When Torrance eventually does sink his ax into Hallorann's heart, we scarcely care: Good, now get on with the chase!

The Shining's last reel is the Q.E.D. of Nicholson's performance. He has been pushing the story's supernatural envelope until he predictably bursts out of it into the reality of clinical mania. Nicholson has been criticized for the intensity of his acting—a polite way of insinuating that he goes over the top. He does. But this is the only place left to go. The exceptional, rather than excessive, vigor of his performance, his overemphatic, malignly overeloquent acting, exaggerated by the Steadicam's intense acceleration as Torrance pursues Danny through the maze, all serve to rush him toward his own destiny; anything less would not be enough. Nicholson's body language is in the outsize tradition of the old High German silent cinema, an art form filled with monsters, golems, and fiends in human shape: savage, extravagant, halfway to mime. Torrance goes from man to Minotaur, bellowing, "Danny, Danny, Danny . . ."—the word dying on his lips, becoming animal-like screeches loosed into the freezing air.

The son escapes his father's vengeance; it's the father who pays the penalty. The Oedipal lesson of *Barry Lyndon* is once more inflicted on the older antagonist. Only this time Torrance doesn't limp off on his one good leg into the future. He is allowed to shelter in the refuge of the past: Kubrick's final—and most controversial—surprise.

After Danny has rejoined his mother, and both have taken off in the snowmobile abandoned by the murdered Hallorann, Kubrick cuts savagely to a close-up of Torrance, frozen to death in the dawn's bright light. It has the shock of a sudden full stop. Then comes the recoil. Slowly, gracefully, in one smooth, unbroken tracking shot, the camera withdraws into the Overlook, down the central corridor, distant dance music filtering in, the symmetry of its gliding progress firmly sustaining the tension. The camera selects a framed photo hanging in the dead center of the wall. A couple of dissolves and we are "in" the group picture of a crowd in evening dress. In the front rank is a younger, more elegant Torrance in black tie and dinner jacket, smiling—no, *smirking*—at the lens like a hanger-on at a Gatsby-era party. The camera pans down to the picture's descriptive label: "Overlook Hotel, July 4th Ball, 1921."

Soon after the film's New York opening, Kubrick removed the

coda showing a hospitalized Wendy being congratulated by the Overlook's manager on surviving her horrendous ordeal. The scene had followed Torrance's deep-freeze demise in the maze and his reincarnation at the Independence Day ball. This suppression of all concern for Wendy is in keeping with the story's patriarchal bias. But more important, it keeps the thematic line intact: metaphysical survival, not physical escape, is *The Shining*'s subtext.

In a film constructed around the reality of physical "space," and what happens to the sanity of an individual afflicted by too much of it and not possessing the resources to fill it, the concept of "time" asserts itself as a late but crucial metaphysical element. The past incites Torrance to murder his future, his posterity. That he fails to do so shows we are not in the grip of the past. This is the optimistic side of the film. But to a confirmed skeptic like Kubrick, who believes man has little capacity to learn from his past and none at all to shape a rational future for himself, the best that can be said is that it's an illustration of random odds at work, whose outcome is a little less pessimistic than might have been predicted.

Torrance fails to obey "orders," and pays the penalty for it; but as the photo suggests, reincarnation is an open-ended escape. Death doesn't come as the end, simply as a junction. Time, as the scientist Einstein and the philosopher Vico speculated, may be "bent," and its cyclical "shape" keeps us coming and going, back and forth, to other times, other realms. Each today doesn't lead to a tomorrow, but may consign us to a yesterday. Man's mythical powers don't die with him: each death is a new beginning. A comforting thought, particularly so if, after attempting to murder one's wife and child, one can begin life again at a glitzy Independence Day party.

The Shining suggests that Kubrick himself may have come full circle. The plot may be bloodcurdling penny-dreadful stuff, but the grand design imposed on it recalls the more rarefied pattern of *2001: A Space Odyssey*. Consider: In both films a man falls victim to a fate that awaits him somewhere "out there"; in both, mysterious forces compel him to journey alone into the unknown; in both, he survives a metaphysical/supernatural experience, passing through the Star Gate in the earlier film, the maze in *The Shining*; in both, he emerges from the ordeal transfigured, changed into a different yet still recognizable being, a Star-Child and a 1920s playboy. One heralds hope for the world; the other a refuge from its terrors.

Kubrick never published his shooting scripts, only, sometimes, the continuity script of the movie when completed. So we cannot follow his thinking while he shot *The Shining*, only speculate how his mind may, consciously or not, have reshaped the material and drawn it closer to his own obsessions. For the same reason, we can't answer with any certainty the metaphysical conundrums posed by the film's key scenes. Like the puzzle-pictures of the artist M. C. Escher, they look rational until we look ever more closely into them, and then we see they have been constructed in clever defiance of rationality.

The only alternative, then, is to intuit the mind of the maker, guess (or second-guess) what he was up to. The insoluble theorem is the one with the greatest attraction for the rational thinker: he wished to keep us puzzled.

Full Metal Jacket

Full Metal Jacket still surprises many people. Usually, they aren't quite sure what to make of a film that splits itself so brutally into two parts. Not at all typical of mainstream moviemaking, which tends to offer seamless sensations. To some viewers, it looks like an "instructional short" about army training, followed by a longer "entertainment" feature devoted to the hell of battle. *Full Metal Jacket*, in fact, offers us one movie that might be entitled "The Theory of Killing," followed immediately by another that one could call "The Practice of Killing." As one might expect of a Kubrick film, practice bedevils theory and holds some nasty shocks for the theorists.

Kubrick's twelfth movie is his most paradoxical, his coldest but also his most human. In style, it is also his most abstract, but the nearest he has come to the traditional look of cinema. Its schizoid structure distorts and discomfits perception. What does it all mean? There seems at first to be no link—simply a clean break— between the repetitive actions and obsessional mania of its first forty minutes and the unstructured terrors of its last seventy-six. There is a link, of course; but the way Kubrick puts it, it sounds pitiless—it is about professional indoctrination versus individual motivation. In other words, being taught to function like a weapon is one thing, but putting the lesson to work requires feelings as well. And sometimes feelings, in the interests of humanity, contradict training. "Our rifle is only a tool; it's the hard heart that kills" is the film's interior mantra and the constant chorus of the Marine "grunts" in it. But sometimes the heart has its reasons for not killing—and then the perfect plan malfunctions.

Full Metal Jacket is a Vietnam war story adapted from a first novel of brilliant, vivid compactness by the late Gustav Hasford, who covered Vietnam with the First Marine Division. Published in 1979 as *The Short Timers*, it follows Marine recruits through eight vicious weeks of boot-camp training on Parris Island, South Carolina, a hellhole constructed to test the "phony-tough and the crazy-brave," and then accompanies the survivors on to Vietnam in time for the Tet Offensive and the battle of Hue. Kubrick claims the book found *him*—not he, *it*. Which shouldn't surprise us: Hasford might have written it intentionally for the moviemaker. By now, one is familiar with the ways Kubrick's work has focused obsessively on the variety of influences that control people's perceptions and responses: by the synchronicity of time (*The Killing*), by military ambition (*Paths of Glory*), by the perversities of their own deviant natures (*Lolita*), by a "fail-safe" defense device going haywire (*Dr. Strangelove*), by a "thinking" computer developing a survival instinct (*2001*), by the State's brainwashing techniques (*A Clockwork Orange*), by destiny in collusion with character (*Barry Lyndon*), by the power of the occult (*The Shining*). *Full Metal Jacket* includes just about every theme Kubrick had explored up to then—and more.

Why the change of title? According to Kubrick, *The Short Timers* was a fine title if one already knew it refered to Marines doing a Vietnam hitch and "Magic Marking" the days off on the calendar—a makeshift timetable in the novel. This table of endurance is crudely inked on the back of a flak jacket worn in a pinup by a busty bimbo, a woman-child, her body sectioned into 365 days—plus a "bonus" of another twenty for being Marines, until they could "rotate back to the world." If one didn't know this, Kubrick felt, one could think *The Short Timers* referred to factory workers on a half-day shift. Such an explanation perhaps contains a deliberate pinch of ingenuousness; more likely, the alternative title resonated nicely with his grim cynicism. He explained: "A 'full metal jacket' refers to a bullet design used by police and military the world over in which a lead bullet is encased in a copper jacket. It helps it feed into the gun better. It also keeps the lead from expanding inside the wound: which the Geneva Convention on Warfare makes a point of—I guess," he added ironically, "it's meant to be more humane."

One critic, observing the increasingly isolated and guarded nature of Kubrick's moviemaking, had recently quipped that the director (and notorious stay-at-home) had to find subjects he could shoot within twenty miles of his own front door. And truly meeting such a challenge, Kubrick's preproduction planning turned this taunt into working reality. The "Vietnam" of *Full Metal Jacket* was shot virtually on his own doorstep in southeast

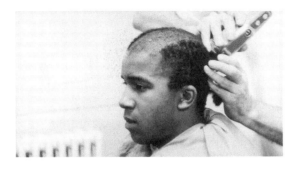

"Goodbye, my sweetheart," says the music track, and it's goodbye to the hair and other individual traits of the new Vietnam Marine recruits. Full Metal Jacket's prologue already converts humanity into the components of a machine.

England. With the help of Anton Furst, an ingenious production designer, Kubrick created the city of Da Nang and the bomb rubble of Hue on one square mile of the Thames Estuary, at Beckton, East London, formerly home to a British gas plant, now scheduled for demolition. Of course, once one recovers from amazement at such chutzpah, it makes perfect sense. *Full Metal Jacket* is not a "jungle" movie but a street-warfare account of battle. News photos showed the real Hue looking as if an atom bomb had hit it. "Sometimes it is easier to build 'reality' than go to it," Kubrick observed; "cheaper, too." His research showed that the French-style industrial architecture of Hue looked like buildings owned by the nationalized British gas industry! Far from requiring construction, the existing "city" needed only be further razed by a wrecker's ball. Commercial advertisements in Vietnamese magazines were discovered in the Library of Congress and microfilmed. Blown up to the size of billboarding and made to look suitably battle-worn, they "dressed" the gigantic open-air set. The Thames-side location's relative isolation permitted immense billows of flame and smoke to fill the air without infringing upon antipollution ordinances, and to be maintained day and night, lending a "descent into hell" feeling to the Marines on their fatal final patrol. The Parris Island barracks were replicated on an industrial estate at Endfield—with British Territorial Army paratroops standing in for U.S. Marine "grunts." Hundreds of Vietnamese were trawled out of their restaurants, kitchens, and ghettos in England and Continental Europe; many hundreds of tropical palms were imported, then "despoiled" and defoliated to look battle-torn. The tumult and the shooting were to last five and a half months.

It was a war that Kubrick must have been fighting inside his head for thirty-five years, ever since he had attempted another film about a "lost patrol," *Fear and Desire*. Clearly, what goes around comes around—but this time with full technical resources. With *Full Metal Jacket* he created a battle zone by and for himself, but now with a clarity of vision about the madness of war that had eluded him the first time.

Kubrick's unusually confident declaration that Hasford's book "found me" suggests how instantaneously he'd seized on it at first reading. In one way, this isn't surprising. In characterization and style, Hasford's Vietnam novel echoes another nightmare dystopia that Kubrick had filmed sixteen years earlier: *A Clockwork Orange*. Hasford's writing is spare, tough, functional, and driven by a first-person narrative as hard and heartless, though not quite so subtly humorous, as that of Anthony Burgess's narrator, the satanic Alex. Hasford's first-person story-teller, a "wise-guy" ex-college kid, possesses the same demonic energy, survival talents, and flagrant but "cool" insubordination of Burgess's antihero. He is nicknamed "Joker" by the sour command of Gunnery Sergeant Hartman, the boot-camp martinet. His fellow "grunts" also sport noms de guerre—"Animal Mother," "Cowboy," "Rafter Man," "Daytona Dave," "Crazy Earl," "Chili Vendor"—recalling the inner-city gang of punkish droogs commanded by Alex. The artificial vocabulary of teenage slang invented by Burgess which he called "Nadsat" is paralleled by the lingo developed by Hasford's mob under the pressure of battle and the contiguity of comradeship. "Vanish, Joker, most ricky ticky," "Doubletime up to the ville and souvenir me one cute orphan, man." Though much diluted in the film, such dia-

The programming begins.

Sergeant Hartman (Lee Ermey) lays down the ground rules and makes sure the new boys "take direction."

logue confers the same jubilant semantic power on the Marines as Alex's suprematist teen-talk did on his vandal generation. Kubrick must have thrilled at finding so much ready-made for him on the page. He adapted it with the credited assistance of Gustav Hasford himself, whom he found not to be an easy coworker. Indeed, what he found was a rather unpredictable and even threatening one. More to his taste—well, certainly safer— was the second-credited coscripter, Michael Herr, who had written one of the Vietnam War's seminal literary works, *Dispatches*. Herr helped flesh out the all-important syntax of military usages and phrases, amoral locutions, and evasive euphemisms. Such dialogue developed, like *Dr. Strangelove*'s War Room exchanges, as an unconscious commentary on the distorting effect that such "officialese" has on the actions of powerful men and the truth of history.

Faces are what register most memorably, first and last, as Kubrick's most hallucinatory creations. The Star-Child gazes benignly down on earth from its angelic bubble in *2001*. Alex, the Devil's child, looks mankind in the eye and grins with satanic relish at the future shock he is about to deliver in *A Clockwork Orange*.

Faces are up-front, too, in *Full Metal Jacket*. The first shots reflect the duality of good and evil, man's divided self, that constitutes Kubrick's perennial concern. That division now finds explicit, if ironic, statement in this film. As the youngsters, incarcerated for their weeks of hellish training at the Parris Island base camp, submit their heads to the barber's shears, they lose personal identity. Before our eyes, they turn into grown-up Star-Child clones—later to be transformed again, this time into Alex's

"I got your name, I got your ass. You will not laugh.
You will not cry. You will learn by the numbers."

droogs in jungle green. The next forty-odd minutes of concentrated filmmaking are dedicated to one continuous theme, a passage
that feels designed with ruler and T square and is as beautiful in
composition as it is damnable in its content. The shaven-headed,
robotic "grunts" are dismantled mentally and emotionally, then
reassembled as killing machines. Nothing like this extended com-
bat-training sequence had ever been seen on-screen, even in army
instructional films. And no "official" films would be as shameless
in what they let us see and, just as important, hear. A leather-
lunged gunnery sergeant, played by a real Marine veteran named
Lee Ermey, sprays the captive, petrified kids with a Rabelaisian
stream of invective that first attacks the very roots and append-
ages of their manhood. Then, when they are ripe for remotiva-
tion, Ermey bonds them physically, mentally, and morally to the
artillery rifle as if it were a substitute for their shrunken, droop-
ing penises. The humor is bitter; the humiliation shocking; the
disorientation surreal; the dehumanization total. Kubrick is in
his element.

His discovery and deployment of Lee Ermey in this prologue is
a masterstroke. He didn't at first appreciate the full resources that
Ermey would bring to it. "Stanley told me one thing, 'Lee, I want
it real,'" Ermey has recalled. "I said, 'I wouldn't give it to you
any other way.'" In fact, Ermey gave him much more than "reali-

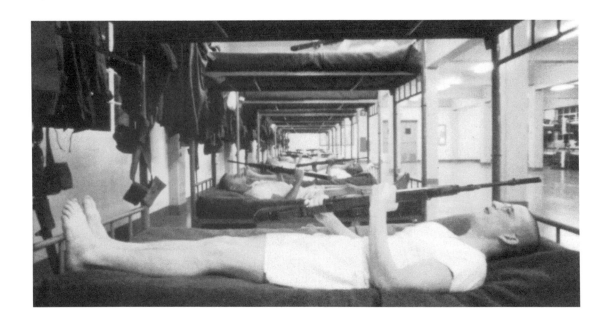

ty." Quickly, Kubrick realized he had a "natural," an actor of impressive self-control and—even more gratifying—dramatic inventiveness. Ermey adapted intuitively to that Kubrick imperative, the "crucial rehearsal period." In this mode of working together, director and player transcend the script's directions, joining in an exploratory venture into character and action which can transfigure a character or scene and enrich a movie with a sense of epiphany. Ermey has related how his supporting role gradually became, under Kubrick's guidance, a moving and shaping one—at first, by accident. In an incident early on in filming, Ermey demonstrated that the Marine Corps had been as valuable to his performance as a course in Method acting. One day he momentarily lost his way in the script during one of those lengthy, unstoppable monologues, when, in his role as drill instructor, he strides along before ranks of terrified adolescents,

"This is my rifle. This is my gun."

One is for fighting, one is for fun, but Kubrick shows how the killer instinct and the sexual urge can be combined.

deriding their looks, names, and sexual completeness and admonishing them with a stream of earthy insults and salty expletives. Ermey blanked but he did not falter, much less halt. To do so would have ruined the long, blustering take. Instead, drawing from a vast reservoir of boot-camp scatology, his tongue fired off words even more direct and revolting than the script called for. "I bet you're the kind of guy that would fuck a person in the ass and not even have the common courtesy to give him a reacharound." He later recalled: "When Stanley called 'Cut,' he ran up . . . and said, 'Lee, what's a reacharound?'" If Kubrick blushed—unlikely—on being informed of the meaning of this defecatory term, it was probably out of pleasure at the outrageous originality of the "additional dialogue."

Thereafter, Ermey's talent for inventing (or remembering) invective was siphoned out of him—until it filled a 250-page ref-

As in a laboratory, the new "animals" are conditioned
by their trainers' program.

erence book of "samples" and a sound track amplified into a barrage of mental attacks in which some heard clear echoes of Kubrick himself. Ermey drills the enlisted men like a film director. He insists on "take" after "take" until his "players" reach the peak of performance—and deliver.

The look of the movie is alarmingly reductive. People who wait for "the story" to start are destined to wait . . . and wait. Kubrick insists on the rigorous patterning of repetition; camera movements are blueprinted as if on a drawing board. His cast are at first almost individually indistinguishable. In their pure-white

The master plan goes badly wrong. Private Pyle
(Vincent D'Onofrio) executes his instructor and him-
self. As with the computer HAL 9000 in 2001, so with
a programmed human—the flaw in the machine brings
destruction and death.

skivvies, T-shirts, and boxer shorts, they resemble a pallid pack of identical shopwindow dummies waiting to be "dressed." They nevertheless possess the otherworldly aspect of replication, which harkens back to Kubrick's fascination with the storeroom of naked mannequins in *Killer's Kiss*, set up for assault and mutilation by combatants with weapons even more brutal than Lee Ermey's tongue. The Marine Corps instruction manual, designed for processing human beings into a disciplined unit, is thus transformed into the kind of installation to be found in a cutting-edge art gallery with a deconstructionist agenda. No wonder early audiences asked, where's the story—where's the star?

The nominal star of *Full Metal Jacket* is Matthew Modine. His subsequent career has not kept pace with his promise. At this time, however, he *had* appeared in several films that might have been rehearsals for Kubrick's: Robert Altman's *Streamers* (1983), a single-set barrack-room study of raw recruits on the verge of shipment to Vietnam; and Alan Parker's surreal *Birdy* (1984), an allegory about a Vietnam mental casualty literally trying to rise above his psychic injury in a free-flight fantasy as a bird. *Full Metal Jacket*, however, forces Modine to remain as anonymous as the rest of the "grunts" until well into this extended training sequence. It is fully seventeen minutes before any conversational tone, any human intimacy, is permitted between him and any other character. While Kubrick assimilates jokes into scenes involving this mass of "maggots," Modine must suffer literally in silence, the negation of conventional star value. It was a feature that tested his youthful fans to the limits. The disorienting effect is increased by the way the emphasis of interest is placed on two other characters: on Ermey and on his chosen victim (and ultimate nemesis), the fat and dysfunctional Private Pyle, played by Vincent D'Onofrio. Displacing a "money" star like Modine by an unknown and—in this role—unappealing character actor, even temporarily, was a huge risk for a high-budget movie. But it launched D'Onofrio's career.

Pyle is the latest incarnation of Kubrick's pessimistic belief that if something can go wrong in the individual, or the cosmos, it

surely will. Pyle is the flaw in the machine, the grit in the clock-work. "I love working for Uncle Sam/Let's me know who I am," the Marines chorus. The corps does not want robots, Ermey reiterates; simply killers. But Pyle becomes the robot who has killing thrust upon him until it rebounds on the system. To reverse a famous shibboleth of architectural design, Pyle's function fails to follow rule-book form. His purely locomotive functions can't take instruction: he fails his physical training and draws the withering fire of Ermey's sarcasm. When one Marine fails the test, goes the rule, all must suffer. Thus when a jelly doughnut is discovered in Pyle's footlocker—food is barred in the dormitory bays—the rest of the squad are sentenced to push-ups while Pyle, in a parody of parade-ground degradation, is compelled to stand among them eating his illicit pastry. The doughnut incident doesn't occur in Hasford's book, but is highly characteristic of Kubrick's inventiveness. It epitomizes the lunatic disparity so often drawn in earlier films like *Dr. Strangelove* between individuals and institutions. Madness emerges when authority is consumed by trivialities. The jelly-doughnut joke has ominous consequences. "Nobody hates you, Leonard," Joker tries reassuring Pyle, "you just keep making mistakes." Modine's sane tones, his total reasonableness, recall Keir Dullea's cosmonaut in *2001* attempting to allay the first small wave of stressful uncertainty being experienced by HAL 9000. HAL's reaction is an attempt to murder him. Eventually HAL has to be dismantled, having malfunctioned so seriously that he is a life threat to his controllers. Pyle's punishment for his error is delivered with disproportionate cruelty devoid of comprehension; his reaction will be exactly the same as HAL's—and somewhat more successful.

In the eeriest scene in the prologue, filmed with muffled sound and in a bluish light, as if underwater, with music that sighs and groans like labored breathing, dozens of Pyle's comrades converge on his bunk and beat him with soap bars wrapped in knotted towels.

"The dead know only one thing: it is better to be alive."

Private Joker (Matthew Modine) sums up the Vietnam lesson, but . . .

. . . some are incapable of learning from it. The living look down on a lime pit filled with the dead.

Colonel: "You write 'Born to Kill' on your helmet, but you wear a Peace button?" Joker: "I think I was trying to suggest something about the duality of man, sir."

The combat zone finds a place for Kubrick's irony.

In-country in Vietnam. A grass-roots setting, but Kubrick frames it in a way that recalls the concentric architecture of the spaceship in 2001.

Man in the mass will revert to primate behavior and turn on the weak when group solidarity comes under threat. But even the "Dawn of Man" sequence in *2001*, when apes discover the tools of aggression and become sentient assailants, feels like an accidental discovery, an evolutionary jolt, compared with the conditioned regression represented by Pyle's beating. That Kubrick did indeed have this evolutionary "memory trace" in mind was confirmed when he told the film critic Penelope Gilliatt: "Probably way back [aggression and xenophobia] did serve a survival purpose. One way to improve the survival of the hunting band is to hate any suspect outsiders." Once one becomes aware of this, Pyle's big-bodied physique calls up his simian origins—though hardly simian dexterity.

Totally asexual in conventional terms—or even deviant ones— a Marine's training is grounded in the creation of a sexual dependency between man and machine. A kind of marriage is arranged between a "grunt" and his gun. Given a feminine name, the lethal weapon mutates into a sex object: it becomes its owner's phallic surrogate and eroticized escort; a masturbation symbol and a compliant mistress. He takes it to bed and drills with it while supine on the mattress; field-strips it and caresses its parts; and solemnizes the place it holds in his love life by belting out a

Animal Mother: "You talk the talk. Do you walk the walk?"

Dialogue in Full Metal Jacket *projects the enmities that war fosters, even among compatriots.*

Kubrick re-creates the urban jungle of Vietnam in the back lot of an abandoned gas works in Britain.

promise of almost sexual fidelity to it as he marches along clutching his genitals: "This is my rifle/This is my gun."

Surprisingly, Pyle is a crack marksman. The ability to hit a human target without moral scruples is presented with such cold-blooded matter-of-factness that it extinguishes all risk of satire—though the line is a fine one. The "heroes" of the corps, eulogized by Ermey for their marksmanship, include a real-life random killer who shot a dozen people on a Texas campus, and also Lee Harvey Oswald. Both assassins were ex-Marines. Kennedy's murderer was skilled enough to kill the President "at 250 yards . . . with three rounds . . . in six seconds . . . and score two hits, including a head shot." That's something to brag about! And it's not only Presidents that Marines send to heaven. "God must have a hard-on for the Marines," runs the gunnery sergeant's salty eulogy. "We show our appreciation. . . . We keep heaven packed with fresh souls." Two more souls are now ready for delivery.

The brutal double killing that follows seems somehow shocking, appropriate, and cathartic all at the same time. Why? Because the film has followed, step by Euclidean step down to the final Q.E.D., the proposition that every perfect system incorporates its own fatal flaw. Pyle, the bunkhouse butt, now grade A sharpshooter, suffers a severe and irreversible breakdown. At this point the photography of D'Onofrio's physique renders him as positively monumental while at the same time reflecting his reversion to the mind, body, and ominous dysfunction of a self-absorbed child.

The "world of shit" out of which Marines in the larval or maggot state are hatched echoes throughout *Full Metal Jacket*'s dia-

The World War II documentary Why We Fight, *updated to Vietnam:*

"They send the tanks in and blow the place to hell."

"We're getting killed for these people and they don't even appreciate it."

logue. Now it almost comes physically on-screen, too: the show-down occurs in the latrines. This all-white void, tiled and plumbed, repeats Kubrick's long obsession with the ominous effect of symmetry. The toilet bowls stand in double rows, con-fronting each other without grace or modesty like soldiers on parade, a hygienic setting that turns horrific. *The Shining* proba-bly taught Kubrick a thing or two about the tense, unsettling nature of scenes set in men's lavatories. In Hasford's book, the fatal confrontation between Ermey and Pyle occurs in the bunkhouse. The location switch to white sanitary-ware has a chill that also recalls *The Shining*'s snows and their dizzying sense of the Nietszchean abyss. One huge close-up of D'Onofrio is like a flashback to Jack Nicholson's demonic grimace, as the lumpen Pyle confronts the lithe Ermey. Each acts with a total disregard for consequences that would be comic if not so painfully sus-penseful. Pyle aims his gun; the gunnery sergeant aims his invec-tive. "What is your major malfunction . . . didn't mummy and daddy show you enough attention when you were a child?" The vocabulary, especially that intrusive "major," has the inappropri-ateness of someone seeking to deny the emergency that's taking place, rather than delay it: it reminds one of Quilty's flippant sparring with Humbert Humbert as he is about to be executed in *Lolita*.

One 7.62-millimeter high-velocity copper-jacketed bullet knocks the Marine sergeant backward. Then Pyle turns his gun on Joker. But the corps maxim that it is "the hard heart that kills, not the weapon" saves the latter: in this case the heart is a defec-tive instrument. Pyle aims the gun at himself. *Bang!* The blood blotch on the obscene cleanliness of the lavatory tiles serves the

"They don't have one horse in this country—there's something basically wrong with that."

"I wanted to meet interesting and stimulat-ing people of an ancient culture—and kill them."

function of a full stop—end of prologue. Now "the story" proper can start.

As noted, we are used to films today which have a unitary structure. A movie that formally "breaks" itself in two, and into stylistically different segments, evokes audience unease, even a suspicion that its maker may have miscalculated. *Full Metal Jacket* still draws fire from those critics who object to its uncompromising division of narrative and style. Yet any disjuncture disappears once one grants that the practice of killing outside the "laboratory" conditions of base camp is going to be brutally different from its theory. The long second section, set in Vietnam, out in the world, is a reversal of lessons learned, as it were, at (or over) father's knee. Lee Ermey's DI had been a monstrous father figure with "the children." Now that the troops have arrived in Vietnam, he quickly comes to look like a reassuring old tyrant compared with the formless, drifting, ubiquitous fear and loathing that shapes life and death here.

The Marines have got back their hair and (some of them) their humanity. Ermey's bullying humor has become characteristic of the "group gripe" of disillusioned "grunts" and of Joker's laconic commentary. Up until now, Joker has spoken only three short, factual sentences—about place, time, and training progress, the sort of responses a captive soldier might be authorized to make under enemy questioning. The screenplay remains faithful to Hasford's outline of a hellish war, but now it is filled out by Kubrick's painstakingly researched army locutions (official and "underground") and the "attitudes" incorporated in the hundreds of service magazines circulating up and down the war lines. Some of these publications are overtly propagandist, like *Stars and Stripes*, for which Joker works; others are subversive critiques of American commanders. In Joker, the two meet. The old military quip "We have met the enemy and he is us" is ironically relevant. The subtext of virtually every scene is a merciless, often hilarious dissertation on how officialese was employed in Vietnam to hide folly and hypocrisy. Specialized jargon distorted the facts, concealed calamitous judgments, plastered cosmetic

A symbol reappears? A monolith shape (like the omen in 2001 forms the background to the ambush.

The sniper's rifle. The only time that the war is seen from the enemy's viewpoint.

The hidden enemy. Marine rules have their limitations when the enemy has one pinned down.

Hitting back: Instinct, not indoctrination, now aims the gun.

cover-ups onto mortal wounds, and generally infected the rank and file with alienation and their commanding officers with self-delusion.

Since the film's beginning, Matthew Modine has not so much acted as observed. Now he gains his voice—and his personality. His strength as an individual character is a surprise that Kubrick has daringly held back until the second half of the film.

Modine is put to work. Joker's punch lines are Kubrick's moral statements, typically delivered with sardonic temper. He wears two emblems—a "Born to Kill" logo on his helmet and a "Peace" button on his jacket. When a hidebound officer challenges the latter, "How's it gonna look if you get killed wearin' that symbol?" he retorts, "I think I was trying to express something about the duality of man." While this is not the most subtle of Kubrick's expositions, it is helped by the officer's straight-faced reprimand,

Hunting the elusive sniper, the men venture into the underworld of war.

They meet the enemy and it is she. *Gender lends its complications to the man-made rules of war.*

But now, men who are not programmed for mercy must make a moral choice.

"We must keep our heads until this peace craze blows over." Kubrick fares better with black humor than with gray paradoxes about the coexistence of compassion and destructiveness. "Inside every gook"—Vietcong militant—"is an American trying to get out," affirms a colonel. Such self-congratulatory comment on America's imperialist war hits home.

The psychopathology of everyday war permeates all of the second section. Kubrick's camera now follows contoured battle lines instead of straight lines out of the drill book, and records events in a rolling, impressionistic fresco rather than in a predetermined setup. *Full Metal Jacket*'s extended coda thus becomes his most traditional-looking film to date. The training-camp slave driving, with never a dull or empty moment permitted, is immediately replaced by the chaos of a laid-back battle community. Snatch-thieves and prostitutes exploit their U.S. "saviors" on Hue's main streets, where Joker and his new sidekick, the news photographer Rafter Man (Kevin Major Howard), are reunited with Cowboy (Arliss Howard), the rangy country boy from Texas, where, Ermey sneered, "only steers and queers" come from. The nicknames that Ermey had pinned on his "grunts" are retained, and even used by commanding officers. Naming things, in fact, or rather renaming them, is what this war is all about. The "right" name is good public relations. War correspondents are more valuable than "grunts," Joker is told: "grunts" simply kill the enemy; correspondents win hearts and minds. Joker takes on his new duties, resolving cynically "to make the world safe for hypocrisy."

Michael Herr says that all wars are the same. But this one, for Kubrick, has spawned a semantic evasiveness tantamount to paranoia. At a morning briefing in the Information HQ, the agenda has to do with words and their meanings in the combat zone. The anodyne phrase "sweep and clear" is ordered to become a replacement for the pejorative "search and destroy"; a fine (and self-serving) distinction is made between "refugees" and "evacuees." A morale-boosting visit by Ann-Margret is imminent; but the briefing officer knows what really raises the guys' spirits: "Grunts like reading about dead officers." "How about a general?" Joker volunteers. Such flippancy is in shocking contrast to the barrack-room bawdiness of the Parris Island prologue.

A sudden Vietcong attack heralds the Tet Offensive's onset, which is exploited by Kubrick mainly for its sardonic impact, not its battle spectacle. "Does this mean Ann-Margret won't be coming?" Joker asks, poker-faced. Amidst apocalypse—as in *Dr. Strangelove*'s War Room—crisis management takes its first spin into comic dementia.

The laconic attitude signifies a moral collapse that all the macho language and semantic subterfuge cannot disguise. "It's a huge shit sandwich," concedes Joker's briefing officer, "and we're all going to have to take a bite." For some, though, it's a picnic. As Joker is sent up-country in punishment for insubordination, the action pushes closer to Hue and the advancing war front. Killing loses its training-camp precision, becoming ever more random, casual, impressionistic. Everything below the Jolly Green Giant of the chopper carrying him and Rafter Man is a free-fire zone for the door gunner. High on pot, the gunner picks off peasants in the paddy fields like a kid playing a high-score video game.

Michael Herr's authorial voice, the voice of *Dispatches'* sober reportage and moral meditation, is rarely heard amid Kubrick's

"I got the sniper. I blew her away. . . .I am a heartbreaker."

zanier vision, but when it is heard, it sticks in the memory. A mass grave, covered with a biodegradable dusting of lime, prompts Joker's memorial comment: "The dead know only one thing: it is better to be alive." A platitude, but at least words that bear the meaning that life, not a rewrite man, gave them. Kubrick has said: "Vietnam was such a phony war in terms of technocrats fine-tuning the facts like an ad agency, talking of 'kill ratios' and 'hamlet pacification' and inciting the men to falsify a 'body count' or at least total up the 'blood trails' on the assumption they'd have led to bodies anyhow." In *Dr. Strangelove*, the Pentagon "hawks" used words with Olympian detachment to mask the horrors of atomic war; in *Full Metal Jacket*, the "grunts" now toss them about like live grenades. Thirty-four years before, speaking about *Fear and Desire*, Kubrick had reflected: "For all its horror, war is pure drama, probably because it is one of the few remaining situations where men stand up for and speak up for what they believe to be their principles." Not any longer. There are no principles to stand up for here: all is cynicism, and cynicism sharpens men's tongues.

Reaching the battle front, Joker and Rafter Man hook into Cowboy's platoon, a bunch of battle-hardened men whose psyches are open wounds. Animal Mother (Adam Baldwin) is the most chillingly dysfunctional: a madman "grunt" with the

337

"She's praying."

glassy-eyed grin of a blood-drunk killer. If Animal Mother ever "rotated back" into the world, he would show up in *Natural Born Killers*. Before the platoon's bodies begin to bleed from real wounds, Kubrick interpolates three sequences that impose a distancing perspective on events and offer a respite. In the first, an army camera crew enters the frame sideways, moving crablike with weird purposefulness along a line of resting "grunts." Each soldier, like some Busby Berkeley chorus-line babe, throws a disillusioned jibe at Kubrick's camera (the camera-in-the-film) as it passes him by.

The sequence is paralleled a moment later, but now with fraternal awkwardness as surviving "grunts" pay tribute to their dead lieutenant. Each man's one-liner defines his own moral or amoral position: "You're goin' home now" . . . *"Semper fi"* . . . "We're mean Marines" . . . "Go easy, bro" . . . until one reaches Animal Mother and his awesomely blunt epitaph: "Better you than me." The last of these commentary sequences features a variety of Vietnam combatants addressing sound bites directly to the camera. The sequence resolves into a blackly comic parody of the

"Let's get out of here."   *"What about her?"*

gung-ho interviews enlisted men give for TV when their officers' eyes are on them. Only this time the men's true feelings about the war are exposed in deftly graded degrees of sophistication and cynicism that bring the Vietnam War's dialectic back home to America. Joker's quip is predictably the most laconic: "I wanted to meet interesting and stimulating people of an ancient culture, and kill them. I wanted to be the first kid on my block to get a confirmed kill."

The film now slides into its last, most momentous sequence—one that took enormous bravado and knocks the bloody stuffing out of the viewer. It is the most uncompromisingly painful sequence in Kubrick's oeuvre. The platoon meets enemy fire in a dreadful coda that inverts every rule in Lee Ermey's training manual; an unseen sniper pins the Marines down and methodically reduces the gung-ho firebrands of the film's first section to whimpering rags of crippled impotence as winnowing fire rips through bone and flesh, lopping off their extremities, crippling their limbs, perforating organs other than the vital ones with what looks to be torturous rather than terminal intent.

"Shoot me,"
she pleads. . . .

This sequence ends the book as well, but in the novel there is no resolution, no outcome; the survivors never pinpoint their mocking and deadly tormentor. In the film, they do. Kubrick and his cowriters appropriated Hasford's documentary account of the ghastly destructiveness that the invisible sniper's bullets wreak on the human body. Then they turn the immolation into a grimly ironic payoff when the men locate her. Yes, *her*. An impression of a "laughing skull" is all that Joker in the novel is privileged to glimpse: a shape without masculine or feminine gender. In the film, the enemy is scarcely more characterized, but definitely female. The discovery takes a terrible toll on the Marines' well-seasoned reflexes. Conditioned at Parris Island to regard their carbine as the love-lust of their life—"the only pussy" they are going to get—they are now confronted by an adversary whose own gender flows through the barrel of a gun. Once, and once only, Kubrick adopts the enemy's point of view, showing a weapon taking aim at the platoon. As the bullets cut down "grunts" unfortunate or foolhardy enough to expose themselves, Kubrick records their horrifying lacerations through a telescopic lens—avoiding close-up voyeurism, but enhancing the helplessness of wounded men separated from their possible rescuers.

The scene takes place in a rubble-strewn urban wasteland against a backdrop of squat, boxlike buildings that gunfire has reduced to concrete shells. One of these structures caused Kubrick some anxiety when he came to edit the sequence. Though its scarred facade looked little different from any in the immediate environment, the building's commanding site, dead center of the screen, lent it a spurious "importance" that reminded the director of one of the monoliths appearing in *2001* at crucial moments in the story to effect a transfiguration in the life or death of the characters. It's fairly safe to say that Kubrick's worry isn't shared—or even perceived—by the average audience for

"Shoot me."

Showing mercy means delivering a death sentence.

Joker shoots the woman sniper—his first kill.

Full Metal Jacket; but its fretful presence in his mind signifies how the ambiguous monolith haunted even its begetter!

Eventually, the men locate and cripple the sniper. For long moments, they stand silently around her, figuratively unmanned by her gender. Hell's fires flicker all round them. The wounded girl sprawls at their feet, whimpering and murmuring. "What's she saying?" someone asks. Joker replies, "She's praying." Kubrick holds Modine's face in tight close-up, a neutral mask looking down at her, expressive of neither hate nor pity. Now that the foe is at his mercy, Joker's attitude to the duality of war battles inwardly with itself. We wait agonizingly to see if conditioning will defeat humanity—if the peace sign or the war cry will be in the moral ascendant. Given the film's thesis, it can never really be in doubt. Joker's single shot, when at last it comes, joins the two that ended the prologue. These shots form an ironic trio of events that subverts the official indoctrination: the cumulative body count adds up to one murder, one suicide, and now one mercy killing—all very unofficial.

Full Metal Jacket's box office was to suffer from this film's release so close to Oliver Stone's Vietnam film, *Platoon*. Yet in every way they are opposites. Stone's film is a flamboyant illustration of battlefield machismo—and an inferior work. He represents Vietnam as a reflection of social division and personal psychosis that could have existed anywhere in peacetime. The director's own, well-advertised father-son conflict appears as part and parcel—or, perhaps, body bag—of his hero's persecution by a psychotic sergeant, an older man whom he ultimately shoots in cold blood. A classic Freudian catharsis. Kubrick's film has no catharsis. It reveals a fatal human flaw in bodies inflexibly programmed to obey orders. Stone's film is more theocratic than

In a hell of their own, the Marines hump down for the night.

technocratic; it seems to extrapolate its pitiless finale from the God-given examples of the Old Testament. It certainly constitutes a powerful report from the combat zone; its acknowledged autobiographical content—Stone was a decorated Vietnam veteran who killed the enemy—also provides its personal pathology. Kubrick's film, on the other hand, is an argument constructed, figuratively and literally, on wasteland and represents its maker's dispassionate overview of what war does to men. Thirty years earlier, *Paths of Glory* illustrated the ambitions that tempt men to sacrifice their fellow men in war; with *Full Metal Jacket*, Kubrick pushes further along the path, past the point where glory might be found, and turns human venality into nihilism. Only one consolation is offered to us: "The dead know . . . it is better to be alive."

In the final, curiously tranquilizing sequence, Joker and what remains of his platoon hump down toward the Perfumed River, where they will set down for the night. "We have nailed our names in the pages of history. Enough for today," runs Joker's spare commentary, shorn of any sentiment, any requiem note for the dead. "I am so happy I am alive. . . . I am in a world of shit. Yes. But I am alive, and I am not afraid." Night falls around the characters until they lose definition and become silhouettes against the endlessly burning fires. In *Paths of Glory*, a girl sang to the World War I troops preparing to go up-line into battle, and the men's faces became those of tired children reacting to a bedside lullaby. More fools they, the director could be saying; but at least that movie allowed us a sentimental out. In *Full Metal Jacket*, the childlike motif is repeated, this time with the theme song from Saturday morning Mickey Mouse club days piping innocently from the lips of the survivors. It is the movie's most human moment—but the descent into infantilism doesn't bode well for history, or mankind.

Marching to the cadence of a chant extolling Mickey Mouse. Just as the soldiers in Paths of Glory *found comfort in a song before battle, so too, in* Full Metal Jacket, *Kubrick's exhausted warriors revert to the tranquilizing certainties of childhood.*

Eyes Wide Shut

Kubrick's thirteenth and, as it tragically turned out, his last film proved that his long search for a new subject had not sapped his capacity to surprise. An exhilarating and unexpected image — unexpected for him, who had hitherto been wary of overt sexuality—opens the film. A young blonde woman stands there in a black sheath dress, back to us. Even clothed, she radiates an aerobic tension. At any second, one feels she could explode into the erotic. Suddenly, she lets her dress slither to her feet and, for a fleeting moment, is brazenly naked. Then: the screen blacks out, as if an eyelid had closed reflexively to mask what the retina had glimpsed. Exposure and denial, temptation and retreat: such are the recurring motifs of what follows. The very title Kubrick gave his film implies it: *Eyes Wide Shut*.

Such self-contradictory words also fit the narrative stream of events that occupy the next 156 minutes. "Eyes wide shut" connotes a spellbound state: the state of a waking dream. The film's mysterious incidents occur in a plausible Manhattan. (Its streets have been meticulously and brilliantly constructed, save for establishing shots, on Pinewood Studios' back lot.) But even so, this is a generic city: a townscape of dream. Here Alice and Bill Harford, her doctor husband, venture first independently and then in uneasy relationship, as their perception of each other changes and sexual fantasy encroaches on the enviable lifestyle of an affluent, apparently happy couple—the kind we used to call the Beautiful People.

The literary source of *Eyes Wide Shut* was at first kept a closely guarded secret. But those who recalled that Kubrick had considered filming Arthur Schnitzler's *Traumnovelle* as long ago as 1971 soon guessed it. He had returned to his old ambition to film what

Bill and Alice (Tom Cruise, Nicole Kidman), the happily married Manhattan couple, set out for a Christmas party. Sophisticated domesticity, framed in one of Kubrick's favorite "corridor" compositions, will soon give way to sexual dalliance and marital disharmony.

the mind could see, but the eye could not. *Traumnovelle* dealt, in particular, with the unconscious jealousies that live within all of us, even apparently happily married people. The announcement by Warner Bros., in 1997, that Frederic Raphael would be composing the screenplay clinched the suspicions that the director was eager to venture into the sexual minefield, an area avoided except in *Lolita*, and then gingerly because of the constraints of film censorship prevailing at the time.

Schnitzler had been inspired to write *Traumnovelle*, or *Rapture: A Dream Novel* as its English publishers more enticingly retitled it, by knowledge of his fellow Viennese Sigmund Freud's work on the roles that dreams played in people's sleeping and waking life. Set in the Hapsburg Empire's Austrian capital of Vienna, its protagonists are a rich society doctor and his wife, who are compelled to question their state of conjugal bliss after being separately propositioned at a fashionable ball. The wife confesses

Alice's importunate encounter with the amorous Hungarian (Sky Dumont) at the Christmas party puts erotic temptation in her way . . .

to earlier infidelities, real or imagined; the husband embarks on his own sexual adventures—are *they* real?—culminating in an orgy from which he barely escapes with his life. Doctor and wife resume life together, apparently refreshed, but in fact more like lovers than young marrieds.

For such a film theme to succeed, Kubrick felt a need for stars of the first magnitude: two who could supply the cumulative wattage of roles played in other movies, as well as media curiosity about their "real" lives offscreen. Good fortune befell him when the script interested not only two of the industry's most successful actors, but a married couple: Tom Cruise and Nicole Kidman.

They assented at once, not guessing that, for most of the next three years, their lives would be hostage to the characters they played in *Eyes Wide Shut*. To their credit, neither Kidman nor Cruise ever complained. Their reach as actors, they felt, should exceed their grasp. The film provided that chance. Kubrick was to construct Shnitzler's fantasy around their personae, pushing their talents into areas of emotional self-revelation that neither player had ever attempted.

The celebrity that Kidman and Cruise radiate endows the film with an immediate interest transcending the merely voyeuristic—though that element, given their real-life marriage, is present too.

Eyes Wide Shut ushers in its principal characters immediately: there's no "getting to know you" approach, no prologue. Cruise and Kidman are *there* in the opening shot, in their elegant Central Park West apartment—its walls hung with paintings by Christiane Kubrick and her daughter Katharina Hobbs. We're carried into the home life of Bill and Alice Harford without pause for speculation about who they are. We watch them dress for a night out, moving about with the unconcerned intimacy of a married couple well used to one of them using the toilet while the other smartens himself up in the bathroom mirror nearby. No secrets, you'd say; no worries. The soundtrack music, Victor Sylvester's orchestra playing dance melodies that might have descended collaterally from Strauss, is like an aural evening wrap

. . . while her husband, accosted by two strange and flirtatious girls (left, Stewart Thorndyke; right, Louise Taylor), finds himself starting his own sexual adventure.

"Why haven't you ever been jealous of me?" Alice, on the rebound from her own sexual encounter at the party and high on pot, brazenly reveals a past infidelity to her husband. White walls focus the eye on her defiant stance; then, as her confession inflames Bill, they are supplanted by red drapes that key the film's dominant hue of sexuality.

a woman would wear: light, elegant, pleasurable. Only the Steadicam and its wide-angle lens hint that this domestic scene already has its frontiers in dreamland, by the way the camera establishes a floating visual rhythm both smoother and more effortless than the start-and-stop agenda of an ordinary married couple with child and babysitter moving briskly toward a night out.

Moreover, it is Christmas, no ordinary time. Trees twinkle with baubles and colored lights, as they do throughout the movie. Cruise and Kidman seem bathed in their reflected radiance.

Finding this director in so festive a mood is a surprise and an omen: Kubrick-watchers, a suspicious bunch of pessimists, will be asking, "How long can it last?" Longer, actually, than we expect. Kubrick continues to indulge us pleasurably as the "perfect couple" leave their apartment as if caught in the condo-doorstep cameras of a *Vanity Fair* photo spread. The slight figures that Cruise and Kidman both cut work in this direction. They

Nick Nightingale (Todd Field), Bill's medical school buddy turned Sonata Café pianist, tempts his friend into the act of rashness that will cost a life. The up-lit illumination from natural sources recalls Torrance's sinister encounter with the barman in The Shining.

possess a chic never seen in a Kubrick film: she in her backless semi-transparent evening gown, worn with the self-confidence of someone who doesn't carry a spare inch of flesh; he slightly cocky in tux and black tie. Schnitzler's Vienna has come to town, courtesy of two of America's most dazzling achievers.

But it is from this early moment that the film's production designers (Les Tomkins, Roy Walker) begin to edge it away from reality. The private party that Bill and Alice are headed for is being held in a Fifth Avenue mansion much like the Frick Museum crossed with the Helmsley Palace Hotel lobby, a dazzling *palazzo*, almost dissolved in the wattage of its own interior illumination. Its walls are less than solid: a waterfall, rather, of tiny lights and polychrome Christmas illuminations. These "rich and famous" guests dancing with the stars to easy-listening music might soon be enveloped into some time warp like that in *The Shining*, doomed to repeat their pleasurable, purposeless distractions to time without end.

Bill has his first chance encounter: with Nick Nightingale (Todd Field), his one-time buddy in medical school, now a drop-out working nights as a band and café pianist. As the men pump and punch each other like guys who need to give their greetings tangible expression, Alice wanders into an adjacent salon, slightly tipsy on champagne, and sets her glass down on a console table. For a moment, the crystal flute creates a tension—then a supremely confident older man, an elegant Hungarian (Sky Dumont), coolly appropriates it, drains it as if planting a vicarious kiss on Alice's mouth, and, within seconds, is propositioning her. Imperceptibly, husband and wife are being diverted from each other, parted by minor events of chance that become imbued with mystery, possibly danger. Bill, too, has been accosted by a couple of laughingly flirtatious girls. Each takes an arm and seeks to draw him away on some unspoken mission of their own choosing.

Alice's chance acquaintance is more direct. "One of the charms of marriage is deception," he tells her: "a necessity for *both* parties." Women in his part of the world get married in order to lose their virginity. Then they can enjoy illicit relations with men other than their husbands. Such advice in present-day America (and elsewhere) might sound as old-fashioned as great-grandmother's recipe book; but in this setting, it doesn't seem inappropriate. Decadence is shimmering in the veils of light. A pinch of late-nineteenth-century Austro-Hungarian cynicism, like paprika, adds an alien sharpness to the American milieu. Like those immigrants from the sexual hunting grounds of Hapsburg Europe who became U.S. filmmakers—Von Stroheim, Curtiz, Wilder, Preminger, to name a few—Kubrick, whose family came from those same regions, is raising the odds in the games of love and

In search of sexual excitement and release, Bill, disguised in cloak and mask, gains entry to the orgy—and is detected.

"I felt ashamed." Alice confesses the lascivious dream she has had while her husband was at the orgy. Home safely after his imprudent venture into private vice, he finds it brings him no comfort.

seduction, revising the rules to favor predators. The Schnitzler novella exerts its sexual pull.

It is jerked back, though, to mainstream America by an incident in an upstairs bathroom where Bill has been urgently summoned by his millionaire host, Victor Ziegler (Sydney Pollack), a man who looks as if he could buy anything, or buy off anyone. "A little accident" has occurred: in other words, a girl has OD'd.

Bathrooms and their ceramic conveniences occupy a central and ominous place in Kubrick interiors: the scene where Jack

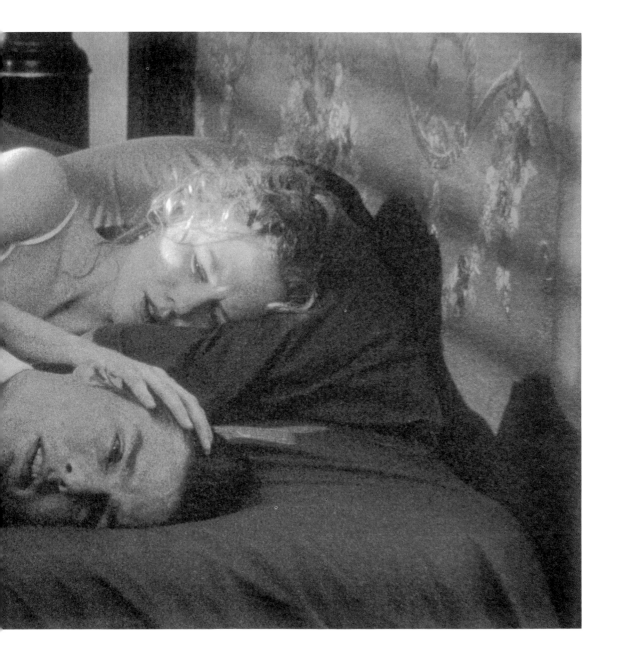

Nicholson's Torrance encounters the messenger from his past life and foresees his fate in *The Shining*; or the site where Vincent D'Onofrio's demented Marine in *Full Metal Jacket* blows his brains out seated on the toilet. Ziegler's immaculate bathroom is now the place where Bill, in his professional capacity, treats a naked girl slumped in narcoleptic posture like a collapsed marionette. This girl will shortly become his "redeemer" in a life-threatening confrontation where he himself is the helpless victim.

All sex in the film is coupled with a compulsive death wish as

"That's not the end of it—why don't you tell me the rest of it." Shaken by his own experiences in the real world, Bill starts to wonder whether his wife was a part of it in her dream state—or in reality.

it was in Schnitzler's work, implying a fateful link. Even *La Ronde*, with its linked series of romantic assignations, was originally a metaphor for the spread of the social disease syphilis. Later on, Bill makes a courtesy house call on one of his patients whose father has just died. His elderly corpse occupies the bed in a French Empire–style suite in a manner that subliminally recalls the penultimate enigma in *2001* when *its* bedridden tenant morphs from dying mortal into a reborn angel child. While Bill offers his condolences to the grief-stricken young daughter, she impulsively plants a voluptuous kiss on the doctor's mouth. But by that time, Bill's sexuality has been disturbed by events in his own home.

The most extraordinary and complex sequence Kubrick directed in his later years occurs after Bill and Alice have returned from the Christmas party—both of them, aroused by encounters there, scarcely waiting for bed before making love. But later, as

Husband and wife reach an uneasy rapprochement: but the sex life of each of them has been too deeply infiltrated by experience and imagination to resume as before.

they smoke pot and quiz each other about the "partners" that fate has cast in their way, their verbal foreplay makes a bizarre detour. From erotic tenderness, it crosses the white line on the high road of conjugal convention. Each increases the pressure of probing curiosity about the other's encounter. Then, as if they've ceased to be a married couple and become lovers, each jealous of the other, the tone turns accusatory.

Does Bill get aroused by female nudity when examining his patients, Alice wants to know. He protests: sex may be too near to death for the patient to become inviting to her doctor. Unsatisfied, Alice taunts him with the episode of her Hungarian importuner at the party. "Why haven't *you* ever been jealous of me?" She makes it sound as if she ought not to be congratulated for her marital fidelity, but condemned for not taking the chance of an affair. Bill replies: "I know *you* would never be unfaithful to me." A fatal error. Marital propriety is resented for its undertone of proprietorship. In seconds, the marriage partnership becomes mutual enmity, in which there can be only one winner. Kubrick awards the scene to Kidman, framing her in a posture of near-naked defiance, clad only in undergarments that emphasize a constitution of sculptural tautness, then allowing her to subside into a confessional position of almost fetal rebirth as Bill's "wife" and "mother" of his child claims she committed an act of infidelity that asserts her own sexuality as a "woman."

"Oh, if you men ever knew what we women think and do." Kidman phrases her emotional outburst almost as if ejaculated in breathless puffs of pure feeling; Cruise generously consents to assume the unresponsive close-up pose of the rejected husband—now even worse than rejected. Haltingly, as if she were seeing before her eyes the sex act she re-creates in her monologue, Alice describes an intense fantasy she imagined with a naval officer she saw across a room one summer. Can one have sex with a stranger and at the same time continue to love one's husband? Usually this double standard is a male prerogative; inverted here, it becomes the woman's claim.

Throughout *Eyes Wide Shut*'s extended shooting schedule, the usual rumors circulated: Kubrick was putting his two stars through an infinity of retaken scenes and script additions. If true, it looks worth the pains taken and given. Their performances come from mind as well as gut. Kubrick has wrenched Cruise and Kidman away from the placenta of their customary starring roles, making them seem to think for themselves and feel grief, guilt, shame, and jealousy, too. Shortly after the film finished shooting, Kidman appeared on the London stage in David Hare's play *The Blue Room*, coincidentally an updated version of Schnitzler's *La Ronde*, in which she impersonated a multiplicity of women having sex with different ranks and conditions of men. Her stage-playing won plaudits from British critics. It is reasonable to wonder if her success was a product of months spent on Kubrick's set, in the belly and brain of her role.

When Bill's jealousies recur subliminally, Kubrick gives shape to them in black-and-white photography, as Bill's mind fastens on his wife's confession. These shots are hardly necessary—though quite effective in revealing Kidman's anatomy in more explicitly erotic activity.

By now, Kidman has been offscreen for quite a long stretch, as if dismissed for her misdeeds, though she remains ever-present in Bill's jealous thoughts. Clearly, Kidman has established Alice's sexual longings, real or imaginary, as the matrix of the story. Bill's own amorous misadventures as a young stud searching for

Retracing his steps, Bill visits the theatrical costumer (Rade Sherbedgia) who supplied his disguise, and finds the man's daughter (Leelee Sobieski) only adds to the mystery.

action have a hard job competing with his wife's report on her dream world.

Sometime later, accosted by a hooker offering him "a little fun," he nevertheless can't think what kind of fun he wants—and leaves it to her. "What do you want to do?"—"What do you recommend?" She promises a surprise; but we, like Bill, never discover what. His mobile phone—that intruder alarm in so many movies nowadays—literally calls his conscience home. Alice is waiting: maybe penitent, more likely sobered.

The Kubrick-Raphael screenplay follows Schnitzler's narrative closely, often—though not always—finding a satisfactory modern analog to incidents and minor characters in nineteenth-century Vienna. The prostitute is a victim of the plague in both novella and film script: of syphilis in the former, AIDS in the latter. Nick Nightingale, the band pianist who plays at the Sonata Café, is a reasonable counterpart for Nachtingall, the novella's pianist who

Lifestyles of the rich and decadent: Bill's millionaire friend (Sydney Pollack) tries to convince him that the night's happenings were more innocent than he imagines. But who would trust a man with a red billiard table?

plays blindfolded at a masked orgy in an out-of-town *schloss*. In the film, he is a facilitator who smuggles Bill into a Gothic country house in upstate New York where well-heeled guests hidden behind Venetian masks copulate with naked women in every corner of the cavernous room. This sequence is visually striking, but nearer to Schnitzler's Vienna than Manhattan's out-of-towners. The Forbes 500 set caught with their pants down always tends to look slightly ridiculous, though Kubrick choreographs the revels with all the sinister solemnity of an impending sacrifice and peoples the standard cowled celebrants of Gothic romance with some phantasmagoric creations out of Max Ernst's sado-sexual canvases. Bill is recognized as an interloper, interrogated, threatened with torture and death, but "redeemed" by the self-sacrifice of a masked woman reveler. As Bill later discovers in a morgue scene, he has been saved by the girl he treated for an overdose in

Ziegler's bathroom. His later detective work to discover the "reality" of his night out and his savior's death ends in ambiguous "probabilities," not "certainties."

Returning to Alice, chastened but still in moderate heat, he discovers her in a terrified state: she has had lewd dreams of her own that appear to intersect with his own nocturnal brush with sex and death. Now it is Bill's turn to "redeem" his marriage, to demonstrate his vulnerability. As if Alice has unmasked his nature, she places the mask he had worn to the orgy, and mislaid there or at home, on their bed pillow. Gracefully, he accepts to let sleeping suspicions lie: better to shut one's eyes to what lurks in the mind than to open them and face the truth. But it is an escape clause, not an ending. What does life hold for them next? They question each other while shopping with their child for Christmas presents. Alice's reply has a manipulative bluntness to it that she expresses in the script's final word—a four-letter one. The conjugal balance has been tilted in her favor. Henceforth, she will be the dominant partner. And not much dreaming will be done.

Although Kubrick produced and directed a film that creates a world within and yet apart from the one his characters inhabit, the real triumph of *Eyes Wide Shut* lies in the performances he has coaxed out of his stars, particularly Kidman. For the first time, she and Cruise seem to be acting without relying on the safety net of their reputations for protection. That such unevasive playing sprang from the quality of Kubrick's direction, they would be the first to acknowledge. Kubrick has often been accused, though never convicted, of an incapacity to reveal the "warm, human stresses" in his subject matter because of a flaw in his own sympathies. This valedictory production gives the lie to that. *Eyes Wide Shut* is his appropriate victory—if, sadly, a posthumous one.

Finally, a few personal thoughts about Stanley Kubrick. I know that word "personal" would have made him bristle. People who knew Stanley "personally," or thought they did, must confront the enigma that now cloaks his gifts with an aura of mystery. He liked to keep it that way. At times I suspect he would have liked to be written out of his own life, like Welles's Mr. Arkadin. Rather than be written about, he would have wished to be left alone to spend his days and nights in filmmaking incognito, unobserved, unreported. Yet it was not to be.

Years ago I discussed Greta Garbo with him, another notable recluse whose path literally used to cross my ski tracks in Klosters, Switzerland, where she spent part of the year. I said to Stanley that she had invited the world into her life by attempting to shut it out. He has been as diligent as Garbo—and far more ruthless—in playing the exclusion game. But his penalty for inadvertently feeding the myth of the movie industry's most secretive and power-driven outsider has been proportionate, too.

The explanation for such obsessive seclusion is sometimes surprisingly simple. Garbo's distance between herself and others extended logically from the tactics she had found so effective in her film career at MGM. Faced with her bosses' demands, hers was the triumph of the apathetic will. Garbo preferred *not* to do anything she didn't want to do, and ignored the possible consequences of her refusal. She was an aberration in a Hollywood where mutinous stars soon fell into line, subdued by the threat of suspension or perhaps loss of privileges, protection, and—the most feared punishment—money. But Garbo simply didn't care. Her work didn't matter to her. If it had brought her world fame, so what? The studios' legal armories contained no weapon against a star who didn't care. Garbo won.

Stanley Kubrick did care, however. His work so obsessed him that nothing was allowed to distract him from it, disturb or destabilize him. Everything in his daily agenda was arranged with that singular aim. And, of course, to his annoyance, the world didn't always comply with his wishes. Just as Garbo was pursued by the paparazzi of her era, the world assailed this other icon, this man who simply asked to be left alone, to get on with things. Occasionally, his modest demand generated a blackly comic side. I'm thinking of the slightly sinister con man who received a great deal of media attention in London in the 1990s by passing himself off at parties and in restaurants as "Mr. Stanley Kubrick." His imposture was only possible because few people had recently seen the real Kubrick. Even up-to-date photos of him were rare. The masquerade gratified the imposter's vanity and perhaps a mild measure of mania. But to Kubrick-watchers, it represented an eerie feeling of destiny, reminiscent of Edgar Allan Poe's tale of William Wilson, in which the haunted narrator eventually meets his doppelgänger.

However, when I read a report that the impostor had "waved gracefully" on bidding goodbye to the people he had deceived—including some journalists, who should have known better—I realized at once that he couldn't have been Stanley. Stanley's life-style was one that could hardly be called graceful. Functional, yes. Intense, yes. Tortuous, yes. But never graceful. It was arranged without regard to anyone else's sensibilities, in order to facilitate the one aspect of existence that defined the man—his work. Images were Kubrick's life.

I once thought Kubrick's extreme reluctance to meet journalists had something in common with the way primitive peoples—or Hollywood celebrities—fear that the cameras of the tourists or the paparazzi may steal a part of their soul, or their fame. But the real reason, I suspect, is starker. Cameras held no terrors for Stanley, but words created considerable unease in him—other people's words. They couldn't be controlled.

As friends, we went back nearly forty years. I had seen *Killer's Kiss*, and then *The Killing*, and written to the films' British distributors, United Artists. Why, I wanted to know, had such hugely original action-thrillers been relegated to tawdry little London screens instead of playing in first-run cinemas? The UA publicity director—also a Kubrick fan—promised that the new film he was making, *Paths of Glory*, would definitely open big. "It has stars," he added. (Oh, dear.) I used this letter as my sympathetic "calling card" when next in New York. Kubrick was living on the Upper East Side. The area at that time—the early 1960s—was a German-American enclave. We ate dinner in a local restaurant with a *Bierkeller* bias to its menu (Wiener schnitzel, I remember), in order to escape the debris of Kubrick's apartment, which was currently being joined to the one next door: a sign of his expanding activities and need for space.

A little after midnight we went back to his apartment so that I could collect my topcoat. Bright tin cans of film were being off-loaded from a delivery truck into his lobby elevator. I squinted at their titles. They were in Japanese, but a few words here and there in English provided a clue. "Are you going to make a film about outer space?" Even then Stanley gave me that swift, wary glance of his I later came to know. *"Please, be careful what you write."* I *was* careful, for ten years or so I was careful, until there was no need to be careful anymore: *2001* was under way. Later, I surmised that he'd ordered up the Japanese sci-fi films to study the state of the art in special effects. But secrecy—Stanley would call it security—even then was tight. Control was becoming a dominant passion.

Kubrick eventually won formidable contractual control of his films. He owns, for instance, virtually any film he makes after an initial fifteen or so years of commercial exploitation by their distributors. But even before he grew so powerful, Stanley had innate ways of exercising control. At times, on the set with him or on location, even a visitor like myself feels himself to be the object of a palpable concentration of willpower. Certainly this force affected the artists and crew. Nothing malign. But a kind of cerebral intensity expressed through his voice, which is low but curt, and his eyes, large and dark. When it wants to, the voice can turn irresistibly enticing. But the eyes are the commanding feature. They lock one into their owner's system like a radar beam tracking a UFO.

John Richardson, in his superb and monumental biography of Picasso, refers to his subject's *mirada fuerte*—literally, his "strong gaze," an all-consuming stare, that fixes people and objects and claims ocular possession of them. Richardson quotes a study by a colleague, David Gilmore, of the machismo nature of people raised like Picasso in Andalusia, in whom "[the] eyes are fingers holding and probing. . . . The *mirada fuerte* has elements of curiosity, hostility, and envy. But the sexual element is present also. . . . The light of the eyes is highly erotic." Granted, Stanley Kubrick and Pablo Picasso come from a different latitude, faith, and creative genre. Even so, they use an extremely similar physical and mental manner to dominate their work, possess and transform it. Like Picasso, Kubrick, too, has a wit with a streak of refined amusement in it, both taunting and self-protective.

In the 1950s, during the early years of the Cannes Film Festival, Picasso sometimes descended from his home in the Mougin hills to join a few of us for late-night drinking. We critics were already in thrall, but to the man who was the festival's *président d'honneur* in those days, Jean Cocteau, an early and sycophantic Picasso crony. While we snacked and drank and Cocteau talked and talked, Picasso would idly, silently, play with crayons, sketching our likenesses on the bar's paper tablecloth. Then, the wine bottles empty and even Cocteau drying up, the bill being called for, the artist would whip the cloth off the table and ask with amusement, part imp and part demon, "Which one of you would like to buy your portrait?" Which one of us could afford to! No bidders:

the paper "canvas" was shredded before our eyes with malign glee. I think that if Stanley had witnessed Picasso's little comedy, he would have recognized a soul mate. Arnerà, who printed Picasso's etchings, used to say of the artist that "he took an aggressive delight in encountering an obstacle and surmounting and conquering it." That seems a perfect description of Stanley's modus operandi, too.

One of Stanley's associates, Julian Senior, of Warner Bros., once told me he telephoned him to report a good box office for Kubrick's most recent film in some distant part of the world. There came a pause as this bit of news was received and analyzed. Then: "Why tell me something I can do nothing about?"

Occasionally I tried to break the spell Kubrick cast by telling him something I knew would divert him, some anecdote or piece of trivia. Quite often I then found my passing intervention acquiring a baleful relevance to some basic interest of his own, usually to do with the exercise of power, and being filed away for future use. Thus I once told him how Wernher von Braun, the engineering genius behind the Nazi's guided-missile program—and America's—made it a rule never to hire anyone who reached for the saltcellar before tasting his food. I suspect this "test" then went on to repose, along with others designed to split people open for inspection, in Stanley's memory bank. Lucky—and rare—were those who were invited to break bread with Kubrick. And when the occasion did arise, they would have been well served to watch the salt!

Another time I suggested he look at the memoirs of Albert Speer, Hitler's architect and munitions minister. Speer had just published them after twenty years' incarceration for war crimes in Spandau prison, along with other high-ranking Nazis who had been spared execution. In Speer's account, these men, once the most powerful in Europe, are reduced to whiling away their days stalking grasshoppers in the prison yard, feeding flies to spiders, or quarreling with each other to maintain their phantom rank and status. This struck me as marvelous material for a grotesque comedy along the lines of *Dr. Strangelove.* "You could get Speer to design it," I added, perhaps too glibly. Stanley saw the possibilities, but vetoed my suggested production designer. Speer? He would be too expensive.

To Stanley, all talk had to contain vitamins and calories. I don't think he would have missed food of the routine kind if he had to do without it. Napoleon, another irregular and abstracted eater, with no table manners to match his eminence, was the same way: people with weighty matters on their mind don't pay much attention to what's on their plate. But people who provide talk have to be precise. "Garrulous" is the word Stanley used—not unkindly, though—to describe a close associate from the past (*not* Arthur C. Clarke, I hasten to add). This was a man with wide knowledge in many fields, but who, according to Stanley, hadn't gotten his conversational priorities right. Not that Stanley's own conversational priorities always had to do with filmmaking.

Finding Jack Nicholson sitting near me and alone at the 1995 Venice Film Festival, waiting for his hosts to arrive at the luncheon table, I reintroduced myself. (We'd met on the set of *The Shining* fifteen years earlier.) Almost immediately, our lines of dialogue overlapped: "Have you been in touch with Stanley?" He's been on to me almost every night, Nicholson said. About a new movie? No, to find out how O.J.'s trial went that day.

People trying to contact Stanley experienced frustration, and generally ended up defeated and irritable. One person who did get through is reputed to have been met with: "To what low criminal act did you stoop to get this number?" The story may be apocryphal, but the remark is in character.

The situation, however, is very different when Stanley did the calling. One Christmas, in the Swiss ski resort of Mürren, the proprietor of my small hotel woke me up around 1:30 a.m. A telephone call from England. I took it where it had come through, in the bar, which was still occupied at that hour by a few of the owner's hard-drinking cronies. It was Stanley calling. He had tracked me down through the Swiss tourist office in London, having systematically eliminated the (admittedly few) hotels where I might be staying. The call was about a series of his films which British television was planning to show in the New Year. "Stanley," I said, "it's not even Christmas yet." To make this call had involved putting in an earlier one to a private yacht cruising in the Caribbean, carrying Alan Yentob, then chief of the BBC-TV channel that was going to show the Kubrick movies. The yacht was under charter to one of the Saatchi brothers, the British advertising moguls: Stanley had reached Yentob by radio-telephone. All this to coordinate how I was going to introduce and comment on the films. A few hours earlier, on the same night, after I had gone to bed, an American airliner had crashed in the Scottish village of Lockerbie. Stanley broke this news to me. He didn't then know the disaster's horrifying extent, or whether it was accident or sabotage; but if the former, he was already speculating on the potential metal fatigue to be expected in an aircraft of this vintage.

On finishing the call some twenty-five minutes later, I broke the news of the disaster to the Swiss, who had sat silent, listening to the one-sided conversation with half an ear cocked. "Lockerbie," at that time, meant as little to these Alpine dwellers as it did to most people in Britain. The real conversation-stopper was the name "Kubrick."

I worked for Stanley only once, unpaid and briefly. He sought my journalist's know-how to help him compose "period" news items for a montage sequence intended for *The Shining*. He wanted me to invent fifty years of ill-omened events at the Overlook Hotel, happenings great and small—sudden deaths, murders, arson, suicides, financial swindles, marital scandals, bizarre accidents—all suggesting a fateful ambiance in the place. The reports had to be "dressed up" to look as if they'd been culled from Colorado newspapers during the first half of the twentieth century. "But what do I know of newspapers in Colorado over one week, never mind fifty years!" I exploded. The reply was: You supply the items, I'll supply the papers. It reminded me of William Randolph Hearst's famous order. Hearst proposed to send a photographer to cover hostilities somewhere on the globe: What hostilities? the man protested; there is no war. Came the answer: You supply the pictures, I'll supply the war.

A few weeks later, I got home to find cans of film containing thirty-five-millimeter photocopies of the front pages of the *Denver Post* and *Rocky Mountain News*. These cans and a reading machine, a device then the size of a small domestic refrigerator, pretty well filled my front hall. It took me six weeks, working on my knees in the hallway—the "reader" was too big to fit into my workroom—to scan newspaper reports of events in Colorado between 1900 and 1955. The task was large, for once I found the kernel of a likely story, I had to invent my own mini-dramas, fabricate headlines in a variety of period styles—the newspaper's makeup changed over the half century—and add subheads, bylines, intros, and subsequent paragraphs. (I had warned Stanley that someone, someday, would freeze-frame the video of *The Shining* and read the stories that supposedly were conveying the hotel's malign reputation to Jack Nicholson: it wouldn't be enough to have just an opening paragraph.)

I like to think I created a sense of hellish doom for the Overlook which Dante—well, Stephen King, at least—would have been proud to claim. Stanley thought it . . . okay. None of it was ever used—the sequence showing Nicholson discovering the scrapbook was abandoned as overly obvious—though the book, as mentioned, can still be glimpsed at Jack's elbow while the "blocked" writer vainly labors at his typewriter.

Disappointed? A little. But I had learned that heartbreak was a hazard of working with Kubrick.

Stanley was a man of instinctual kindness and generosity. He never forgot an anniversary. He repaid the loyalty of his aides when they left his employ. Once he even intervened with Jerry Brown, then governor of California, on behalf of the late Gustav Hasler, author of the novella that underlies *Full Metal Jacket*. Hasler had been convicted in the United States of purloining a vast quantity of books from several London libraries, and sentenced to a term in a California correctional facility. (Brown was sympathetic, but let the sentence stand.)

But an individual's feelings—any individual's—counted for little when Stanley went after what he wanted, or didn't want, or perhaps may have wanted. All options were covered, most rejected. Sometimes people took it hard. Hence the occasional intimations of "ingratitude" that seep through the otherwise cautious recollections of some who've been closest to Stanley while filming.

I have not always agreed with him. To tell the truth, I would have been happier if *The Shining* had cut all ties with the supernatural. Its powerful illustration of how a man is driven mad by his own demons was terrifying enough clinically without conjuring up the occult to gratify the Stephen King ghoul club.

Madness appeals to those who see the world as an asylum. The protagonists' warped perception of life supplies an energy, comic or tragic, that drives several of Kubrick's finest movies. He was particularly fascinated by the mundane things that counterpoint the madness of great events. They fed his ironic pessimism about how the world is organized. I remember his grim amusement on learning how Pierre Salinger and Dean Rusk had allegedly passed the time when hastily summoned back from Hawaii after President Kennedy's assassination in 1963. They had played poker. And Salinger won seven hundred dollars—"quite a lot then," Stanley mused. "You may think it terribly bad taste, playing poker at such a time," he went on, "but looked at another way, it is just the thing that men numbed by momentous calamity would do. It gives a macabre perspective to events that you couldn't get if you portrayed the world-shaking consequences of Kennedy's murder."

The theme of "containment" or "entrapment" also exercised a persistent fascination for Stanley, even outside the thematic content of his films. I glimpsed this at first hand.

He was with me on the afternoon I took possession of the first home I owned in London, a newly built, very modern apartment with wall-sized windows. These afforded me a pleasant view of the outside world, but being near the ground, they were already arousing fears of what unpleasant things might come through them uninvited.

Stanley's off-the-cuff remedy was brutally simple: put up steel grilles. "You mean live behind bars!" I said. Oh, it's not so bad: you'll soon get used to it, was his answer.

Well, it wasn't . . . and I did. With slatted, Venetian blinds covering the rigid metal grids, and double glazing, I was scarcely aware of the iron I have lived behind ever since—so far securely. Stanley, I imagine, could thrive in a cell, given reasonable comforts and, of course, communications with the outside world.

I sometimes think fondly of a film he held in amused esteem, as do I—Fritz Lang's 1932 expressionist thriller, *The Testament of Dr. Mabuse*. In it, the mad criminal who's locked in a lunatic asylum manages to dominate his keeper by sheer willpower and communicate with his gang outside, writing down his orders and tossing them out of his cell window. If incarceration does not cure madness, neither must it inhibit communication.

Julian Senior, a Warner Bros. vice-president based in London and for many years Warner's valued link with Stanley, compares him to a medieval craftsman whose home was his workshop. It is an apt analogy. Stanley clustered his biological family around him, but lived with—and for—his work. His was not a setup you often find in Beverly Hills, or even in the more outlying (and pleasant) bits of America where "A"-list filmmakers take refuge from the importunate demands of the movers and shakers who rule Hollywood. These out-of-towners go in for a comfortable setup, all right; but unlike Stanley, they don't build the studio around themselves.

Stanley lived in England for nearly forty years and made every film since (and including) *Lolita* there. He found the life comfortable and free from the intolerable pressures that would have been on his doorstep in America. In England, he was known as a "name," of course, but not subjected to the obligations of a celebrity. His home was a large country mansion with many rooms, big enough to incorporate a ballroom (now used as her artist's studio by Christiane, his third wife). It's situated on a private estate once owned by a wonderfully elegant Edwardian dandy and millionaire racehorse owner, who won the Derby with his favorite, Golden Miller, way back in the 1930s. I encountered this very character at someone's dinner party and, since my horse-racing expertise would hardly get me past the starting post, I made small talk, noting that Mr. Kubrick was living at his former property. "Oh, yes," the old boy drawled in the fruitiest of

Edwardian accents. "He makes films—horror ones, I believe." I told Stanley this later. I think he was relieved not to have been more clearly identified.

The stables at Stanley's country house are big enough to sport their own miniature bell tower as well as a whole pack of Derby racehorses, but they were converted instead for use as production offices. It's crucial to understand that what other people view as a "hermitage," he only saw as a severely functional work base.

Though stereotyped as a "recluse" by the media, he was far less reclusive than other creative people with famous names but almost unidentifiable faces, who have kept public curiosity at bay: J. D. Salinger, for example, or Thomas Pynchon and Harper Lee, are all refugees from the media, guarded by family and friends with the zeal of high priests shielding a divinity from the stares of the mob. Unlike these literary isolates, Kubrick if he appeared in public was more easily recognizable—notwithstanding the story of his opportunistic doppelgänger. His invisibility was not so absolute as theirs. In fact, reclusiveness wasn't even a rational decision. It just grew up around him. He was not disingenuous about it, however. He knew it had uses, such as the publicity value that giving no public interviews paradoxically achieves. In fact, Kubrick did give interviews—to the print media, anyhow, though very, very few—as each film was ready for release. His distributors were not treated any more generously where his time and presence was concerned. They have sometimes had a perilously short time to devise a full-scale publicity campaign for a new film. The details, even so, were supervised at a distance by the absentee filmmaker, with every decision subject to explanation and validation.

What other filmmakers might consider a disadvantage, Stanley, I think, saw as a safeguard. Such tight scheduling ceded him control of the way his work was presented, and thus perceived.

All this power was possible only because it was "in the contract." Patience, persistence, risk taking, and self-denial won it for him over the years. When lawyers met to haggle over some point Stanley Kubrick raised, time just as well might have taken unpaid leave. He didn't allow himself to be worn out: he wore out others.

He is rumored not to have liked traveling and never to go abroad. This was not quite true; but when he did travel, it was not with the purpose of relaxing. He had been to Germany for his wife's family bereavement. Another trip was to Normandy's beaches where the Allies invaded Fortress Europe in 1944. He had apparently been further east still, though date and destination are obscure. Christiane Kubrick once let slip to an interviewer that she and her husband had been watching an open-air play—also unidentified—in a Black Sea resort when the arena was suddenly flooded "by five hundred bearded extras all looking like Stanley." "Abroad" for Stanley usually remained a concept of the mind, not a destination. Why go abroad when the world could be brought to his screen?

I once visited him in Ireland during the shooting of *Barry Lyndon*—one of the occasions when historical necessity compelled him to travel more than twenty miles from home. I found him in a rented mansion near Dublin looking at the biggest TV screen I'd ever seen. An episode from the distinguished documentary *The World at War* was just winding down. He gestured to me to sit down and wait. . . . "I want to see how it ends."

"Stanley," I said, "we win." The irony fell flat. The twentieth century was all of a piece with the eighteenth century he was then filming. Wherever he was, Stanley remained a time traveler —not a tourist.

It's a cliché that great artists with their minds on work scarcely know the color, shape, or cut of the clothes on their backs. Stanley proved the truth of this. His otherwise nondescript clothes reflected the man in only one way—a frequent military provenance in his daily wear. If pants and jackets were meant for battle, they were good for filmmaking's crisis management. Though concerned to conceal the workings of his own mind, it is the notion of "works" in the widest sense that continuously fascinated him and so gives some insight into that mind. His obsession with "systems" and the way they function didn't eliminate an aesthetic response.

On a recent occasion, I visited him at home and noticed a gleaming white Porsche parked in the mansion's forecourt—a thoroughbred among the workhorse Range Rovers and U.S. Army surplus trucks he kept in the adjoining stable yard. Stanley was famously concerned with physical safety. He viewed speed with skepticism. He was known to ring off on his car phone when approaching an intersection, then call back once he had negotiated the crossing. So it surprised me to find that the high-speed Porsche belonged to him. Yet looked at another way, the Porsche is a piece of superb machinery, the ultimate in engineering systems. Thus the car makes a statement about its owner that has nothing to do with speed, still less with status. It is "the works" in it that he admired and aestheticized.

Over the years, Kubrick mustered a domestic apparat that placed his immediate family at the core of his extended filmmaking one. Their talents fed into his. Christiane is an exhibiting artist whose considerable gifts place her in the *intimiste* manner of such painters as Bonnard and Vuillard. Her subjects are usually still lifes or outdoor views, rendered with subtle, colorful, and sensuous detail. Stanley appeared, as a saturnine presence framed in beard and brooding brows, in some of her earlier interiors. He does not appear in the later ones I've seen. At home, or outside it, as far as personal credits are concerned, Kubrick didn't play favorites. Christiane Kubrick has contributed to the design of his films, usually uncredited. Stanley's brother-in-law, Jan Harlan, a member of a distinguished stage-and-screen dynasty in prewar Germany, was his executive producer. His son-in-law, Philip Hobbs, was his associate producer on *Full Metal Jacket*. Tony Frewin, a published novelist and authority on H. L. Mencken, and Leon Vitali, who played the venomous young aristocrat in *Barry Lyndon*, acted as Kubrick's assistants round the clock. They logged all calls, kept contact with New York or the Coast, ran interference for him, and, when filming began, assisted in untold ways. Vitali, for instance, often operated a video camera to trawl through possible players for minor roles, relieving Stanley of preproduction chores as well as the pain involved in facing performers he would have had to turn down.

Katharine, the Kubricks' eldest daughter by Christiane's first marriage, is married to Philip Hobbs and is a professional-standard photographer in her own right. Anya, the Kubricks' first child by the present marriage, is a successful opera singer. As mentioned, the youngest daughter, Vivian, has composed music for some of her father's films and kept the "family album" on Super 8 film and later on video. She is the only person so far entrusted to record her father at work. This she did, in a short but intense documentary of him directing *The Shining*. To some viewers it presented a disturbing picture of Kubrick as both "daddy" and "demon"—a darkly sardonic if not actually satanic presence, but also someone who could suddenly be sweet-tempered, even self-amused. Kubrick the family man contrasts oddly with his image in the myths that have collected around him like Gothic shrouds. Take my word for it: they conceal no monster.

If I were invited to record one single vision of Stanley, my mind would go back to a moment when I saw most clearly his daunting concern for detail.

The night before *The Shining* was to open in New York, I called at Elstree Studios, on the outskirts of London, where Stanley had his production offices. I was picking him up for supper. It was nine o'clock at night, a late hour for studio visiting. "Anyone working?" asked the security man checking me through the front gate. "One is," I said, with sinister emphasis, as if to imply he was keeping the lot open only for Stanley. The guard laughed: he knew who.

I found Stanley in the storage block he was renting, his general-command post. Its sole identification: a forbidding notice saying HAWK FILMS—KEEP OUT. Its open-plan space was already cluttered up with all the paraphernalia of a film company: trestle tables, typewriters, stacks and stacks of documents, the congealed remains of half-eaten food on paper plates, the high-tech coexisting with the unhygienic. Stanley sat in a pool of light, hemmed in bunkerlike by rack upon gleaming rack of bright film canisters containing every single take he'd shot, whether used in the film or not. He wore his usual combination of mismatched items that might have been left over from the last war—or issued in preparation for the next. He was holding a telephone to his ear and an outsize magnifying glass to his eye. It looked as if he were directing his forces on some distant battlefront. I didn't speak, he simply nodded to me—sit down.

Spread in front of him was what proved to be a copy of that day's edition of *The New York Times*, couriered in an hour or so earlier from London airport. It was open at a full-page advertisement for *The Shining*. Stanley was talking in low, well-contained but intense tones, clearly angry. But he was reprimanding an unhappy soul at the other end of the line with the force of irony, not ire. "Doesn't it strike you as strange that you're three thousand miles away in New York, and here I am in London telling you that the 1 a.m. extra performance of *The Shining* has been left out of the movie ad in today's *Times*?"

Did it strike me as strange to be there listening to this disclosure? Not really. What other moviemaker, I asked myself, having devoted three years of his life to create on film the fantasies in his mind's eye, could have mustered the energy to monitor the small print of an ad—one part of a line—for a movie house three thousand miles distant? I already knew the answer: only Stanley Kubrick.

I last heard from Stanley at Christmas, 1998. He always sent a gift, usually art books, this time an album of the great French photographer Lartigue. "Let's try to meet next year." I recognized the greeting, wry and laconic: the "not forgotten" reassurance of a friend who knows he needn't apologize for his elusiveness, as it's in his nature, not an oversight, and thus eminently pardonable. But it was not to be.

Julian Senior, Warner Bros. closest link with Stanley, called me on his mobile around 3.30 p.m. on March 7, his voice hard and urgent with concern. Stanley had died earlier that day, in his own bedroom, of an embolism. Sick at heart, I sat down to write his obituary as calls—redirected by Warner Bros., I suspect—started flooding in to me from the world's radio and TV media. Stanley's death was made all the more dramatic by its timing, a bare 24 hours after his last film, *Eyes Wide Shut*, had finally been seen by outsider's eyes, few though they were: just Terry Semel and Bob Daly, Warner Bros. co-chairmen, Tom Cruise and Nicole Kidman, in a New York screening room. The projectionist—Semel confirmed this—was ordered to turn his back to the screen once the film had begun and only turn around again for the reel change. Several obituaries commented that it was as if, having finished his work, Stanley had finished with life. That, of course, is nonsense, Stanley was never really finished with a film, and therefore would not have yielded his life without a struggle.

The momentum generated by his passing, and all the duties of recording it for interviewers, carried me through the week until, at 3:00 p.m. on the gray and wintry afternoon of Friday, March 12, I drove to Stanley's country home—this time to see him buried. It was hardly a "ceremony": more a gathering of family, friends and associates when Jan Harlan, his brother-in-law and long-time executive producer, characterized as "the world's greatest assembly of Stanley Kubrick experts." That set the tone: ineluctable loss mingled with the grateful relief of levity. Never, never, let it be said that the mood was funereal. "You know I hate funerals," Stanley would have said, in his low, insistent voice, "forgeddit." We couldn't; yet, over the next 105 minutes, we did, seated in an arc of chairs (a bottle of Evian water beside each), well over 100 of us—so much for Stanley's being a hermit!

It was a private gathering—the media were kept at bay, over a mile away down the long manor drive with its white picket fences; a police van stood by to reinforce the message that no misbehavior would be tolerated. I hope I do not trespass on family sensibilities in the next few paragraphs; but Stanley's last hours spent in spirit with his friends should not generate the myths and falsehoods that so easily spring up where privacy meets secrecy and there is no eyewitness account. It was a "family farewell": Stanley's children and grandchildren, gifted cellists, clarinetists and singers, provided the song and music: Bach's 2nd cello suite Sarabande; the 2nd movement of Brahms clarinet Sonata in F Minor; Ravel; the Adagio from Rachmaninov's Sonata in G Minor; and one of his favorite pieces, the Adagio from Schubert's String Quintet in C. The only overtly religious note was the Kaddish.

Perhaps the oddest feeling was generated by our being in a vast pavilion, as long as a cricket pitch, erected on the lawn outside the friendly family kitchen where I had last had supper with the Kubricks. There was no grass beneath our feet, but a carpet of green baize-like color, which I imagine roused some concern as Stanley hated that particular hue. Too late, though, to change it. I thought at first the florists had been too generous; then I realized these trees and shrubs were actual growing plants. Stanley was to be interred in his own garden.

What struck me suddenly was the symmetry of it all. One particular tree of a very formal shape filled the center. A grand piano counter-balanced the shrubs opposite it. On the far back wall of the pavilion hung a painting of Stanley by Christiane which I had often seen: a domestic interior, in tones of orange and blue, with Stanley in his black-bearded early middle-age posed beside a window through which slanting snow or sleet fell into a garden much like the one we were in. It was exactly as Stanley would have arranged the scene for a shot. His face looked out at us from the Order of Service on each chair, now wearing a more benign and patient expression, the beard a gray fringe, looking over rimless spectacles, almost professorial—a snapshot taken by Christiane in September 1998.

I hate the word "eulogy." Stanley's unique strengths and lovable eccentricities all formed the text of memory, spoken with affection and feeling but also with many a sly "dig" at the quirks in the man's ways of doing things. Terry Semel followed Jan Harlan; then Steven Spielberg, Nicole Kidman, Tom Cruise. It was the testimony of craftsmanship and friendship, not awe or greatness. For me—for many of us, I'm sure—the most moving moment had been when Stanley's casket was carried in on the shoulders of his grandchildren, supported, too, by Tom Cruise, with Emilio d'Alessandro, Stanley's loyal Italian major domo over many years, following behind it. It was placed on two trestles in the far background and when the time came for it to be lowered into the grave, we all lined up, the 100-odd of us, and each drew a scarlet rose from the huge spray that had been placed on the plain dark-wood coffin and dropped it into the grave along with a pinch of earth from four small bowls, one at each corner of the pit. Stanley's favorite dogs, retrievers in the main, occasionally wandered in and out, no doubt perplexed by the absence of their master, a homely touch in a harrowing moment of eternal separation.

Then we ate, drank and chattered away to each other in the

huge kitchen and conservatory. In Beverly Hills, this would have been a heavy-duty occasion with bodyguards, velvet ropes, VIP enclosures: here, it was almost like an English picnic. The grand-children had asked us to "look at the sky...at the 'magic hour,'" and, as we did, it was illuminated by brilliant fireworks. Then the evening mist crawled up toward the house, and we went home.

Filmography

Day of the Fight (USA, 1951).
Director, Photography, Editor, Sound, Stanley Kubrick.
Commentary, Douglas Edwards.
Documentary short on Walter Cartier, middleweight prizefighter.
Running Time: 16 minutes. Distributor: RKO Radio.

Flying Padre (USA, 1951).
Director, Photography, Editor, Sound, Stanley Kubrick.
Documentary short on the Reverend Fred Stadtmueller, Roman Catholic missionary of a New Mexican parish of 400 square miles.
Running Time: 9 minutes. Distributor: RKO Radio.

Fear and Desire (USA, 1953).
Production Company, Stanley Kubrick Productions. Producer, Stanley Kubrick.
Director, Photography, Editor, Stanley Kubrick. Script, Howard O. Sackler.
Frank Silvera (Mac), Kenneth Harp (Corby), Virginia Leith (The Girl), Paul Mazursky (Sidney), Stee Coit (Fletcher).
Running Time: 68 minutes. Distributor: Joeseph Burstyn.

Killer's Kiss (USA, 1955).
Production Company, Minotaur. Producers, Stanley Kubrick, Morris Bousel.
Director, Photography, Editor, Stanley Kubrick. Script, Stanley Kubrick, Howard O. Sackler. Music, Gerald Fried. Choreography, David Vaughan.
Frank Silvera (Vincent Rapallo), Jamie Smith (Davy Gordon), Irene Kane (Gloria Price), Jerry Jarret (Albert), Iris (Ruth Sobotka), Mike Dana, Felice Orlandi, Ralph Roberts, Phil Stevenson (Hoodlums), Julius Adelman (Mannequin Factory Owner), David Vaughan, Alec Rubin (Conventioneers).
Running Time: 64 minutes. Distributor: United Artists.

The Killing (USA, 1956).
Production Company, Harris-Kubrick Productions. Producer, James B. Harris. Director, Stanley Kubrick. Script, Stanley Kubrick, based on the novel *Clean Break*, by Lionel White. Additional Dialogue, Jim Thompson. Photography, Lucien Ballard. Editor, Betty Steinberg. Art Director, Ruth Sobotka Kubrick. Music, Gerald Fried. Sound, Earl Snyder.
Sterling Hayden (Johnny Clay), Jay C. Flippen (Marvin Unger), Marie Windsor (Sherry Peatty), Elisha Cook (George Peatty), Coleen Gray (Fay), Vince Edwards (Val Cannon), Ted de Corsia (Randy Kennan), Joe Sawyer (Mike O'Reilly), Tim Carey (Nikki), Kola Kwariani (Maurice), James Edwards (Car Park Attendant).
Running Time: 83 minutes. Distributor: United Artists.

Paths of Glory (USA, 1957).
Production Company, Harris-Kubrick Productions. Producer, James B. Harris. Director, Stanley Kubrick. Script, Stanley Kubrick, Calder Willingham, Jim Thompson, based on the novel by Humphrey Cobb. Photography, George Krause. Editor, Eva Kroll. Art Director, Ludwig Reiber. Music, Gerald Fried. Sound, Martin Muller.
Kirk Douglas (Colonel Dax), Ralph Meeker (Corporal Paris), Adolphe Menjou (General Broulard), George Macready (General Mireau), Wayne Morris (Lieutenant Roget), Richard Anderson (Major Saint-Auban), Joseph Turkel (Private Arnaud), Timothy Carey (Private Ferol), Peter Capell (Colonel Judge), Susanne Christian (German Girl), Bert Freed (Sergeant Boulanger), Emile Meyer (Priest), John Stein (Captain Rousseau).
Running Time: 86 minutes. Distributor: United Artists.

Spartacus (USA, 1960).
Production Company, Bryna. Executive Producer, Kirk Douglas. Producer, Edward Lewis. Director, Stanley Kubrick. Script, Dalton Trumbo, based on the book by Howard Fast. Photography, Russell Metty. Additional Photography, Clifford Stine. Screen Process, Super Technirama-70. Color, Technicolor. Editors, Robert Lawrence, Robert Schultz, Fred Chulack. Production Designer, Alexander Golitzen. Art Director, Eric Orbom. Set Decoration, Russell A. Gausman, Julia Heron. Titles, Saul Bass. Technical Adviser, Vittorio Nino Novarese. Costumes,

Peruzzi, Valles, Bill Thomas. Music, Alex North. Music Director, Joseph Gershenson. Sound, Waldon O. Watson, Joe Lapis, Murray Spivack, Ronald Pierce.
Kirk Douglas (Spartacus, Laurence Olivier (Marcus Crassus), Jean Simmons (Varinia), Charles Laughton (Gracchus), Peter Ustinov (Batiatus), John Gavin (Julius Caesar), Tony Curtis (Antoninus), Nina Foch (Helena), Herbert Lom (Tigranes), John Ireland (Crixus), John Dall (Glabrus), Charles McGraw (Marcellus), Joanna Barnes (Claudia), Harold J. Stone (David), Woody Strode (Draba), Peter Brocco (Ramon), Paul Lambert (Gannicus), Robert J. Wilke (Captain of Guard), Nicholas Dennis (Dionysius), John Hoyt (Roman Officer), Fred Worlock (Laelius), Dayton Lummis (Symmachus).
Original Running Time: 196 minutes.* Distributor: Universal Pictures.
*The running time of the film shown in Britain was three minutes shorter. Later, when the film was in general distribution, Universal cut it to 183 minutes for all countries and subsequent releases. The scenes eliminated concerned mostly a very understated attempt by Marcus Crassus to seduce his slave Antoninus. The cuts make nonsense of their relationship.

Lolita (Great Britain, 1961).
Production Company, Seven Arts/Anya/Transworld. Producer, James B. Harris. Director, Stanley Kubrick. Script, Vladimir Nabokov, based on his own novel. Photography, Oswald Morris. Editor, Anthony Harvey. Art Director, William Andrews. Set Design, Andrew Low. Music, Nelson Riddle. Theme Music: Bob Harris. Sound, H. L. Bird, Len Shilton.
James Mason (Humbert Humbert), Sue Lyon (Lolita Haze), Shelley Winters (Charlotte Haze), Peter Sellers (Clare Quilty), Diana Decker (Jean Farlow), Jerry Stovin (John Farlow), Suzanne Gibbs (Mona Farlow), Gary Cockrell (Dick), Marianne Stone (Vivian Darkbloom), Cec Linder (Physician), Lois Maxwell (Nurse Mary Lore), William Greene (Swine), C. Denier Warren (Potts), Isobel Lucas (Louise), Maxine Holden (Receptionist), James Dyrenforth (Beale), Roberta Shore (Lorna), Eric Lane (Roy), Shirley Douglas (Mrs. Starch), Roland Brand (Bill), Colin Maitland (Charlie), Irvin Allen (Hospital Attendant), Marion Mathie (Miss Lebone), Craig Sams (Rex), John Harrison (Tom).
Running Time: 153 minutes. Distributor: Metro-Goldwyn-Mayer.

Dr. Strangelove, or How I Learned to Stop Worrying and Love the Bomb
(Great Britain, 1963).
Production Company, Hawk Films. Producer-Director, Stanley Kubrick. Associate Producer, Victor Lyndon. Script, Stanley Kubrick, Terry Southern, Peter George, based on the novel *Red Alert*, by Peter George. Photography, Gilbert Taylor. Editor, Anthony Harvey. Production Designer, Ken Adam. Art Director, Peter Murton. Special Effects, Wally Veevers. Music, Laurie Johnson. Aviation Adviser, Captain John Crewdson. Sound, John Cox.
Peter Sellers (Group Captain Lionel Mandrake, President Muffley, Dr. Strangelove), George C. Scott (General "Buck" Turgidson), Sterling Hayden (General Jack D. Ripper), Keenan Wynn (Colonel "Bat" Guano), Slim Pickens (Major T. J. "King" Kong), Peter Bull (Ambassador de Sadesky), Tracy Reed (Miss Scott), James Earl Jones (Lieutenant Lothar Zogg, Bombardier), Jack Creley (Mr. Staines), Frank Berry (Lieutenant H. R. Dietrich, DSO), Glenn Beck (Lieutenant W. D. Kivel, Navigator), Shane Rimmer (Captain G. A. "Ace" Owens, Copilot), Paul Tamarin (Lieutenant B. Goldberg, Radio Operator), Gordon Tanner (General Faceman), Robert O'Neil (Admiral Randolph), Roy Stephens (Frank), Laurence Herder, John McCarthy, Hal Galili (Members of Burpelson Base Defense Corps).
Running Time: 94 minutes. Distributor: Columbia Pictures.

2001: A Space Odyssey (Great Britain, 1968).
Production Company, Metro-Goldwyn-Mayer. Producer, Stanley Kubrick. Director, Stanley Kubrick. Script, Stanley Kubrick, Arthur C. Clarke, based on the latter's short story "The Sentinel." Photography, Geoffrey Unsworth. Screen Process,

Super Panavision, presented in Cinerama. Color, Metrocolor. Additional Photography, John Alcott. Special Photographic Effects Designer and Director, Stanley Kubrick. Editor, Ray Lovejoy. Production Designers, Tony Masters, Harry Lange, Ernie Archer. Art Director, John Hoesli. Special Photographic Effects Supervisors, Wally Veevers, Douglas Trumbull, Con Pederson, Tom Howard. Music, Richard Strauss, Johann Strauss, Aram Khachaturian, György Ligeti. Costumes, Hardy Amies. Sound, Winston Ryder.
Keir Dullea (David Bowman), Garry Lockwood (Frank Poole), William Sylvester (Dr. Heywood Floyd), Daniel Richter (Moonwatcher), Douglas Rain (Voice of HAL 9000), Leonard Rossiter (Smyslov), Margaret Tyzack (Elena), Robert Beatty (Halvorsen), Sean Sullivan (Michaels), Frank Miller (Mission Control), Penny Brahms (Stewardess), Alan Gifford (Poole's Father), Edward Bishop, Glenn Beck, Edwina Carroll, Mike Lovell, Peter Delman, Dany Grover, Brian Hawley.
Running Time: 141 minutes.* Distributor: Metro-Goldwyn-Mayer.
*The original running time of *2001: A Space Odyssey*, when previewed on April 1, 1968, in New York, was 161 minutes. Kubrick himself subsequently took the decision to trim about twenty minutes. He commented: "It does take a few runnings to decide finally how long things should be, especially scenes which do not have narrative advancement as their guideline." He had previously trimmed *Paths of Glory* between preview and release, and, of course, *Dr. Strangelove* had its intended pie-throwing ending taken out by Kubrick for reasons referred to in the text.

A Clockwork Orange (Great Britain, 1971).
Production Company, Warner Bros./Hawk Films. Production-Director, Stanley Kubrick. Associate Producer, Bernard Williams. Assistant to Producer, Jan Harlan. Script, Stanley Kubrick, based on the novel by Anthony Burgess. Photography, John Alcott. Editor, Bill Butler. Production Designer, John Barry. Production Assistant, Andros Epaminondas. Art Directors, Russell Hagg, Peter Sheilds. Special Paintings and Sculpture, Herman Makkink, Cornelius Makkink, Liz Moore, Christiane Kubrick. Costumes, Milena Canonero. Electronic Music, Walter Carlos. Music, Henry Purcell, Gioacchino Rossini, Ludwig van Beethoven, James Yorkston, Arthur Freed, Nacio Herb Brown, Sir Edward Elgar, Nicolay Rimsky-Korsakoff, Erika Eigen. Songs, Gene Kelly, Erika Eigen. Sound, Brian Blamey. Executive Producers, Max Raab, Si Litvinoff.
Malcolm McDowell (Alex), Patrick Magee (Mr. Alexander), Michael Bates (Chief Guard), Warren Clarke (Dim), John Clive (Stage Actor), Adrienne Corri (Mrs. Alexander), Carl Duering (Dr. Brodsky), Paul Farrell (Tramp), Clive Francis (Lodger), Michael Gover (Prison Governor), Miriam Karlin (Cat Lady), James Marcus (Georgie), Aubrey Morris (P. R. Deltoid), Godfrey Quigley (Prison Chaplain), Sheila Raynor (Mum), Madge Ryan (Dr. Branom), John Savident (Conspirator), Anthony Sharp (Minister of the Interior), Philip Stone (Dad), Pauline Taylor (Psychiatrist), Margaret Tyzack (Conspirator), Steven Berkoff (Constable), Lindsay Campbell (Inspector), Michael Tarn (Pete), David Prowse (Julian), Jan Adair, Vivienne Chandler, Prudence Drage (Handmaidens), John J. Carney (CID Man), Richard Connaught (Billyboy), Carol Drinkwater (Nurse Feeley), Cheryl Grunwald (Rape Girl), Gillian Hills (Sonietta), Barbara Scott (Marty), Virginia Wetherell (Stage Actress), Katya Wyeth (Girl), Barrie Cookson, Gaye Brown, Peter Burton, Lee Fox, Craig Hunter, Shirley Jaffe, Neil Wilson.
Running Time: 137 minutes. Distributor: Columbia Pictures/Warner Bros. (U.K.), Warner Bros. (USA).

Barry Lyndon (Great Britain, 1975).
Production Company, Warner Bros./Hawk/Peregrine Films. Production-Director, Stanley Kubrick. Executive Producer, Jan Harlan. Associate Producer, Bernard Williams. Script, Stanley Kubrick, based on the novel by William Makepeace Thackeray. Photography, John Alcott. Editor, Tony Lawson. Production Designer, Ken Adam. Assistant Producer, Andros Epaminondas. Art Director, Roy Walker. Makeup, Anne Brodie, Alan Boyle, Barbara Daly, Jill Carpenter, Yvonne Cloppard. Costumes, Ulla-Britt Soderlund, Milena Canonero. Wigs, Leonard. Music, Leonard Roseman, Johann Sebastian, Bach, George Frideric, Handel, Frederick II, Wolfgang Amadeus Mozart, Giovanni Paisiello, Franz Schubert, Antonio Vivaldi, The Chieftains. Choreography, Geraldine Stephenson. Historical Adviser, John Mollo. Gambling Adviser, David Beglas. Fencing Coach, Bob Anderson. Horsemaster, George Mossman. Armorer, Bill Aylmore. Stunts, Roy Scammel.
Ryan O'Neal (Barry Lyndon), Marisa Berenson (Lady Lyndon),

Patrick Magee (Chevalier de Balibari), Hardy Kruger (Captain Potzdorf), Stephen Berkoff (Lord Ludd), Gay Hamilton (Nora Brady), Marie Kean (Mrs. Barry), Diana Koerner (Young German Woman), Murray Melvin (Reverend Runt), Frank Middlemass (Sir Charles Lyndon), Andrew Morell (Lord Wendover), Arthur O'Sullivan (Highwayman), Godfrey Quigley (Captain Grogan), Leonard Rossiter (Captain Quinn), Philip Stone (Graham), Leon Vitali (Lord Bullingdon), Dominic Savage (Young Lord Bullingdon), David Morley (Little Bryan), Anthony Sharp (Lord Harlan), Pat Roach (Toole), Norman Mitchell (Brock), Roger Booth (George III), Michael Hordern (Narrator).
Running Time: 187 minutes. Distributor: Warner Bros. (U.K.), Warner Bros. (USA).

The Shining (Great Britain, 1980).
Production Company, Warner Bros./Hawk/Peregrine Films. Producer-Director, Stanley Kubrick. Executive Producer, Jan Harlan. Script, Stanley Kubrick and Diane Johnson, based on the novel by Stephen King. Photography, John Alcott. Steadicam Operator, Garrett Brown. 2nd United Photographer, Douglas Milsome. Sound, Ivan Sharrock. Editor, Ray Lovejoy. Production Designer, Roy Walker. Art Director, Les Tomkins. Makeup, Tom Smith. Costumes, Milena Canonero, Leonard. Hairdresser, Leonard. Assistant to Mr. Kubrick, Leon Vitali. Music, Wendy Carlos, Rachel Elkind, György Ligeti, Béla Bartók, Krzysztof Penderecki, Henry Hall.
Jack Nicholson (Jack Torrance), Shelley Duvall (Wendy Torrance), Danny Lloyd (Danny), Scatman Crothers (Hallorann), Barry Nelson (Ullman), Philip Stone (Grady), Joe Turkel (Lloyd), Lia Beldam (Young Woman in Bathtub), Billie Gibson (Old Woman in Bathtub), Barry Denen (Watson), David Baxt, Manning Redwood (Rangers), Lisa and Louise Burns (Grady Children), Kate Phelps (Receptionist).
Running Time: 120 minutes (original length, 146 minutes). Distributor: Warner Bros. (U.K.), Warner Bros. (USA).

Full Metal Jacket (Great Britain, 1987).
Production Company, Warner Bros./Natant Films. Producer-Director, Stanley Kubrick. Executive Producer, Jan Harlan. Coproducer, Philip Hobbs. Associate Producer, Michael Herr. Production Coordinator, Margaret Adams. Casting, Leon Vitali. Script, Stanley Kubrick, Michael Herr, Gustav Hasford, based on the novel *The Short Timers* by Gustav Hasford. Photography, Douglas Milsome. Aerial Photography, Ken Arlidge. Steadicam Operators, John Ward, Jean-Marc Bringuier. Video Operator, Manuel Harlan. Editor, Martin Hunter. Production Designer, Anton Furst. Set Dresser, Stephen Simmonds. Makeup, Jennifer Boost, Christine Allsop. Costumes, Keith Denny. Music, Abigail Mead, Johnny Wright, Nancy Sinatra, The Dixie Cups, Sam the Sham and the Pharoahs, The Rolling Stones, The Trashmen, The Marines' Hymn. Sound, Nigel Galt. Technical Adviser, Lee Ermey.
Matthew Modine (Private Joker), Adam Baldwin (Animal Mother), Vincent D'Onofrio (Private Pyle), Lee Ermey (Gunnery Sergeant Hartman), Dorian Harewood (Eightball), Arliss Howard (Cowboy), Kevin Major Howard (Rafter Man), Ed O'Ross (Walter J. Schinoski), John Terry (Lieutenant Lockhart), Keiron Jecchinis (Crazy Earl), Kark Taylor (Payback), Tim Colceri (Door Gunner), John Stafford (Doc Jay), Bruce Boa (Page Colonel), Ian Tyler (Lieutenant Cleves), Papillon Soo Soo (Da Nang Hooker), Ngoc Le (Vietcong Sniper).
Running Time: 116 minutes. Distributor: Columbia-Cannon-Warner (U.K.), Warner Bros. (USA).

Eyes Wide Shut (Great Britain, 1999).
Production Company, Polestar/Hobby Films Ltd. Producer-Director, Stanley Kubrick. Executive Producer, Jan Harlan. Coproducer, Brian Cook. Script, Stanley Kubrick, Frederic Raphael. Inspired by the novella *Traumnovelle* by Arthur Schnitzler. Photography, Larry Smith. Steadicam Operators, Elizabeth Ziegler, Peter Cavaciuti. Editor, Nigel Galt. Production Designers, Les Tomkins, Roy Walker. Art Director, John Fenner. Costume Designer, Marit Allen. Assistant to the Director, Leon Vitali. Assistant to Stanley Kubrick, Anthony Frewin. Sound, Eddie Tise. Music, original music composed by Jocelyn Pook. Original Paintings, Christiane Kubrick, Katharina Hobbs.
Tom Cruise (Dr. William Harford), Nicole Kidman (Alice Harford), Sydney Pollack (Victor Ziegler), Marie Richardson (Marion), Rade Sherbedigia (Milich), Todd Field (Nick Nightingale), Vinessa Shaw (Domino), Alan Cumming (Desk Clerk), Sky Dumont (Sandor Szavost), Fay Masterson (Sally), Leelee Sobieski (Milich's Daughter), Thomas Gibson (Carl), Madison Eginton (Helena Harford).
Running Time: 156 minutes. Distributor: Warner Bros.